THEIR LIVES

THEIR LIVES

THE WOMEN TARGETED BY THE CLINTON MACHINE

CANDICE E. JACKSON

World Ahead Publishing, Inc.

World Ahead Publishing's books are available at special discounts for bulk purchases. World Ahead Publishing also publishes books in electronic formats. For more information, visit www.worldahead.com.

First Edition

ISBN 0-9746701-3-8
LCCN 2005924358

Printed in the United States of America

10 9 8 7 6 5 4 3 2

To Judith,
Without your steady guidance
I would have nothing to say.

CONTENTS

ACKNOWLEDGMENTS

ERIC JACKSON is a visionary entrepreneur I had the privilege of getting to know when we were economics students at Stanford together. Publication of this book is just one of the projects at World Ahead Publishing, Inc. that owes its existence to Eric's exceptional talent and hard work, and I am deeply grateful for the opportunity to work with him and each of the extraordinary people at World Ahead. David Hodel's contributions are equally important; his input brought structure to what began as a muddle of ideas for this book. Arthur Willner provided insightful critique at a critical stage of the manuscript, and whatever advice I didn't take, I probably should have.

Shelly Jackson, Tami Kumin, and Jim Fite planted seeds for this book, whether they realized it or not, and I am extremely appreciative even though the result may not be what they had in mind. Bill Anderson and Doug Shoemaker are the best research and business partners a girl could hope for, and any successes of mine are due largely to their brilliance and friendship.

Friends and family who stood by me in this effort are too numerous to name. I hope you all know who you are, and how much I love that you love me even when my ideas make you wonder why you do. I can't resist a shout-out to Jen, Jason, and Mary; you guys are the gems of my life, and I can't imagine trudging this road without you. And I am truly blessed with parents, Rick and Jeanine, and two brothers, Richard and Jonathan, who continually inspire me with their passion and conviction.

Much to her dismay, I can't spare Patty Campbell the humiliation of open association with this book. Her support for me during this process knew no bounds, even though after reading the first chapter she wanted a blurb on the book jacket to say: "If God is a Democrat—and I believe He is—then Candice Jackson will burn in hell." Hopefully I won't find out if she's right for a good long while, and in the meantime her love and laughter make life worth all the ups and downs. The Campbells, Sayhounis, and Houlihans triple the fun and have become my second family, and I love them dearly

Finally, each of the women I write about in this book has my genuine respect. Whether they agreed to be interviewed for this book or not, each woman has touched my heart and earned my admiration for their courage and inner strength. I owe them a personal debt of gratitude for standing on the side of truth no matter the consequences they suffered.

INTRODUCTION

WHY ANOTHER book about Bill Clinton? Well, in a memoir the length of *War and Peace*, Bill Clinton got the chance to tell us about himself. He told us about his personal and political life. He told us about people who influenced him—his parents, his wife, his political allies, and even his enemies. But some people were glaringly absent from Clinton's best-selling *My Life*, and this omission was no accident. Yet understanding the effect Clinton had on these unnamed lives is critical for exposing his supposed pro-feminist agenda and gaining insight into the source of his undeniable misogyny: liberalism.

Revisiting the stories of several women who have come forward over the years about their experiences with Bill Clinton is not an exercise in right-wing moral condemnation or political bitterness. As a libertarian, I have little sympathy for the Clinton-bashing performed by moral conservatives throughout the 1990s. But as a feminist, I have a deep interest in reminding myself and others of the serious violations of women's rights Bill Clinton committed in his personal life. This behavior, from a man whose political career was characterized by most feminists as a giant step toward gender equality, is baffling. The explanation for this seeming paradox apparently escaped both the left and right during Clinton's presidency.

Most conservatives missed the political point we'll examine in this book. Instead, the right jumped at the chance to argue for Clinton's impeachment and prosecution for lying and attempting to cover up his affair. On the other hand, most liberals quickly dismissed Clinton's bad behavior as "personal failures" that somehow didn't reflect on his politics. They found it all too easy to write off the women linked to Bill Clinton as "bimbo eruptions."

The women profiled in this book may not have been Ivy League graduates or leaders in their fields, but they didn't deserve to have their jobs threatened, their reputations smeared, or their tires slashed just because they crossed paths with Bill Clinton. Although many of these women confess to consensual affairs with Clinton, several disclose sexual harassment and even assault. As a recovering victim of sexual assault myself, I understand the pain involved in coming to terms with such an experience. But I cannot imagine the terror involved when your perpetrator is the Leader of the Free World with countless resources at his disposal.

As Clinton, his wife, and their team of political loyalists gear up to promote the paperback release of his memoirs and celebrate the opening of a presidential library geared at securing his "legacy," it's time to discover the chapters Clinton left unwritten and the lives left upended in his wake. Before we laud his presidency or send Hillary in his footsteps to the Oval Office, let's spend some time with seven remarkable women to see how their experiences shed light on the character and politics of a man who once assured us he could feel our pain.

CHAPTER ONE

STRAYING OR PREYING?

I N MANY WAYS, Bill Clinton came across as a hallmark of our times—cocky, fun-loving, able to handle himself in a fight. He seemed interested in doing the right thing, whatever that was at the time, but not uptight about it. During the 1992 campaign no one in the mainstream media wanted to talk much about the rumors wending their way out of Arkansas. A few cautionary voices were already trying to warn us about the spotty personal history of the man who would be president, but he played the saxophone on late night television, for crying out loud. What's not to like? Unfortunately, jamming with the Arsenio Hall band would not be the extent of presidential firsts visited upon us by Bill Clinton.

Not that Clinton single-handedly introduced indiscretion to the office. Accusations of infidelity sullied at least a dozen administrations, and John F. Kennedy's peccadilloes have become the stuff of legend. Moral outrage in Washington, D.C. often has as much to do with whose ox is being gored as with genuine moral sensibilities. The rules have changed in recent decades, partly due to the fallout from the Watergate scandal. In an unprecedented power shift, investigative reporting brought down a sitting president, and for better or worse our tripartite balance of governmental power saw a fourth institution grafted into the accountability structure. Now an official's private life receives detailed attention, and the modern tradition of mercilessly trying candidates in the press is firmly entrenched. A person's private life is not merely a matter of reputation and public opinion; with a sufficient public outcry, special prosecutors can be summoned and the full weight of the judicial branch can come down on a politician with devastating consequences. It's hard to imagine JFK sitting before a congressional committee or grand jury defending his sexual behavior. Maybe Bill Clinton was just born forty years too late.

◊

In retrospect, the socio-political, economic, and cultural indicators as they stood in 1990 should leave us unsurprised that we woke up one day late in January 1993 to the sight of Democrats at their inaugural rally, giddily singing off-key while the words of Fleetwood Mac droned *ad nauseam*, "Don't stop thinking about tomorrow..." from rented speakers. Communism had been defeated in the Soviet Union, Iraq had been halted in its violent bid to annex Kuwait, and the national malaise from the Carter years was dispersed by eight years of booming prosperity and national pride under Ronald Reagan. Most Americans were feeling good about their place in the world, and it was time to turn attention back to problems at home. With the financial rush of the 1980s quickly fading and a voting public irritated at having their taxes raised by a president who explicitly promised he would do no such thing, Clinton's good-natured appeal in 1992 should have been obvious.

Those same factors also help explain the abrupt shift from twelve years of Republican leadership to a Democratic victory. Just over half the presidential elections since 1824 have yielded a winner with more than 50 percent of the popular vote, and only four presidents in U.S. history have ever won 60 percent or more of the popular vote (Republicans Warren Harding and Richard

Nixon; Democrats Franklin Roosevelt and Lyndon Johnson).[1] With control of the White House consistently hinging on such an even split in the popularity of Republicans and Democrats, it takes relatively little pizzazz for an individual candidate to persuade enough voters to swing an election.

And Clinton possessed nothing if not pizzazz. From his MTV appearance disclosing his underwear preference to his down-home renditions of his humble youth, Clinton offered an energetic, charismatic alternative to old-style politics. To hear those who have met him, his charisma is a palpable thing. He has a gift for making a person feel like the most important person in the world when speaking one on one. He is an engaging public speaker and exudes a humor and generosity that many found appealing, especially in contrast with GOP stodginess. His wife, describing seeing him on the Yale Law School campus for the first time in 1970, gushes, "He also had a vitality that seemed to shoot out of his pores."[2] Styling himself a New Democrat and promising to reinvent government, Clinton capitalized on dissatisfaction with the recession of the early 1990s and charmingly won his chance to rule the world.

◊

Clinton was not on the national scene for long before rumors and evidence of impropriety began cropping up in earnest. Before long, some people began to realize that Clinton's boyish charm had a flip side—a weakness for sexual indiscretions that even by 1992 had already produced a string of women with tales of extramarital affairs.

The Clintons and their long-time political friends had discussed how to handle Clinton's reputation for philandering well before Clinton's 1992 campaign. Whether Clinton had a "Gary Hart problem" that could derail his plans for ascending to the presidency was a frequent topic as far back as 1987, when Clinton seriously considered running for president. Biographer

David Maraniss reports that by 1990, when Clinton decided to seek re-election as governor of Arkansas and simultaneously began pondering a 1992 presidential run, he was irked each time his close political advisors raised concerns about whether he was in danger of imploding like Gary Hart.[3]

In 1988 after Gary Hart had dropped out of the Democratic primary amidst evidence of his extramarital sex life, Clinton and his long-time aide Betsey Wright privately discussed the Hart debacle.[4] According to Wright, Clinton "wanted to believe and advocated that it was irrelevant to whether the guy could be a good president."[5] Much to the chagrin of many on the right, Clinton probably had the pulse of most Americans on that one. Philandering, as such, is rarely a barrier to public approval of an official's job performance. Following the advice of political consultants by admitting early on to marital rough spots while appearing hand-in-hand with Hillary permitted Clinton to benefit from Americans' long history of drawing a distinct line between officials' public and private lives. "If Hillary's okay with it, we should be okay with it," became a familiar tune in editorials, op-eds, and the press. The repeal of many state adultery laws throughout the twentieth century and the infrequent prosecution of adultery in the states that continue to criminalize it[6] seems to reflect an American attitude in favor of sexual privacy and the classification of adultery as more of a personal, spiritual issue than a public, legal one. Gary Hart's downfall was something of an anomaly brought about in large part by his incredibly foolish grandstanding—he expressly denied extramarital activity and challenged the press to put a tail on him to prove him wrong. They did, and his career never recovered.

In his memoirs Clinton writes of Gary Hart, "I thought Gary had made an error by challenging the press to tail him…but I felt bad for him, too…. After the Hart affair, those of us who had not led perfect lives had no way of knowing what the press's standards of disclosure were."[7] He continues, "Finally I concluded that anyone who believed he had something to offer should just run, deal with whatever charges arose, and trust the American people."[8] Apparently for Clinton, Hart's error was not philandering but playing truth-or-dare with the press about it. The women's stories revisited in this book make clear exactly what Clinton meant by "deal with whatever charges arose" — Clinton and his crew proved themselves skilled at a disturbing game of defense and offense best described as "Deny and Smear." As for his ostensible determination to just "trust the American people," the following chapters detail just how much Clinton mistrusted us, preferring always to lie rather than come clean when confronted with misdeeds.

In 1991 Bill and Hillary appeared together at a gathering of Washington political press corps elites amid speculation about his imminent candidacy. Clinton told the press that he and Hillary were "committed to their marriage," having worked through "some problems."[9] Trusting this strategy, a combination of whitewashing the actual nature of their marital problems and posing Bill as a contrite wanderer, the Clintons escaped Hart's fate and landed themselves the Top Job.

Clinton's memoirs devote three paragraphs to his decision to appear with Hillary to comment on their marriage before he ran for president.[10] He's not sure if he did the right thing by addressing the questions about his infidelities. "Character is important in a president," he writes, "but as the contrasting examples of FDR and Richard Nixon show, marital perfection is not necessarily a good measure of presidential character."[11] In other words, we shouldn't care about a president's marital faithlessness. Even if he's right, he misses the point. If Clinton's behavior amounted only to *The Bridges of Madison County*-style love affairs, perhaps his wife and daughter would be the only women with rights to complain. But that isn't the case. The women profiled in this book reveal Clinton not as a philanderer, but as a sex addict, sexual harasser, and sexual abuser. It's the difference between straying and preying, and it's a huge difference. Clinton's mistreatment of women is surely part of his "presidential character" we should care about. Further, if a correlation exists between his view of women and view of politics, then he deserves classification as a liberal misogynist and should be used to illustrate the dangers inherent in modern liberalism, a political philosophy espoused by another Clinton with apparent presidential ambitions.

◊

If Clinton had merely joined the venerable ranks of presidents who also happened to be philanderers, his sex life would have been followed like a soap opera in our voyeuristic society but his behavior would not have provided material for this book. Unfortunately for the many women mistreated by him, Clinton's interactions with women spanning his political career place him outside the category "philanderer" and into much more serious categories like "sex addict," "sex offender," and "misogynist."

I don't use those terms lightly. Dictionary definitions of "philanderer" include one who engages in many love affairs, especially with a frivolous or casual attitude; one who has casual or illicit sexual relations with many women; or, one who is sexually unfaithful to his wife. The word comes from an obsolete word, *philander*, which used to mean "lover." Philandering may be about men who "love" women too much, but sexual abuse, sex addiction, and misogyny have nothing to do with love and everything to do with power and control, often based on a view of women as objects.

A working definition of "sex offender" is a person who commits a sex crime—i.e., inflicting sexual contact on someone without their consent, by force or threat. Sexual abuse isn't about love or even sexual gratification. It's about feeding a pathological drive for dominance and control. As one sexual abuse victim's program puts it, rape and other sex offenses are about sexualized violence, not about violent sex.[12]

The word "misogynist" literally means "one who hates women," from the Greek words *misien* ("to hate") and *gyne* ("woman"). Encyclopedia entries for misogyny use the additional definition "[A]n exaggerated pathological aversion toward women." Far-left feminists have co-opted the word misogynist to denigrate any person who disagrees with their political agenda. For example, journalist Richard Goldstein's leveled the catchy accusation that the George W. Bush Administration practiced "stealth misogyny" by stationing female faces in high-level administration posts while "closing women's offices in federal agencies, defunding programs that monitor discrimination, appointing people who oppose affirmative action and welfare for single mothers to policy-making posts," and waging an "assault on choice" (i.e., abortion rights).[13] Liberalism's monopoly on defining women's issues has emboldened leftists to hurl the label "misogynist" at virtually everyone who opposes abortion, reproductive rights, affirmative action, the welfare state, or any other part of the current left-liberal political agenda. That distorted application of the word goes way beyond the core meaning of "misogynist." As I use the phrase here, a "liberal misogynist" is a person who supports women's rights *politically* yet repeatedly mistreats women *personally*. Of course, not all misogynists are liberals and vice versa. Yet liberal misogyny is a specific manifestation of misogyny that deserves closer inspection.

In the article "Sexual Addiction: Diagnosis and Treatment,"[14] Dr. Aviel Goodman describes sexual addiction as a condition where some form of sexual behavior is repeated in a pattern, marked by "recurrent failure to control the sexual behavior," and "continuation of the sexual behavior despite significant harmful consequences." Based on the behavior we'll examine in the following chapters it's not much of a stretch to surmise that Bill Clinton fits the description of a sex addict more closely than that of a mere philanderer. In a 1998 article, *The New York Times* quoted Dr. Jerome D. Levin, a psychotherapist and author of a book entitled *The Clinton Syndrome: The President and the Self-*

9

Destructive Nature of Sexual Addiction as advising the president to invoke the 25th Amendment and enter a rehabilitation program for sex addiction treatment.[15] Dr. Don Fava posted on-line a short analysis stating about sexual addiction:

> A lack of lasting relationships or frequent changes in parental figures during early childhood leads to the development of a faulty conscience. Such persons cannot experience true love, but rather use others to gratify their own narcissistic needs, i.e. to prove to themselves that they are capable of being loved....It is interesting to study the psychodynamics of sexual addiction because many of the same dynamics associated with this disorder lead to a preoccupation with power and admiration as a way of denying shame and humiliation....Is this our president Clinton? I don't know, but you can bet that a lot of people are analyzing the man this very moment....[16]

It's debatable whether Clinton suffers from a clinical sex addiction, and for our purposes, it isn't terribly relevant. Whether or not his behavior merits a clinical diagnosis, much of it matches popular descriptions of sexual addiction. Of course, even an addiction cannot eliminate the element of personal responsibility for one's actions; addictions of all kinds are treatable, provided the afflicted person is willing to admit the problem and accept help for it.

Clinton has publicly admitted to a sexual relationship with Monica Lewinsky, and to at least a brief fling with Gennifer Flowers. He has alluded publicly many times throughout his career to marital problems, but has stopped short of confessing to liaisons with any other specific women. Clinton copped to an affair with Flowers during the same deposition at which he denied a sexual relationship with Lewinsky; perhaps he hoped that coming clean about Flowers would satisfy his truth-telling responsibilities and increase his credibility as he continued to deny an inappropriate relationship with Lewinsky. However, when Lewinsky's story broke in 1998 she had the advantage of scientific evidence—DNA on a certain blue dress—which eventually cornered Clinton into admitting a sexual relationship with her. Clinton's other conquests have only their own stories to tell, leaving them largely on the losing side of a "Bill-says/she-says" battle.

This is the very situation that most victims of sexual abuse find themselves in, and it often discourages women from coming forward. Women's rights advocates have made great strides in legal and social arenas encouraging women's testimony to be taken seriously, making it more difficult for offenders to get away with abuse by denouncing their accusers as "psychos" making it up or sluts who wanted it. Bill Clinton's politics, it seems, actually helped him avoid accountability. Because Clinton was allegedly a political champion for women's issues, the individuals and groups who pose as advocates against misogyny were — with few exceptions — unwilling to stand up for Clinton's women, unwilling to believe their stories, and unwilling to help the rest of us understand that signing legislation strengthening abortion rights doesn't negate the consequences of misogyny in personal behavior, much less the abuse of political power to cover up one's actions.

◊

From Clinton's brief affairs with Elizabeth Ward Gracen and Sally Perdue as governor of Arkansas, to his decade-long recurring affair with Gennifer Flowers, to his alleged unwanted advances thrust upon Paula Jones and Kathleen Willey, to his confessed sexual encounters with Monica Lewinsky in the Oval Office and — if you find her story as credible as I do — his vicious assault on Juanita Broaddrick, Bill Clinton consistently views and treats women as playthings. He has used his ever-expanding positions of power to seduce, entice, cajole, pressure, abuse, smear, and destroy women unfortunate enough to be caught in his gaze. Clinton's encounters with women undoubtedly include many purely consensual affairs; with respect to these women, the real mistreatment began after the affair had ended, when his physical conquests became political liabilities. Other encounters demonstrate actual sexual assault and harassment, often followed by serious violations of these women's lives when they became threats to his political career.

How is this behavior possible from a man feminists supported as the best-ever president for women's rights? Psychoanalysis may provide a partial explanation for Clinton's mistreatment of women, but our focus is on the explanatory reach of Clinton's *politics*. Feminists cheered Clinton's election in 1992, and endorsed his re-election in 1996, albeit a bit less enthusiastically after Clinton had, in their view, sold out the feminist agenda somewhat by signing Republican legislation like welfare reform and the Defense of Marriage Act. With respect to the many allegations of Clinton's sexual misbehavior, even some feminists had no choice but to openly condemn Clinton's behavior. By 1998, Patricia Ireland, then president of the National Organization for Women (NOW), felt compelled to release a statement assuring the public that NOW had taken a stance against aspects of Clinton's behavior toward women. [17]

But the double standard was all too clear. If Clinton hadn't been a politician with the power to advance their political agenda—or worse, if Clinton had been a conservative politician unwilling to advance the feminist agenda—Clinton's women would have been viewed by women's rights advocates as targets of pathological abuse, and their stories of mistreatment by Clinton would have been met with sympathy for them and anger at Clinton. Instead, the Clinton spin machine has quite successfully made jokes of these women, glossing over the plausibility that they suffered real injuries at the hands of Bill Clinton. Revisiting the experiences of the women in this book breaks that spin machine and illuminates the connection between Clinton's misogyny and his liberal politics.

Elizabeth. Sally. Gennifer. Paula. Kathleen. Monica. Juanita. And the man they have in common: Bill. What to make of their stories, and his? The seven women whose stories are recaptured in the following chapters make up a diverse group, each with her unique personality and life experience. There are beauty queens, a singer, an actress, a housewife, a widow, and businesswomen in the mix. Some are quiet and shy, others are loud and ostentatious. Their interactions with Bill Clinton span more than two decades. None of their stories can ever be proved in a court of law, but none has ever been disproved either, leaving the issue of credibility in the realm of Bill says, she says. None of these women went public with their stories until they felt pressured or coerced into doing so. When they did, each experienced severe mistreatment for their trouble. For women like Paula Jones, Kathleen Willey, and especially Juanita Broaddrick, any denigration tossed at them when they came forward only added to the mistreatment they suffered in their actual physical encounters with Bill Clinton. Featuring the stories of Elizabeth, Sally, Gennifer, Paula, Kathleen, Monica, and Juanita necessarily omits other women who have spoken out over the years—and leaves out dozens of others *rumored* to have been similarly mistreated. As tempting as it is to delve into these other accounts, the women profiled here suffice as a representative sample from which to examine Clinton's misogynistic pattern and what it says about his political ideology.

Each woman's experience crossing paths with Bill Clinton sadly illustrates a different dimension of the intersection between personal mistreatment of women and political ideology that makes Clinton a shining example of liberal misogyny. The various forms of mistreatment visited upon these women include disregard for their self-esteem, integrity, and psychological well-being; chauvinism and male superiority; cruel smear campaigns designed to write them off as trashy sluts; objectification, patronization, and seductive destruction; and outright physical violence. Their collective experience is evidence of a pattern of mistreatment by a man whose sexual behavior long ago crossed the line from "mere" philandering into probable sexual addiction, sexual abuse, and misogyny. As we will see, aspects of liberalism that contributed to such mistreatment include: using any political means to achieve a worthy political goal; relying on intermediaries to enforce political demands; judging the message based on the presumed motives of the messenger; elevating groupism over individualism; trusting in government as super-parent; succumbing to government seduction; and most critically, perpetuating the use of force to achieve moral values. Exploring the stories of the seven women in this book will connect the dots between Clinton's misogyny and his political liberalism.

◊

It's only fair to begin our look at these women's stories with a glance at Bill Clinton's version of his own story. Clinton's autobiography, *My Life*, first hit the shelves in June 2004. Twenty-seven years after his affair with Gennifer Flowers began; twenty-six years after he raped Juanita Broaddrick; twenty-one years after he slept with Elizabeth Ward Gracen and shared a fling with Sally Perdue; thirteen years after his crude advances toward Paula Jones; eleven years after taking advantage of Kathleen Willey; nine years after his first sexual encounter with Monica Lewinsky; and just five years after surviving impeachment, Bill Clinton devoted nearly 1,000 pages to telling his story.

Very few of those pages talk about the women in his life. Even his wife and daughter receive scant attention compared with the book's central purpose (in his words): to tell the story of America during the years he grew up and came of age, and the story of what it's like to be the president leading a great country into a new millennium. Realistically, it's impossible for any number of pages to tell a person's full life story. Clinton has told his the way he wanted to, in his voice, with his perspective. The topics he covers, the vignettes and memories he shares, say a lot about his values and beliefs. I encourage readers to spend quality time with Clinton's memoirs because they convey his point of view on the subjects covered in this book: women and politics. Though his view of women is evident mostly by its absence in his memoirs, Clinton communicates in great detail his reasons for adhering to liberal ideology.

It won't spoil his story to take a peek at what Bill Clinton has to say about the women discussed in this book. It won't take long, either, because he doesn't say much about them. No doubt he would like to leave us with the impression that the women profiled in this book impacted his life so negligibly that they don't deserve his attention, or ours. Of course, that attitude lines up perfectly with his misogyny. He had a devastating impact on the lives of women who crossed his path but they meant little or nothing to him. If he had a strategy in how to deal with women in his memoirs it appears to be: don't mention them at all except to illustrate the depravity of your political opponents. Here's the summary: he briefly mentions by name Gennifer Flowers, Paula Jones, Kathleen Willey, and Monica Lewinsky. He offers little by way of excuse or explanation, and he ignores the existence of the other women profiled in this book.

In a television interview promoting *My Life*, Clinton said that one of the reasons his political enemies couldn't just "let it go" with respect to his personal failures was that too many people involved in politics today refuse to let politicians be three-dimensional people; politicians are too often forced into cartoon characters labeled good or evil, heroes or villains. I couldn't agree more with that insight. Coming from Clinton it's both wise and hypocritical. As the following chapters show, Clinton helped squash many women into cartoon characterizations rather than allow them to exist as three-dimensional human beings. But it's a good reminder to place in context whatever criticisms we level against Clinton. He too is a complex, three dimensional human being, and painting him into a caricature only obscures truth and accuracy. Clinton's mistreatment of women exists alongside other, better human qualities like compassion for the downtrodden and passion for solving global problems ranging from AIDS to nuclear proliferation.

That said, Clinton's misogynistic behavior merits exposure as one of the darker aspects of his character, not in order to ridicule or judge him, but to better understand its causes in hope that others can avoid such damaging behavior. As a world leader who will influence countless people for decades in the remaining years of his life and for centuries through his legacy, Bill Clinton the man and the politician should be examined from all angles. For better or worse he is one of the people to whom history will turn to gauge society's successes and failures during the 1990s and on whose shoulders future generations will place praise and blame for myriad developments. When it comes to women's rights, perhaps in time Bill Clinton will be viewed as a person who illustrated some of the risks inherent in liberalism's attempt to ensure gender equality by government coercion.

His story, their stories. His version, their version. His life, their lives. They have no scientific or legal proof with which to persuade you of the truth. But neither does he. Spend some time with Clinton's book and this one, and decide for yourself whom you believe.

CHAPTER TWO

MODUS OPERANDI

A S THE FIRST baby-boomer president, Bill Clinton has been psycho-analyzed to the hilt. Many authors have delved into speculative analysis of how Clinton's childhood affected his adulthood. His biological father died before he was born, he was devoted to his mother, he grew up loving and hating an alcoholic and abusive stepfather, he struggled to rise above poverty, and so on. Clinton himself, in his autobiography, discusses the way his boyhood experiences—good, bad, and ugly—impacted his actions and feelings in manhood. In places his reflection is remarkably candid and worthwhile for gaining an understanding of what kind of boy grew up to be this kind of man.

Even though this book focuses on Clinton's political beliefs, it's critical to remember that politics isn't the only (or perhaps even the most important) factor driving Clinton's misogyny. Young Bill suffered many emotional burdens, and as the bumper sticker says, "Hurt People Hurt People." But our focus here will remain on the way his liberal politics, rather than psychology, influenced his behavior.

Clinton's generalized statements about his feelings toward women, peppered throughout his autobiography, don't divulge anything especially unusual, but they do hint at some self-awareness of a struggle to build meaningful, monogamous relationships. He praises his mother, grandmother, wife, and daughter for their respective roles in his life and also for being strong, independent women. His early experiences with women like his mother and grandmother also imply at least a light-hearted resentment of some kind. For example, when Clinton writes about working on an early political campaign and being assigned to travel the state with the candidate's wife and daughters he says he didn't mind the job because he was "used to being bossed around by women, so we got along well."[1]

He also admits that as he entered junior high school and adolescence he began to get to know himself a bit and "some of what came into my head and life scared the living hell out of me, including my anger at Daddy [stepfather Roger Clinton], the first stirrings of sexual feelings toward girls, and doubts about my religious convictions."[2]

Young Bill was a "secret-keeper" who didn't talk about these common feelings of self-doubt that are part of coming of age.[3] This reluctance to discuss his feelings could help explain how a person who desired to do the right thing could find himself behaving poorly despite an intellectual conviction that women should be treated with respect. He shares a portion of a high school essay he wrote in which he describes himself as "a living paradox—deeply religious, yet not as convinced of my exact beliefs as I ought to be; wanting responsibility yet shirking it; loving truth but often times giving way to falsity....I detest selfishness, but see it in the mirror every day."[4] At that age, Clinton writes that he wasn't sure how to feel about himself. "I didn't do bad things; I didn't drink, smoke, or go beyond petting with girls, though I kissed a fair number. Most of the time I was happy, but I could never be sure I was as good as I wanted to be."[5] He doesn't say whether he ever outgrew that uncertainty or view of himself as a "living paradox," but with respect to his treatment of women perhaps he didn't.

Summing up his years at Oxford, where he studied as a prestigious Rhodes Scholar in his early twenties, Clinton writes: "Just like that, it was over, two of the most extraordinary years of my life....I had traveled a lot and loved it. I had also ventured into the far reaches of my mind and heart, struggling with my draft situation, my ambivalence about my ambition, and my inability to have anything other than brief relationships with women. I had no degree, but I had learned a lot."[6] Those struggles would continually pose the greatest threats to his political career, though he spends little time discussing that throughout the rest of his book.

When Bill proposed to Hillary, she said she loved him but wasn't sure about marrying him. He writes, "I loved her and wanted to be with her, but I understood her reservations. I was passionate and driven, and nothing in my background indicated I knew what a stable marriage was all about. She knew that being married to me would be a high-wire operation in more ways than one."[7] This is one of the few passages that shows a fairly direct acknowledgement of unfaithfulness as a personal character flaw. As much as he claims to love his wife, this passage also shows an unintended callousness tinged with sexism: she knew what she was getting into when she married him.

Interestingly, Clinton seems to equate sexual misconduct with "personal demons." Wrapping up his thoughts on the Monica Lewinsky affair he writes:

> I also came to understand that when I was exhausted, angry, or feeling isolated and alone, I was more vulnerable to making selfish and self-destructive personal mistakes about which I would later be ashamed. The current controversy was the latest casualty of my lifelong effort to lead parallel lives.... During the government shutdowns I was engaged in two titanic struggles: a public one with Congress over the future of our country, and a private one to hold the old demons at bay. I had won the public fight and lost the private one.[8] (p. 821).

Hopefully whatever introspective insight he's gained about his behavior has helped him integrate his parallel lives and avoid feelings of shame and paths of self-destruction. But he still offers no recognition that losing his "private" battles with "old demons" caused very real heartache, hurt, and destruction in the lives of the women who apparently embodied a temptation that he could not resist.

"Old demons" suggests a long, deeply rooted history of struggling with how to treat women, and might be perceived as a typically Clintonesque vague and partial admission that he didn't tell us the whole story. Some women not mentioned in his memoirs, including some of the women profiled in this book, may indeed be part of his struggle with old demons. While he perhaps feels that he owes us no further explanation, we owe it to ourselves and history not to ignore these women's stories, and to learn from them what we can about misogyny, politics, and the impact of both on real people.

◊

As a Southerner, Clinton grew up surrounded by a Bible Belt culture that thrives on the motto, "Sin, repent. Move on."[9] According to the witty, fascinating exposé *Sex in the South*, "The deal in Dixie is that everybody does it but no one talks about it. Because no one talks about it, sex is encased in a plain brown wrapper making everything about it taboo, taciturn, and twisted, with just a smidgen of sin to top it off."[10] Bill Clinton, the book contends, is a perfect example of this attitude toward sex, with his own Clintonian spin on the subject: "sin, repent, and sin again."[11]

In addition to his regional upbringing, Clinton's childhood and youth may also help explain why he gravitated toward the political beliefs he adopted. It is true of most of us that the family, culture, and experiences we grow up with heavily influence our social and political views. I grew up with parents who started their own small business. My early years were full of stories from my parents about how taxes and regulations made it more difficult for them to succeed, so I gravitated toward a conservative Republican orientation. Of course, childhood influences can be cast aside in adulthood, when other life experiences and thoughts take over. For instance, conservative author David Horowitz spent his youth as an ardent Communist, Hillary Rodham Clinton calls herself a former "Goldwater girl" and Young Republican,[12] and I exchanged conservatism for libertarianism soon after college.

Between his personal background and the general social conditions that existed as he came of age in the 1960s, it is unsurprising that Bill Clinton found his ideological home on the left side of the political spectrum. The left's call for peace during Vietnam, its faith in government's ability to provide for the basic needs of all people, its emphasis on racial and gender equality, and its core themes of fairness and social justice, would all have appealed to a young Bill Clinton.

Clinton attached himself at a tender age to far-left campaigns and movements, including the 1972 campaign of George McGovern. He opened up a McGovern for President headquarters in New Haven while attending Yale Law School even though local Democratic leaders were not supporting McGovern in the primary.[13] He delivered New Haven for McGovern at the Connecticut state convention that year, and New Haven was one of the "few places in America that voted for McGovern over Nixon" in the general election.[14] He was immediately, immensely successful at persuading people to see things his way, targeting his efforts for McGovern on anti-Vietnam sentiment.

McGovern ran on getting out of Vietnam and cutting defense spending, using the money saved to fix the domestic problems of "rebuilding our cities, renewing our rural economy, reconstructing our transportation system, and reversing the dangerous pollution of our air, lakes and streams."[15] In good leftist fashion, McGovern wanted to accomplish these things by managing the economy to impose "an adequate money supply, reasonable interest rates, and the selective use of wage and price guidelines."[16] As Bill Clinton the politician would later do, McGovern tried to appeal to America's middle class fears, promising that government could "allay the anger of many working middle-income Americans burned by inequitable taxes, unpleasant neighborhoods, and shoddy goods and services."[17] A true leftist, McGovern also insisted that government could cure every ill, from "the lingering curse of racism" and "the plight of hunger" to "bad housing, and poor health services."[18]

After his early taste of politics Clinton focused on running for office immediately after obtaining his law degree. He lost his first campaign for U.S. Representative in Arkansas, but soon found a place in Arkansas state politics as attorney general and then governor. When it came time for Clinton to run for president, he had taken to heart McGovern's resounding defeat by Richard Nixon. Clinton had discovered how to repackage liberalism to appeal to a winning coalition of interests. He was the New Democrat in a whole new era of American politics.

◊

In the novel and movie *Primary Colors*,[19] we find a remarkable exposé of how it might have gone for the Clintons on the road to the White House. Particularly notable is a speech by Libby, close friend and troubleshooter for fictional candidate Jack Stanton and his wife Suzie. (The Libby character was patterned after Clinton loyalist Betsey Wright, whom we'll meet in the next chapter.) Upon learning that the couple is planning to throw a below-the-belt punch at a political opponent, she marvels at how far the two have fallen from their idealistic youth. Libby threatens to go public with proof that Jack believed he had gotten the babysitter pregnant. Libby closes her tirade:

> You see Jack, she hasn't even heard. She's isn't even upset that you f***ed your seventeen year old babysitter. And you know why? It's never the cheat that goes to hell, it's always the one who he cheated on. That's why you can still talk in that tender hearted voice about being in it for the folks and Suzie here can only talk in that voice from hell about your political career....

Here is a fictionalized description of a liberal misogynist: someone who can use and abuse women in his personal life while claiming his behavior doesn't detract from his political merit because the policies he advocates serve a greater good. Because he's in it for the folks, he and his supporters (and even his wife) can excuse his behavior as weakness for which he can be forgiven. For character Jack Stanton, this means he can commit what is probably statutory rape against a young woman, abandon a child he helped create, and betray whatever trust his wife placed in him, while still claiming to stand for the rights of the little people and women everywhere. This is more than simple hypocrisy.

The essence of this fictional character's outburst amounts to our first identification of a tenet of liberalism that plays a role in tolerating misogynistic behavior.

In modern liberalism, political goals justify any political means to achieve them. For example, leftists uphold the goal of nondiscrimination based on race or gender, and feel completely justified using any and all political means to try to accomplish that goal. The impact of their chosen means on individual people, and the burdens they impose on real people in pursuit of their objective, can be conveniently ignored or dismissed as small prices to pay in pursuit of such a worthy cause. Anyone who objects to the means selected to achieve the goal is attacked as heartless and as a terrible person who *wants* racial and gender discrimination to continue.

Let's pick on a favorite issue that continues to divide liberals from conservatives: affirmative action. Liberal ideology gives pride of place to the goal of racial and gender equality in all areas of society—housing, employment, education, the military, etc. Liberals make no distinction between ensuring nondiscrimination *by the government* against citizens, and nondiscrimination *among private people*. With the target of complete nondiscrimination established, liberals over the past thirty years have included affirmative action programs as one of their favorite political means to achieving their goal.

Sidestepping the debate over whether affirmative action is actually *effective* at accomplishing the objective of eradicating discrimination, liberal advocacy of affirmative action dismisses the very real prices paid by individual people who end up injured by affirmative action. Some injuries are psychical, consisting of having freedom of choice taken away by affirmative action requirements. For example, a company that contracts with the government may prefer for any number of reasons to hire subcontractors who happen to be white or men (or worst of all, white men), but affirmative action policies take this choice away from the contractor regardless of the harm it may cause his business by limiting his subcontracting options. (Loss of freedom of choice is given very short shrift in American politics today, unless the choice lost is one to abort an unwanted pregnancy.)

Other injuries caused by affirmative action policies are of a different nature. Consider a white or Asian applicant to a government-funded college who is turned away because an applicant with similar credentials and test scores got a boost in her application score just for being born African American. The first applicant has suffered a very real loss of opportunity, denied on the basis of something entirely out of her control: race. Willingness to accept inflicting that kind of injury on people is one of the aspects of affirmative action that sharply divides liberal and conservative ideologies. Liberals insist that if such cases do occur, it's worth the suffering of those applicants for the greater good of making sure candidates of racial or ethic minority groups are admitted.

Conservatives and libertarians, on the other hand, maintain that political force (the threat of which compels both the contractor and the university in our example) should only be used in limited circumstances. There are ways to achieve worthy goals that do not involve government compulsion. Liberals, however, see political force as a valid means to any end they deem worthy, regardless of the negative impact use of such force has on individuals who pay the price.

Here is where liberalism dovetails with misogyny. For a man who is psychologically disposed to undervalue, mistrust, or dislike women, adhering to a liberal belief system that views individual injuries as mere sacrifices for a greater good can encourage him to behave as a misogynist. It is easier work rationalizing a trail of human wreckage in the wake of careless one night stands, girlfriends on the sly, unwelcome sexual advances, and infidelity to a marriage, when your politics dictate a willingness to accept the sacrifices of others for the sake of achieving your noble goals.

When any individual woman becomes a threat to your political career, the obvious choice becomes silencing, discrediting, bribing, or threatening her to prevent the downfall of your own rise to power, because, after all, your rise to power is for the greater good. Just think of all the women you'll be helping with your policies; a few real-life casualties of your personal behavior just don't matter all that much. When your politics say that the use of governmental force is a legitimate means to any sociopolitical goal, it's easier to look yourself in the mirror after using personal force as a means to a sexual goal. Armed with the ideological conviction that your exercise of political power is for the greater good, an exaggerated sense of your own importance to the world can ease your conscience when you regretfully have to ruin a few lives to prevent certain women from dragging you off the throne.

◊

Elizabeth Ward Gracen, born Elizabeth Ward on April 3, 1961, in Ozark, Arkansas, was majoring in accounting at the University of Arkansas when she won the title of Miss America in late 1981. By the end of 1982 she had married her high school boyfriend and the couple moved to New York City to study acting. In 1983, when she was 22, she met Governor Bill Clinton while on a visit to see her parents back home in Arkansas. [20] She was doing a public service announcement and he offered her a ride back in his limousine. After a flirtatious limo ride they went to the vacant apartment of a friend of Clinton's at the Quapaw Tower in Little Rock. The rendezvous lasted all of two hours, and by her own account "was not a huge success."[21] Clinton called her when she got back to New York, but she told him she was uncomfortable pursuing the relationship and they never spoke of it again. That should have been the end of her story, but instead it was only the beginning.

Her marriage fell apart the following year but her acting career gained some momentum. When her name surfaced in the 1992 presidential campaign, Gracen issued a public statement at the request of Clinton operatives denying she'd ever had sex with the candidate.[22]

Reportedly, Gracen got her big break in show business a week after her manager met with two Clinton pals, Hollywood producer Harry Thomason and campaign chairman Mickey Kantor, in 1992. The film work took her to Croatia and then Brazil. Gracen initially said she felt offended at the idea that Clinton had anything to do with her job offers and protested, "I've worked really hard for all I've got."[23] The timing of events, however, continued to raise suspicions that Clinton tried to help her in exchange for her silence. She prefers to attribute her sudden career successes to her decision to pose in the May 1992 issue of *Playboy*, but even that nudge helped her career in large part due to her fling with Clinton. Today, her manager insists that contrary to previous reports, her appearance on the cover had been part of the *Playboy* deal from the start, and that Gracen was "very disappointed" that the magazine "used" her interview comments about Clinton to help sell the issue. Mostly because of the *Playboy* publicity, Gracen said, "I was very high-profile at the time," explaining why she was offered a role, without an audition, in the movie *Sands of Time*, filmed in Croatia in 1992.[24] Her current manager tells me that Gracen remains "doubtful" about whether Clinton had any involvement with her career.

In 1993 Gracen landed a guest appearance as immortal con-artist Amanda on the *Highlander* television series. For those of you who are unfamiliar with the series, the tagline for *Highlander* was "There can be only one." One might wish that Bill Clinton followed the same motto. Her television character proved sufficiently popular to bring her back the following season, and she stayed for the run of the show. Her public silence appeared to have paid off, though for years she continued to deny that any career advancement came as a quid pro quo from Clinton—"If the president of the United States was on the phone pulling strings for me, I'd be on *Seinfeld*. I'm not standing on the front of the Titanic with Leonardo DiCaprio, am I?" she retorted to one reporter.[25] Six months later, though, she sounded less sure of Clinton's noninvolvement with her career, admitting that after she agreed to deny the affair in 1992 she "suddenly got a very good acting job, a mini-series in Croatia, and then I got another good, long-lasting role in Brazil."[26]

When lawyers for Paula Jones began trying to serve Gracen with a subpoena in late 1997, her life became a bit more complicated. Her name arose in Paula Jones's lawsuit against Clinton when a friend of Gracen's, Judy Ann Stokes, stated under oath at her own deposition that when Gracen had privately confided in Stokes about the encounter with Clinton, Gracen had been "tearful" and had said the sex was not something she had wanted.[27]

Around Christmas in 1997 a mysterious caller Gracen could not identify warned her that a subpoena was underway and advised her not to be around. She spent the next few months "jet-setting between the Caribbean, Canada and Paris,"[28] trying to avoid being served—and being hounded by more threatening phone calls. She told *The New York Post* she was "physically scared," and has been quoted as saying that while on vacation in New York unidentified men in suits, let in by the innkeeper, ransacked her room.[29] Under this kind of pressure, she hired attorney Bruce Cutler, best known for serving as John Gotti's lawyer.

In 1998, caught in the middle of rumors about being forced into sex with Clinton, Gracen finally came clean and admitted to having a one-time affair with former governor Clinton. During her initial interview about the fling in the spring of 1998, she said, "I had sex with Bill Clinton, but the important part to me is that I was never pressured... We had an intimate evening. Nothing was ever forced."[30] She was coming forward to avoid getting dragged into the Paula Jones case. Since her affair with Clinton was consensual and she wasn't a state employee, her story had no relevance to Jones's claim of sexual harassment and wasn't something she wanted to discuss. "The lies gain credibility every day that I don't address them... This is something I don't want to talk about at all. It's no one's business."[31] When asked what she thought of her friend Judy Stokes's deposition testimony about the sex between Gracen and Clinton being forced, Gracen said, "I never told her that Bill Clinton pressured me or harassed me. I don't know why she said that. It baffles me."[32] She continued, "That never happened. It's completely false. It insults all women who have been sexually harassed."[33] Gracen added, "I was very young, but I always knew what I was doing. It's behavior I wouldn't recommend to any young woman, no matter what degree of glamour or glitter there seems to be at first."[34]

In April 1998, Gracen appeared on NBC and apologized to Hillary Rodham Clinton. "What I did was wrong, and I feel very, very bad about it now.... That's not the way a woman should treat a woman,"[35] Gracen said. That kind of remorse and sense of responsibility Gracen felt as the "other woman" is understandable and even admirable. But if Gracen thought she was playing into the Clintons' good graces by rescuing Bill from allegations of rape and apologizing to Hillary, she was sorely mistaken.

In the summer of 1998, Gracen got another call from the same voice that had warned her about the subpoena, this time telling her she'd better shut up about her affair with the president or she could lose her career or be audited by the IRS. According to her lawyer, letters from the IRS soon began arriving at her parents' address, which was not listed in her tax filings, claiming she hadn't filed returns and threatening to seize her wages and property.[36] One of her lawyers, Vince Vento, said at the time, "She pays her taxes…. She's really square. I don't think anybody wants to take on the government…. She just feels it's completely unfair…. The only person who would benefit would be the president of the United States, unless there's some other agenda out there."[37] Gracen's manager told me that looking back, the IRS incident "was bizarre," but Gracen is "doubtful that Clinton had anything to do with it." Maybe her tax number just came up coincidentally, but maybe not. She isn't the only Clinton woman to receive an unexpected IRS audit after going public—Paula Jones and Juanita Broaddrick, whose stories we'll examine in later chapters, also found themselves on the wrong end of IRS investigations.[38]

In a 1998 interview Gracen said of Clinton, "Every week on the show I battle evil. But all those evil people have a charming side. Have I made my point?"[39] In an interview about her television role on *Highlander: The Raven* in August 1998 she admitted, "It's been a nightmare…. I was dragged into the media; my family and friends were staked out."[40] In another 1998 interview she concluded, "This whole thing is a car wreck. Everybody's damaged…. It's about power, egos and agendas. It's very Machiavellian. It's scary for all the women involved."[41] She regretted that she'd been dragged into what she called "this horrible chess game" and said, "I think Clinton is a very dangerous, manipulative man and I've had to be very careful."[42]

Luckily for Clinton (though not for Gracen), whatever negative impact he had on her life has since been overshadowed by an even more dangerous, manipulative man.[43] Her experience with this man was even more frightening because instead of just a one-night stand, as with Clinton, it was a man she'd allowed into her life for two years. In late 1999, Gracen discovered to her shock that the man who had been her lover and business advisor for two years was actually a conman. While she knew him he used the name Pat Augustus, posing as an investment banker and international businessman who swooped into her life just in time to help her handle the press when the Clinton scandal began to catch up with her. In the end Augustus forced her into bankruptcy and left her terrorized. He went to such lengths to manipulate her, lie to her, and steal from her, that she is left bewildered about the truth of much of what occurred in 1997 and 1998. Once she discovered that Augustus (later arrested and charged with fraud and embezzlement in Paris under the name Pat Austin[44]) was deceiving and swindling her, she had no way of knowing how much of the harassment she'd suffered in 1997 and 1998 had come from Clinton's cronies looking out for his career, and how much had come from Augustus himself.

Looking back now, Gracen's present manager tells me, "Austin [a.k.a. Augustus], not Clinton, was the true villain." Augustus was posing as a protector and friend, but in reality he manipulated and frightened Gracen "into believing she was involved in a political tug-of-war that could threaten her livelihood, her family, her life." Gracen's manager continues, "She will never [know] exactly what happened, but she is certain she was misinformed during the time." He also insists, "She regrets making some of the comments she made in 1997/1998." How much of Gracen's suffering was due to Clinton, and how much to this supposed conman boyfriend, is a question apparently even she cannot answer, but it's still clear that Gracen made a grave tactical error by indulging in an affair with Bill Clinton.

◊

The kind of intimidation and harassment Gracen suffered as a potential witness against Clinton isn't exactly a far cry from Clinton's modus operandi. When it comes to scaring off women who threaten his career, reporter Suzi Parker has her own story about Bill Clinton.

Parker is a freelance journalist in Arkansas. In 1998 she was working with a whistleblower, a physician on contract to provide services in the Arkansas state prison system. Under a pseudonym, this whistleblower had written a fictionalized account of the dangers he observed in the Arkansas prison system's plasma program. Throughout the 1980s and early 1990s (while Clinton was governor) the prison system permitted prisoners to sell their plasma for $7 per pint.[45] The plasma was then sold to Canada. The catch: the prisoners' plasma was so poorly screened that over 42,000 Canadians were infected with Hepatitis C, and thousands more with the HIV virus.[46] Despite attempts by the FDA to shut down the prison plasma program, Governor Clinton and his cronies kept the company collecting and selling the prison plasma licensed and in business.[47] Because the private company (run by a Clinton friend and supporter) kicked back half its profits to the prison system on plasma it sold, "plasma became a profitable enterprise" for the prison system, the prisoners, and possibly Clinton's friends and political supporters.[48]

The Canadian government finally traced the infected plasma back to the Arkansas prison system, yet the American press largely failed to pick up the scandal. Parker worked tirelessly on the story, exposing the history of the plasma program and the involvement of key political figures, including Clinton. After publishing a lengthy piece (one of the first and only stories on this scandal to appear in American media),[49] Parker began receiving mysterious, threatening phone calls in the middle of the night. A couple of months later, Parker published an article about a press conference at which a group of hemophiliacs infected by the tainted Arkansas blood threatened a lawsuit against the Canadian government and possibly against Bill Clinton and other Arkansas officials.[50] While attending the press conference Parker says she knew she was being watched and followed, perhaps by government agents. "It was creepy," she told me, but she continued reporting on the surfacing scandal.

That is, until May 1999, when the plasma scandal whistle-blower's clinic in Pine Bluff, Arkansas was firebombed; on the same night, the hemophiliac group's office in Canada was burglarized.[51] The hemophiliac group had been working closely with the whistleblower to prepare the threatened lawsuit on behalf of Canadians infected with Hepatitis C and HIV from tainted Arkansas prisoners' blood.[52] Between the intimidating phone calls she'd been receiving and the violent arson and burglary patently designed to deter investigation into this scandal, journalist Suzi Parker got the message and backed off.

It's not in a reporter's nature to quit a story, but by 1999 Parker had been in Arkansas long enough to see how Clinton operated and to feel genuinely frightened for her safety. While we may never know who actually set the fires and burglarized the offices, Parker tells me that she is convinced that Clinton and his associates were behind the intimidation tactics. If they were, then they escaped any repercussions. When Canadians eventually filed a lawsuit, they named only Canadian officials and companies. The American press more or less ignored the story—and the connection between this Canadian health care tragedy and the governor of Arkansas who kept the tragedy in motion for so many years.

Whether or not Elizabeth Ward Gracen's career boosts came as a quid pro quo for her years of silence about her affair with Clinton, she moved on with her life and built a successful career for herself. After a friend testified about her having sex with Clinton years after the fact she began receiving an ongoing string of veiled threats, putting her in fear for herself and her family. Only then did she speak out about their affair. Trapped in Clinton's tangled web of women who could derail his career, Gracen found herself hounded, audited, and threatened to the point of stating in one interview that she wanted Clinton to do a cameo on her modern-day swashbuckling show so she could cut his head off.[53] After being taken for a ride by her conman boyfriend, Gracen today is at a loss to know which bizarre, intimidating incidents in her life to attribute to that man and which to Clinton. The details will never be known for certain, but her life-damaging encounter with Clinton is our first illustration of Bill Clinton's liberal misogyny in action.

◊

Nothing about Elizabeth Ward Gracen's liaison with Bill Clinton constituted sexual abuse. He didn't force himself on her, she responded willingly to his advances, and while she regretted her choice to sleep with him, at least it was her choice. Gracen is certainly not alone on a long list of women with whom Clinton had consensual affairs. She's on another list, however, of women whose lives have been significantly damaged by Clinton and his cadre in attempts to prevent them from ruining his career. While Gracen is one of Clinton's women who did not suffer physical abuse at his hands, her encounter with Clinton harmed her in very palpable ways. For her trouble, she isn't even footnoted in *My Life*.

Gracen's story highlights a particular feature of Clintonesque mistreatment of women: when push comes to shove, *his* life is a thousand times more important than *theirs*. For whatever reason, Bill Clinton could not resist climbing into bed with Gracen in 1983, and when he feared that choice could harm his career, he (1) asked her to lie about it publicly, (2) played the benefactor providing career assistance as insurance for her silence, and (3), pressured her with mafia-style anonymous threats and possibly used his political office to sic the IRS on her when (1) and (2) failed to keep her quiet. While we may not be able to prove in a court of law that the threats came from Clinton, it seems almost certain that they came from a Clinton associate looking out for his career. All of it added up to one notion: nothing about Gracen as a person mattered to Clinton nearly as much as his own political ambitions. Not her self-esteem, not her integrity, not her peace of mind, not her financial life. Some hero for women's rights.

At least Clinton called her the morning after (well, soon after). At least when she told him she'd rather not do it again he had the decency to accept the rejection. In a superficial sense, he boosted her self-esteem, perhaps, by expressing his desire to see her again and then taking her rejection in stride. If she felt any temporary feeling of pride or conquest at the chance to rebuff the governor, though, it was short-lived. Nothing about Clinton's subsequent treatment of Gracen exhibited a care in the world for her self-esteem. To the contrary — that this so-called supporter of women's rights relentlessly persecuted her for becoming a potential witness against him surely diminished her personal sense of being competent to cope with the basic challenges of life.

Asking (and expecting) Gracen to lie about their affair also showed a complete lack of regard for Gracen's integrity. Rather than stand willing to face consequences that might flow from his own choice, Clinton expected Gracen to help him cover it up. A well-known Twelve Step program tells its members, "We're only as sick as our secrets." Clinton never intended to permit Gracen the personal autonomy to choose whether and when to share her secret about a sexual encounter; his public image trumped her right to direct the course of her own psychological well-being. As if it wouldn't have been bad enough to ask her to keep quiet, she was pressured to lie about her experience. Most moral codes, whether Judeo-Christian in origin or not, consider honesty a key virtue. Clinton's earnest request that Gracen lie about their affair showed disdain for Gracen's integrity, further illustrating his lack of concern for her as a person.

When the stuff began hitting the fan, the Clinton cadre showed no regard for Gracen's peace of mind or financial security. In fact, they defined the success of their efforts by the destruction of both. Anonymous threatening phone calls and IRS audits put Gracen through mental and emotional trauma. They affected her day to day life by forcing her to hide from process servers to avoid ending up stuck between an intractable judicial system and the thugs responsible for Clinton's dirty work. The Fifth Amendment to the U.S. Constitution protects a person from being forced to testify against herself. The U.S. Supreme Court has explained that the purpose behind this constitutional right is to protect a person from facing the Cruel Trilemma of (a) perjuring herself, (b) telling the truth because she was forced to testify and thus implicating herself, or (c) refusing to testify and then facing contempt of court charges. When Gracen found herself facing these three options, her only way out, as she saw it, was to escape service of the subpoena in the first place.

More than some other Clinton women, Gracen played along with Clinton's game as much as she could. She lied for him, kept quietly going about her life, and tried desperately to escape subpoenas that would have put her in the nasty position of either committing perjury in his defense, or exposing their affair and risking retribution.

Perhaps sensing she would crack under the pressure and go public, or perhaps hearing rumors that Gracen had no intention of lying under oath, the Clinton scandal team took care of business. Amidst threats of personal and financial harm, Gracen took the advice of her lawyer and told her story to the press. Though she may not have realized it, she chose the route other Clinton women have chosen: going public, even years after their sexual encounters with Clinton, in order to raise their public profiles enough to feel a bit safer. Maybe Gracen thought the rumors about Clinton raping her provided her with additional security; by going public she could "help" him by quelling those rumors.

At the same time, she probably hoped that declaring once and for all the consensual nature of her fling with Clinton would encourage the Paula Jones lawyers to lose interest in her as a witness, since her testimony about a completely voluntary sexual interaction shouldn't have been very valuable in helping Jones prove a pattern of sexual harassment. Perhaps that's also why she denied for months that Clinton had helped her career; Jones's lawyers were trying to prove a pattern of Clinton boosting the careers of women who had consensual affairs with him and harming careers of those who refused his advances.

It's hard to blame Gracen for wanting to stay out of the legal mess and be left alone by the media, lawyers, thugs, and IRS. She, and we, will never know whether her life would have been more or less complicated if she had stayed quiet until and unless forced to answer questions under oath at a deposition. All we know is that despite her best efforts to build her own life after crossing paths with Bill Clinton, the experience severely impacted her life for years.

Clinton's behavior toward Gracen says something about his own self-esteem that sheds light on why he mistreated her the way he did. The National Association for Self-Esteem (NASE) has adopted a definition of self-esteem premised on two aspects: competence and worthiness. As psychotherapist Nathaniel Branden puts it, self-esteem is "the disposition to experience oneself as being competent to cope with the basic challenges of life and of being worthy of happiness."[54] Clinton's behavior toward Gracen, on the other hand, closely matches up with the NASE's description of a person with low or false self-esteem:

> [B]ehaviors that might be described as egotistic, egocentric, conceited, boasting or bragging, bullying, taking advantage of, or harming others are defensive behaviors indicative of a lack of self-esteem...[and] should not be confused with authentic, healthy self-esteem.[55]

Clinton exhibited neither a sense of worthiness nor competence in his mistreatment of Gracen, perhaps suggesting a lack of authentic self-esteem on his part. Devoid of a sense of worthiness, any feelings of competence he garnered in bedding a Miss America beauty queen amounted only to arrogance in conquest. Lacking a genuine sense of his own competence to cope with life, he relied on a sense of entitlement to get what he wanted. He succumbed to narcissism and expected good feelings to be handed to him rather than earned. That is, instead of earning the reputation he desired among his constituents, the press, and his family, he acted as if a good reputation was something he deserved regardless of whether his character, demonstrated through his behavior, merited it. When Gracen threatened to tarnish the carefully sculpted reputation he thought he had going for him, he had no qualms about sacrificing hers for his. Clinton the politician may have garnered praise from feminists as a champion of so-called women's rights, but Clinton the man had no trouble treating individual women like Gracen with utter disrespect, expressing through action a belief that he is inherently superior to and more important than his women.

◊

Clinton's mistreatment of Gracen flies in the face of what the women's rights movement has struggled to achieve for over a century. The year 1848 marked a turning point for women's rights in this country. Elizabeth Cady Stanton wrote her Declaration of Sentiments and Resolutions, presented at the women's rights convention held in Seneca Falls, New York.[56] An enduring, eloquent portrait of the struggle for women's rights, Stanton's Declaration of Sentiments called not for government help in obtaining abortions and affirmative action for women in the workplace, but for certain legal reforms to equalize the law's treatment of men and women, like equitable divorce laws, granting women the right to vote, and removal of laws that permitted men to forcibly control and punish their wives. Stanton also appealed to men's consciences for social acceptance of women into all aspects of life, including church and government affairs, education, and the professions.

Outraged by what she viewed as the tyranny by which men ruled over women, Stanton wrote, "He has made her morally, an irresponsible being, as she can commit many crimes with impunity, provided they be done in the presence of her husband... He has created a false public sentiment by giving to the world a different code of morals for men and women... He has endeavored, in every way he could, to destroy her confidence in her own powers, to lessen her self-respect, and to make her willing to lead a dependent and abject life..."

Bill Clinton's mistreatment of women flouts so many of these original feminist goals it's hard to know where to start. We've seen that Clinton's treatment of Elizabeth Ward Gracen contributed to her moral denigration by asking and expecting her to lie for him. Clinton's apparent expectation that *he* can have affairs with impunity but that a woman who dares disclose her part in an affair with him should be publicly and personally hounded helped "create a false public sentiment by giving to the world a different code of morals for men and women." Gracen's experience with Clinton doubtless left her with diminished "confidence in her own powers" and lessened her self-respect. Finally, Clinton demonstrated no belief at all in Gracen's "right and duty" to promote righteous causes of her choosing and participate equally "both in private and in public, by writing and by speaking." Clinton's mistreatment of Gracen embodied what Stanton called an "authority adverse" to the self-evident truth of women's equality "to be regarded as...at war with mankind."

Liberal misogyny is personal in its effect on real-life women, but some of its causes are political. Betraying all the principles women like Elizabeth Cady Stanton fought for, a liberal misogynist like Clinton uses political power to make abortions more accessible while truly treating women as second-class citizens in the sense railed against by the early women's movement. Problematically, the very ideology that equates women's rights with political support for reproductive rights turns a blind eye to personal, misogynistic behavior when it involves one of their favorite sons. Modern feminists have almost completely lost sight of the original goals of the women's movement, twisting the goal of equality of the sexes into political agendas pushing exclusively leftist policies. Liberalism holds that a worthy goal justifies any political means to achieve it. Clinton found this strategy useful; his worthy goal of attaining high office for the benefit of women everywhere justified using any means necessary. With this kind of a mindset, it's easy to understand why he would not hesitate to use intimidation against a former lover like Gracen—not to mention a muckraking journalist like Suzi Parker—to prevent any individual woman from getting in the way of his lofty political aspirations.

Because modern liberalism has strayed so far from the original, exemplary goals of feminism, today's liberal ideology helps create a particular strain of misogyny that praises only *political* intervention in women's lives and glosses over the way women are actually treated on a *personal* level. As a woman, Gracen can thank Bill Clinton for the politically-imposed "protection" of being able to walk into an abortion clinic without harassment from protestors, but sadly, also has him to thank for repeated assaults on her personal equality, integrity, and psychological well-being.

With a protector like this, it's no wonder that this former Miss America once felt it necessary to flee her own country.

CHAPTER THREE

LIKE A GOOD LITTLE GIRL

IN THE SUMMER OF 1992, the Democratic National Convention took place in New York. On July 16, the Democratic Party formally named Clinton its 1992 presidential nominee. The next day on her syndicated television show, Sally Jesse Raphael interviewed a woman named Sally Miller Perdue, then a fifty-three year old former Miss Arkansas who had an affair with Bill Clinton in 1983.

The *Los Angeles Times* ran a biting piece in its calendar section, barely concealing its contempt for "Sally Jesse (There's Nothing She Won't Do for Ratings) Raphael" and blasting her for allowing Sally Perdue to "smear Clinton's character."[1] The opening line: "Oh, my. What's a poor talk show host to do?" On the show, Raphael said she and the show's producers went "back and forth" about whether to do the Perdue interview, deciding to air the show "with a bit of skepticism and a bit of reluctance."[2] The *Times* reporter wrote in mock sympathy, "You could feel her anguish, her humanity."[3] To Raphael, Sally Perdue said she didn't want her story told in a "slimy or bimbo way," nor did she want Republicans to exploit her story.[4] When someone in the audience asked Perdue if she was trying to damage Clinton's campaign, Perdue said she'd never want to do that. When asked if she believed Clinton truly supports women's issues, Perdue answered, "I think he's saying what people want to hear."[5]

Not even a week later, Michael Isikoff reported for *The Washington Post*, "The Clinton campaign is conducting a wide-ranging effort to deflect allegations about the Democratic nominee's private life and has retained a San Francisco private investigator, Jack Palladino to discredit stories about women claiming to have had relationships with the Arkansas governor."[6] Isikoff quoted Clinton aide Betsey Wright (a woman who worked closely with Clinton since their days on the McGovern campaign and who later served as the basis for the aforementioned character Libby in *Primary Colors*[7]) as saying that since the Democratic National Convention earlier that month, nineteen women had alleged sexual relationships with Clinton, in addition to the seven women that were already "being monitored" by the campaign.[8] Wright, who claimed credit for the moniker "bimbo eruptions," dismissed the allegations as "Scud missile[s] on American politics" and the women who leveled them as gold-diggers.[9] Isikoff reported, "In recent months, Palladino's activities have helped the Clinton team douse a number of stories that threatened to revive the issue of the governor's private life."[10]

When Betsey Wright and the Clinton team learned that Sally Perdue was planning to claim an affair with Clinton, Palladino, the investigator, "began calling former associates and estranged relatives of the woman [Perdue] seeking damaging comments about her credibility."[11] Finding at least one such "estranged relative" of Perdue's, the Clinton camp passed that person's name to interested journalists who had begun making inquiries into Perdue's story. Isikoff concluded, "The approach appears to have worked. Although Perdue later told her story on [*Sally Jesse Raphael*], no major news organization has reported the account."[12] Cinching Clinton's ability to quash Perdue's story, Isikoff noted, is that "Perdue has no corroboration for her account, and Clinton denies even having met her."[13] In a move disconcerting to her,

Arkansas state troopers would later corroborate Perdue's account.

In January 1994, just weeks before Paula Jones went public, foreign papers reported Sally Perdue's story as if it were breaking news. Perdue gave an interview to the London *Sunday Telegraph*, disclosing details of her four-month affair with Clinton.[14] From August to December 1983, Perdue told the British newspaper, Clinton came to her home in Little Rock at least twelve times, where the two of them shared their love of music, goofed around, and yes, had sexual relations. At the time, Perdue was a local radio talk show host in Little Rock. Perdue said she used to play the piano at her home, accompanying Clinton on his saxophone. "He had this little boy quality that I found very attractive," she reminisced. "When I see him now president of the United States, meeting world leaders I can't believe it...I still have this picture of him wearing my black nightgown, playing the sax badly.... How can you expect me to take him seriously?"[15]

Clinton had Arkansas state troopers assigned to the government's mansion deliver him to Perdue's house for these rendezvous. "They'd pull up in a wooded area about 30ft from the house and wait there. When Bill was ready to come out he would signal using my patio light, flicking it on and off." This corroborated the stories from state troopers who had alleged in December 1993 that they had been used by Clinton to finesse his extramarital activities. Perdue said the affair ended abruptly over political differences of all things; in 1984 she ran unsuccessfully as mayor of her home town, Pine Bluff, Arkansas. As a Republican. Against Clinton's wishes.

Perdue described Clinton as a "showman," a "brilliant actor," and as a man who "craved approval and needed the constant affection of women." Perdue continued, "I think this whole business needs to come out into the open so that the American people can make up their minds," but doubted that the American press would be willing to help much.

Perdue also came forward with a chilling account of being threatened into silence by Clinton associates. In August 1992, she said, a Democratic party operative named Ron Tucker grilled her and then threatened her not to talk about her liaison with Clinton. If she agreed to behave like a "good little girl" she would be set up for life with a federal job and a regular monthly paycheck. Of course, there was a flip side: "If I didn't take the offer, then they knew that I went jogging by myself and couldn't guarantee what would happen to my pretty little legs. Things just wouldn't be so much fun for me any more. Life would get hard." The FBI reportedly acknowledged that a third party overheard the threats and filed a complaint.[16]

Perdue turned down Ron Tucker's "generous" offer and found herself fired from her job as a college admissions officer at Linwood College in Missouri. After she found her car suspiciously damaged and received anonymous phone calls and hate mail, she kept quiet, "went into hiding," and moved to St. Louis, working in a home for adults with Down Syndrome.[17] Apparently her *Sally Jesse Raphael* interview had not been well-received by the Clinton machine. On coming forward again in 1994, Perdue said "I was forced into the open because troopers mentioned my name last month. The media started pursuing me. I hold no animosity toward Clinton, but I greatly dislike the tactics of Democrats who have tried to portray me as some bimbo. If I speak out now, maybe the truth will come into the open."[18]

Not likely. *The Economist* (United Kingdom edition) reported in February 1994 that "NBC had filmed an interview with Miss Perdue before she spoke to the [London] *Sunday Telegraph*, but it has not yet broadcast it." Apparently, *The Economist* concluded, "The heavyweight American press has considered it beneath its dignity to carry the story."[19] The London *Sunday Times* quoted a *Newsweek* reporter admitting that "the press is willing to cut Clinton some slack because they like him and what he has to say."[20] Not until the press had been through denials about Paula

Jones, Kathleen Willey, and Monica Lewinsky would they later turn on Clinton.

The Boston Globe published an editorial in March 1994 by a staff writer who opined:

> In the past several weeks, much new evidence has surfaced indicating that Bill Clinton consistently and recklessly lied about what one can no longer call his private life. His former bodyguards, the Arkansas state troopers, have told many a bawdy tale of skirt-chasing. Sally Perdue, a former Miss Arkansas, says she was threatened into silence during the 1992 campaign. An Arkansas state employee named Paula Jones says she was sexually harassed by Gov. Clinton in 1991.
>
> Big Media has ignored these stories, which have been relegated to publications popularly (and inaccurately) viewed as marginal: *The Washington Times*; the *American Spectator*; London's *Sunday Telegraph* (!). . . .
>
> It's not that the allegations of sexual misconduct are incredible. On the contrary, "everybody believes the troopers," says one news magazine editor. Rather, it is because many male editors identify with Bill Clinton. Who hasn't had trouble with his marriage, as candidate Clinton candidly confessed before entering the 1992 race?[21]

This editorial summed up the general sentiments of public and press for the first couple of years of Clinton's presidency. In May 1994, not long after Paula Jones emerged on the scene, *The Washington Post* acknowledged that Sally Perdue's story existed—but only in an article denigrating the British press for picking up stories on Clinton's sex life that the American press wouldn't touch.[22]

Sally Perdue rarely spoke up publicly after 1994. In 1996, author Roger Morris (not to be confused with political consultant Richard "Dick" Morris, who worked with the Clintons starting in 1977 and also has written books about them) released a book, *Partners in Power: The Clintons and Their America*,[23] citing Sally Perdue as one of several people willing to admit she had seen Clinton use cocaine. Morris, an experienced political biographer (and a liberal) known for his books on Richard Nixon, Alexander Haig, and Henry Kissinger, wrote that Clinton's biological father and his stepfather had been notorious womanizers, and their behavior was tolerated by Clinton's mother. As Clinton rose to power in Arkansas state politics, Morris reports, Clinton's own womanizing went from bad to worse, and Morris accused Washington's "culture of complicity," including major media and Beltway insiders, of sloughing off evidence that Clinton had physically and verbally abused women.[24]

In an article published by *The Toronto Sun* in July 1996, (apparently American media wouldn't publish him on this topic) Roger Morris revealed more details of Sally Perdue's "break-up" with Bill Clinton:

> When she told him she was thinking of running for mayor of Pine Bluff, Clinton bristled. "You'd...you'd better not run for mayor," he warned her, and the relationship ended in an angry argument. He was clearly upset that she had crossed a line, Perdue remembered. A "good ole boy," as she recalled him, he had wanted a "good little girl" as an intimate. "I don't think he really wanted me to be an independent thinker at that point," Perdue would say.[25]

The "good little girl" line would come back to haunt Sally Perdue when it was thrown in her face as a threat after Clinton had announced his bid for president.

By mid-1997 the Paula Jones sexual harassment lawsuit against Clinton was in full swing, garnering widespread media attention to Clinton's history of encounters with women. Sally Perdue made many lists of women whom commentators speculated the Paula Jones lawyers hoped to depose. By March 1999, even *Investor's Business Daily* weighed in with an article reporting the "diverse" group of women, including Perdue, who "charge that Bill Clinton personally assaulted them, or, through his 'agents' or 'people,' threatened to do them or their families physical harm."[26] *IBD* even quoted the president of a renegade state chapter of NOW that broke ranks with the national organization over Clinton's behavior and warned White House female staffers to be careful: "Mr. Clinton is an abuser of women....Is there anyone there to protect them? Can they report an assault safely, or will they and their families be threatened?"[27] *IBD* cautioned, "To be sure, there is no direct proof that Clinton or anyone working on his behalf bullied women."[28] After running through the long list of women who have openly complained against Clinton or his cadre, *IBD* reached Sally Perdue's name and quoted *Arkansas Democrat-Gazette* columnist Gene Lyons as saying, "Sally Perdue's a nut....I wouldn't believe anything she says."[29] (The following year, Lyons co-authored a book purporting to uncover the right-wing plot to sabotage Clinton's career.[30]) The nuts-or-sluts smear tactic, as the National Organization for Women eventually called it, proved useful against many women.

By January 2001 when *The Weekly Standard* tried to contact the "Women of the Clinton Scandals" to follow up on their lives, staff writer Matt Labash couldn't even track down Sally Perdue,[31] though at one point she had told a media representative she intended to write a book on her encounters with Clinton.[32] She never did publish such a book, and Clinton's autobiography makes no mention of her.

Quietly, outside the public and media radar, she began working in 2001 in Pennsylvania as director of fundraising and public relations for a Quaker organization called the West Chester Meeting of Friends.[33] In late 2004 her name surfaced again. More than twenty years after her affair with Bill Clinton, the experience still adversely affects her life. Using the name Myra Belle Miller (presumably to deflect precisely the sort of negative attention at the heart of her complaint), she filed a federal lawsuit against the Quaker group complaining that her employers have been sexually harassing her after finding out about her affair with Clinton.[34] Now 65 years old, she still battles an image as one of the sluts who seduced the former president.

◊

Sally Perdue—just like Elizabeth Gracen and reporter Suzi Parker—experienced serious mistreatment at the hands of Clinton's intermediaries. In fact, her specific, chilling account of attempted bribery and not-so-subtle threats of bodily injury designed to ensure her cooperation strikes all the same chords as Gracen's and Parker's tales.

As with Gracen's story, Perdue's gives us a couple of "Well, at least . . ." thoughts to consider before dealing with the heart of the mistreatment issue. Well, at least the sex was consensual. Well, at least she holds no grudge against Clinton, blaming instead only the messengers who delivered the bribes and threats. However, by making a talk show appearance during the 1992 campaign Perdue played along a bit less helpfully than Gracen, and received in return a bit more unwanted attention from the Clinton crowd. Running for mayor of her hometown over Clinton's objections was the first way she failed to behave as Clinton demanded. Refusing point-blank to accept any job offers as bribes for her silence during his 1992 campaign was another. Even without the help of major American media, Perdue made her story known, and that was definitely the wrong move for a "good little girl."

Her story was buried by the early Clinton campaign by making direct threats against her personal safety and feeding disparaging statements about her to curious journalists. Looking back, it's striking that journalists inquiring about Perdue with the Clinton campaign would be deterred on the basis of statements about Perdue made by admittedly "estranged relatives" of hers. I daresay most of us can think of a few relations who would be willing to air a little dirty family laundry in a similar situation. No journalists except Sally Jesse Raphael publicly talked to Perdue's family members and friends who believed and supported her. The Clinton campaign's spin machine worked hard to malign Perdue and bury her story, and when that didn't stop her from talking to the press, switched from name-calling to attempted bribery. When that didn't work, they moved on to intimidation.

Remember that our look into the stories of Clinton's women isn't about whether his extramarital affairs should have disqualified him with voters from becoming president, or whether his adultery should have made him impeachable once in office. This isn't even about whether his adultery and ensuing cover-up included abuses of power (like using state resources to facilitate his liaisons) that should have knocked him out of the race or out of office. If Sally Perdue had simply told her story back in 1992 and Clinton had responded, "So what? That's between me and Hillary," he might still have become president of the United States. If the press had widely reported her account we all would have had a few giggles at the thought of Bill Clinton playing the sax in Sally's black nightgown, but, well, as editors across America concluded, who hasn't had marital problems? Unfortunately for Clinton, for the public, and especially for Sally Perdue, it didn't go down quite like that. The feature of Perdue's story that transforms Clinton's behavior toward her from mere philandering to real mistreatment is his use of smear and scare tactics to bully her into keeping quiet.

Wait, you might be saying, Clinton didn't threaten her personally. Perdue only told us about some Democratic party thug who threatened her. True enough. Except for their break-up, when Clinton made it clear that he wanted her to be a good little girl and not do anything so independent as run for office in Arkansas, Clinton didn't do the dirty work himself. It's even possible that Clinton never personally "ordered" anyone associated with him to take specific actions with respect to shutting up Sally Perdue. Who allegedly recruited Ron Tucker to threaten Perdue may never be known. (For the record, Tucker has denied involvement with the threat against Perdue.) Clinton's personality and position of power suggest that it would be more typical for him to just expect the people around him to take care of that kind of unpleasantness. People like Betsey Wright, whose primary professional goal for a solid decade was keeping Bill Clinton out of hot water.

When Clinton seriously considered running for president in 1988, it was Betsey Wright who sat Clinton down and made him list every woman who could cause problems for him, trying to make Clinton "get past what she considered his self-denial tendencies and face the issue squarely."[35] Biographer David Maraniss writes of Betsey:

> For years, she told her friends later, she had been covering up for him. She was convinced that some state troopers were soliciting women for him, and he for them, she said. Sometimes when Clinton was on the road, Wright would call his room in the middle of the night and no one would answer. She hated that part of him, but felt that the other sides of him overshadowed his personal weaknesses.[36]

After making the list with Clinton, "[s]he went over the list twice . . ., the second time trying to determine whether any of the women might tell their stories to the press."[37] This was in 1988, and "[a]t the end of the process, she suggested that he should not get into the race. He owed it to Hillary and Chelsea not to."[38] He might have taken her advice in 1988, but by 1991 he knew he would enter the 1992 race. Those closest and most loyal to him would have to fend off the inevitable stories of his relationships with women to the best of their ability. And they did, to the detriment of women like Sally Perdue.

◊

Conservative author, intellectual, and activist David Horowitz said in an interview once that the supposed "New left," of which he was a part in his youth, "pushed the Democratic party pretty far to the left and got rid of the Hubert Humphrey wing more or less," though even he and his card-carrying Communist comrades of the day had been quite disillusioned with actual communism after Khrushchev revealed

Stalin's brutality.[39] Mr. Horowitz's involvement with leftist and conservative movements, in different periods of his life, gives him valuable perspective on the inner workings of each.[40]

When asked his thoughts about the relationship between today's liberalism and communism, Horowitz quoted James Burnham as saying, "The difference between the Communists and the liberals is that the Communists know what they're doing."[41] (Burnham was the intellectual force behind *The National Review* and author of many books, including *The Managerial Revolution*, which warned against the dangers of exchanging individual freedom for an increasingly bureaucratized, managed society.) Horowitz continued:

> Liberalism often departs from the Communist left in terms of its choice of means. They want the same ends but they don't have the stomach for the brutality that's necessary along the way. ...Liberals are people who do believe that society causes all the problems.... And all that means is that they're going to get the government to stick its hands in your pockets and pick out what you've earned and give it to somebody who couldn't or wouldn't earn it themselves.[42]

Horowitz's insights help us arrive at our second identification of a tenet of liberalism that can engender misogyny in someone like Clinton already predisposed to undervalue women.

Modern liberalism relies on intermediaries to take care of the unpleasant tasks of enforcing the means to their political ends. Liberal ideology, like socialism and communism, focuses on "social ills" it believes can and should be cured by government intervention. Modern liberals in the United States are generally complacent about permitting business, trade, and social interactions to occur freely—but not too freely. Most liberals aren't outright socialists demanding government *ownership* of the economy, but they use legislation and regulation to establish nearly-plenary government *control* over the economy. This kind of backdoor string-pulling doesn't stop with business; today's liberals also advocate legislation and regulation that increasingly controls private behaviors from smoking cigarettes to owning firearms; from what you can build on your own property to whether you can let slip an off-color joke at the office.

The control that liberal ideology demands be exercised over every aspect of the world in which we work and play is always for the good of some down-trodden group or class of people who "need" such intervention on their behalf in order to have a fighting chance. Laws banning smoking in restaurants and bars across the country, for instance, were partly justified as measures necessary to protect waitresses who apparently found themselves victimized by unwanted second-hand smoke and unable to find jobs in non-smoking environments.

Laws and regulations make amazing, almost magical tools, in the hands of liberals. Angry at a corporation for tearing down that community center and stacking an office building in its place? Get a zoning board to regulate that kind of decision. Frustrated at skyrocketing rent in your neighborhood? Nothing that a little government-imposed rent control can't fix. Feel sorry for the single mom who can only find work at McDonald's? Help her out by forcing companies to pay minimum wages and overtime. Of course, some laws and regulations are more effective than others at actually achieving their own aims. Even the effective ones, however, impose heavy costs on those obligated to spend time and money complying; and it's barely worth trying to raise the cost issue in terms of diminished freedom of choice, autonomy, and happiness to people forced to comply. As Ludwig von Mises, one of the most influential economists of the twentieth century, once wrote, "If a man *forces* his fellow citizens to submit to his own standards of value, he does not make them any happier."[43]

There are entire schools of philosophical, economic, and political thought that insist that society functions best when people are allowed maximum freedom to make their own decisions and interact with each other on a voluntary basis. That premise is not embraced by liberal ideology. Modern liberalism insists that every aspect of our lives is up for grabs in terms of regulating our actions so that we'll make decisions liberals think are best. When David Horowitz said "Liberals are people who do believe that society causes all the problems," note that "society" really means all of us going about our daily business, interacting with one another as we see fit. In other words, *we* cause the world's problems, and *we* need to be regulated and conformed to liberal ideals of how human beings should act and treat each other.

In a representative government like ours, all liberals have to do is convince enough politicians to agree about how "we" should behave, and presto! A new law or regulation appears, and our sphere of autonomy over our own choices shrinks correspondingly. Of course, our Constitution supposedly takes some areas of choice out of the eager hands of politicians, but liberals (and some conservatives) are guilty of ignoring that when they feel passionately enough about their particular cause. For example, modern liberalism, with its roots in the progressive movement of the late 1800s, eventually convinced the Supreme Court to abandon its protection of economic freedom by declaring "freedom of contract" practically a dead letter. This allowed the proliferation of economic regulation as we know it today, from occupational licensure laws to federal guidelines on carpal tunnel syndrome. Social conservatives, for their part, are currently up in arms demanding that the Constitution be revised to preclude gays and lesbians from marrying. The concept of personal autonomy takes a back seat to the desire of some to control the behavior of all.

Horowitz's differentiation between liberalism and communism highlights a crucial feature of liberal ideology. In his words, liberals "don't have the stomach" for the brutal means utilized by communism to achieve the social equality that lies at the core of each ideology's vision. Turned off by the thought of an outright dictatorship that openly, relentlessly, disproportionately, and often arbitrarily enforces its edicts at the point of a gun, liberals—who hate guns anyway—use intermediaries to carry out their demands. Institutionally, these intermediaries consist of government courts and agencies. Our long history of peaceful exercise of political power in this country has engendered a deep respect for the sanctity of the law. Most people eschew private violence for obtaining revenge, justice, or redress and instead turn it over to the justice system. Likewise, most people charged with wrongdoing submit to the authority of courts, agencies, boards, and committees. Misuse of the legal and regulatory system to punish people for technical wrongdoing that hasn't inflicted any real injury on others may be inciting a growing disrespect for the law in this country, but even today most people feel fairly confident in our justice system.

On a micro level, the intermediaries liberals rely on to enforce their wishes consist of nameless, faceless civil servants whose job it becomes to keep tabs on us, write us up, collect our required paperwork, and of course call us to task for breaking any of the rules. Aside from the showy, pompous "congressional hearings" that occur incessantly and give politicians the chance to grill and humiliate anyone they want to pick on, it's never the liberal ideologues themselves who *personally* order us to pay fines, tell us we can't remodel our homes without their permission, strip someone of her occupational license for a red tape violation, or drag someone off to prison for an extra-long sentence because of his *presumed thoughts* (i.e., "hate crimes").

Unlike communists, liberals don't barge into our homes in the middle of the night searching for evidence of wrongdoing or take it upon themselves to literally shoot first and ask no questions later if one of us doesn't comply with their desires or dares question their authority. No, liberals use institutions and individuals as intermediaries to enforce their demands on us. These intermediaries create a veneer of civility and softness covering their control mechanisms, leaving us with more of a sense of freedom than would life in the old Soviet Union.

We've already seen in our first identification of liberal ideology that once liberals deem a goal worthy, any political means are fair game to accomplish it. Our second identification of a tenet of liberalism builds on that to help explain the politics behind Clinton's liberal misogyny: with a worthy goal in mind, making sure it gets accomplished is left to intermediaries. Your hands and conscience can stay technically clean when you can rely on others to do whatever it takes to get the job done.

◊

In 2001, a political science professor and a business consultant published an article analyzing the Clinton presidency, asking whether Clinton lived up to his 1992 promise to govern as a "New Democrat."[44] Comparing Clinton's presidency to those of Democrats and Republicans throughout the twentieth century, these scholars concluded that Clinton broke ranks with traditional Democrat policies and governed more conservatively—more like Republican administrations—in several major policy areas including macroeconomic policy, fiscal policy, and monetary policy The only major policy area in which Clinton's New Democrat credentials were "relatively weak" was regulatory policy.[45] The authors surmise that Clinton's approach to inflation, unemployment, discretionary spending, interest rates, and the money supply took the Democratic Party in a "more conservative, New Democrat direction" but his attitude toward regulation "maintained a commitment to certain aspects of the liberal agenda" and ideology.[46]

The authors concluded, "The president needed an acceptable arena in which to pursue liberal policies. Regulatory policy provided it."[47] Budgetary concerns in Washington prompted by the skyrocketing deficits of the 1980s made regulation a more viable, acceptable, and effective method of implementing liberal goals than overt spending and wealth distribution, particularly to achieve aims like government activism in health care, education, and the environment. The study pointed to Clinton-era regulatory measures like "[g]oing after Microsoft and tobacco, regulating the health-care sector, calling for minimum-wage hikes and strict ergonomic standards, and favoring new environmental regulations" all of which helped shift the cost of government activism to private entities, preserving the image of governmental fiscal restraint.[48] And that doesn't even count the Clintons' failed attempt to overhaul the entire health care industry and place it under micromanaged government control.

The New Democrat approach is the same old liberal ideology; it's just relegated itself to certain avenues of activism to accomplish the heart and soul of its program. Forcing us to behave the way liberals think we should has become a task of regulation rather than direct manipulation of the economy FDR-style. Shifting the financial burden of accomplishing the liberal agenda to the private sector through endless federal regulations and bureaucratic hoops has become the favored means for New Democrats to achieve their goals.

An astoundingly astute politician, Bill Clinton learned early in his political career to align himself as a New Democrat, sensing the American public tiring of traditional tax-and-spend liberalism. That's why then-first term Governor Clinton supported Jimmy Carter over Ted Kennedy in the Democratic primary of 1980. When it came down to "practical politics," both Clintons supported Carter's unsuccessful bid for re-election that year, to the surprise and disappointment of some of their left-wing friends who thought Ted Kennedy had the right ideas.[49] Clinton could see that an alliance with Ted Kennedy could do nothing to help him in his own re-election as governor in 1980, so he supported Carter. Both Clinton and Carter lost their jobs to the "Reagan Revolution" in 1980, although Clinton won back the governorship in 1982. After these 1980 defeats, Clinton focused on "what it would take for an activist Democrat to make it to the White House,"[50] as biographer David Maraniss put it.

By the time he reached the White House, Clinton the politician had figured it out. The left couldn't criticize him too much as long as he continued using regulation to achieve far-left goals, yet his presidency appeared fiscally responsible, slashing the deficit and constraining government spending. Aside from his 1993 tax hike raising the top marginal rate to 39.6 percent, tax rates stayed about even through the '90s and he introduced many tax credits that lowered the overall tax burden. Perhaps he had hoped that sweeping health care reform would have been to his liberal legacy what Medicare was to LBJ's, but that dream was quashed by Congress. Regulation and Executive Orders were the most viable outlets for Clinton's liberal agenda.

As early as 1944, the economist Ludwig von Mises commented on the trend toward bureaucratization; how "Congress has in many instances surrendered the function of legislation to government agencies...and it has relaxed its budgetary control through the allocation of large appropriations for expenditures...."[51] Until the New Deal era the Supreme Court regularly declared it unconstitutional for Congress to leave too much rulemaking and decision-making to unaccountable agencies, commissions, boards, committees, etc. This "non-delegation" doctrine has been nearly eviscerated now, permitting what some legal scholars have aptly called our fourth branch of government: administrative agencies. Mises warned, "On the other hand, we must realize that delegation of power is the main instrument of modern dictatorship. It is by virtue of delegation of power that Hitler and his Cabinet rule Germany."[52] Writing in the midst of Hitler's inexorable fist of power over the German people, Mises tried to call our attention to the simple fact that extensive control requires extensive babysitting.

Liberal politicians intent on fixing all society's problems have only to command, "Save those spotted owls!" and it's up to civil servants to carry out the demand and confront anyone whose plan for their own property conflicts with the liberals' goal of protecting the birds. Liberals can say, "It's such a shame that so many people get repetitive stress injuries at work; let's require employers to provide breaks and ergonomically-designed equipment," and leave it up to government employees to audit offices, field complaints from disgruntled workers, and hold administrative hearings to discipline offending businesses. Implementation of their commands becomes someone else's job, leaving them free to pat themselves on the back for furthering their worthy cause without ever having to see up close the toll of compliance on individual people.

◊

All Sally Perdue experienced *directly* from Clinton was boyish charm and the excitement of a forbidden love affair with a powerful man. When she became a threat to Clinton's ambitions, it wasn't Bill Clinton who showed up on her doorstep threatening her safety. It was a complete stranger, a political operative. Speaking vaguely about some powerful people wanting her to keep quiet, this intermediary warned her that only good little girls get to keep their pretty little legs. He was just doing his part to further Clinton's noble quest for power, for the benefit of everyone. Everyone except Sally, that is.

Think of it from her point of view in that moment. You've carried on an affair with the governor. The governor angrily broke it off with you when you made it clear you didn't intend to play the role he demanded of you. Someone patently representing his interests found you. This stranger is now telling you he and others know you go jogging by yourself, and that there's no telling what could happen to you unless you behave yourself. You're deeply offended and have no interest in taking this "federal job" your intimidator is going on about. You're scared, too. But what good is it to go to the police when you know that state law enforcement officers were the ones who had facilitated Clinton's visits to you in the first place?

If you're Sally Perdue, you start to regret your decision to appear on *Sally Jesse Raphael* and you quickly opt to keep quiet. You keep a low profile for a year and a half, until those damn troopers drag your name back into the spotlight. Not wanting any part of the scrutiny that's beginning to come your way, you try to preempt it by going back to the media to tell again of your brief affair with Clinton and disclose the threats you received last time. Maybe that will call off the dogs. When a woman named Paula Jones gets the whole thing rolling again later that year, you do your best to avoid interviews and subpoenas. If Clinton had enough gall and clout as a state governor to treat you the way he did, imagine what he has at his disposal as president of the United States.

Every once in a while, you feel a ripple of anger at being so mistreated. Behave like a good little girl? Just who does he think he is? You may have been a beauty queen in your youth, but you have built yourself a decent, meaningful life. You have goals and ambitions of your own, though none quite as lofty as becoming president. You find yourself on endless lists of "bimbos" and "gold-diggers" even though you never made a dime off your story and naively thought the American people deserved to know some personal history of a man they might want to elect president.

Telling Perdue to be a "good little girl" drips with condescension and disrespect for her as a person. Showing no sense of appreciation for her as a living, breathing human being with rights equal to their own, Clinton's "people" treated her as a shell of a person who could and should be bought off or scared off. It's no wonder that Perdue claimed that Clinton was "saying what people want to hear" when it came to women's issues.

Clinton needed to become president in order to do all the good things he envisioned for so many people. None of those good things could be done if someone tarnished the public's image of him too much. Could that "someone" have been Sally Perdue? Probably not, but it wasn't worth the risk. After indulging in his fun with Perdue, Clinton was off and running toward his ultimate goal again. With Pennsylvania Avenue as his benefi-cent goal, Clinton's politics primed him to be able to count on other people, intermediaries, to do whatever it took to keep him on track. He couldn't resist going to bed with Perdue, but her independence and security meant nothing to him. In this case, he didn't even have to think about her or know what was happen-ing to her. He'd set a goal—for the greater good, obviously—and left implementation of that goal to those around him. Liberals rarely have to witness the frustration, pain, and burden suffered by real people trying to comply with their demands. Clinton, too, never had to see Sally Perdue's face when she was badgered and threatened in order to safeguard his goals.

At least twice in ten years, Clinton or his cadre left Sally Perdue under orders to be a "good little girl." The phrase reveals much about how they viewed this woman. The phrase is at once parental and chauvinistic, insinuating that *he* knows best; *her* thoughts aren't valuable; there are things that girls just can't or shouldn't do. Early and modern feminists alike would justifiably bristle at being told to act this way. It's demeaning, and it re-moves the person at whom it's directed from full personhood into a constricted realm of stereotype. Compliance is demanded of the "girl" not because it's right but because *he* demands it.

Whatever his political positions on abortion and other so-called "women's issues," Clinton's treatment of Perdue demon-strated personal disrespect and an attitude of superiority, especially evident when he angrily told her she'd better not run for mayor. *His* ambitions counted; hers didn't. *His* goals needed to be achieved at any cost; hers didn't. When she emerged as a potential threat to his plans, neither her reputation nor her physical safety mattered. He might have enjoyed sleeping with her, but her interests didn't count compared to his. Perdue was just another *she* Clinton used. She was replaceable, expendable; a body, not a person.

Clinton's attitude toward and treatment of Perdue gelled under the influence of multiple interwoven factors, some emotional, some psychological. And many ideological.

CHAPTER FOUR

MADE FOR EACH OTHER

I N OCTOBER 1991, Arkansas's youngest-ever governor made the most ambitious career statement a person can make: "I am declaring my candidacy for president of the United States."[1] Still youthful at forty-five, Bill Clinton had already weathered seventeen elections in Arkansas, including primaries and run-offs. When he threw his lot in with the pack of Democratic presidential hopefuls that year, Clinton and his team figured their radar screens already revealed the range of potential problems for the national campaign and doubted any real bombshells could explode. His Arkansas opponents had long ago dredged up charges of infidelity, and an Arkansas journalist for a small paper had already coined the nickname "Slick Willie."[2]

Surprisingly, it was actually not a woman who stirred up the trouble in Arkansas that tainted Clinton's national reputation from the minute he announced his candidacy. State employee Larry Nichols, fired in 1988 for making unauthorized phone calls to aid Nicaraguan rebels, sued Clinton in 1990 over his termination and included names of specific women he alleged had affairs with the then-governor, facilitated by state resources like law enforcement personnel and state vehicles. Nichols eventually withdrew his lawsuit, but only recanted allegations of affairs with one of the five women he named.

Clinton denied the allegations along the way, but left enough wiggle-room in how he phrased his denials to force major newspapers from the very start to add comments such as, "Many of the rumors are demonstrably false. Clinton, however, has never flatly denied accusations of past infidelity, saying he should not be measured against a standard of 'perfection.'"[3] That kind of equivocation did more than anything else to keep the press gingerly mentioning Clinton's "problem" as he entered the national race.

The Larry Nichols lawsuit lingered in Clinton's background as more of a nuisance than a danger until a New York tabloid picked it up and ran with it in January 1992. The tabloid named names, and the media began to fret about how to cover the story when no woman allegedly involved had come forward. Of course, when women did come forward the question quickly became how they could "substantiate" or "corroborate" their stories, which in a he said, she said situation is rarely possible. As we've previously seen, Sally Perdue had tried to break her silence in the summer of 1992, but her story was successfully squashed before it picked up steam due to the efficient efforts of the Clinton scandal team. Other women, like Elizabeth Ward Gracen, were helping Clinton by keeping quiet and even issuing written denials of involvement with him in order to satisfy inquisitive reporters and would not come forward until years later.

Before any womanizing charges had hit the national media as more than whispers of rumors, Bill and Hillary had appeared before reporters to preempt such lines of inquiry. Clinton had long faced down a reputation of philandering around Arkansas, and just before officially entering the presidential race, he and Hillary told the press together that they'd worked through problems in their marriage and intended "to be together thirty or forty years" more.[4] It proved a useful tactic, discouraging the press from prying further into this man's past personal issues when he'd (sort of) already come clean about not being perfect.

The same strategy had worked in Arkansas to save Clinton from an ignominious end to his political career before it had really begun. When Clinton first assumed the governorship in 1978 the position ran for a term of only two years. By his re-election bid in 1980 he had angered voters with a license plate fee hike for education reform that helped cost him the election. He campaigned out of office for the next two years and introduced his official campaign for governor in the 1982 cycle by buying television time for a one-minute *mea culpa* telling voters that "his daddy never had to whip him twice for the same thing" and if they gave him back his job he'd never make the same mistakes again.[5] It worked like a charm, immunizing him during the 1982 race from almost every criticism leveled at him by his opponents. Political consultant Dick Morris, the man behind this almost-apology strategy, recalled, "The polls showed a tremendous backlash of sympathy for Clinton because he had already apologized…. People said, 'What's Tucker [Clinton's strongest primary opponent] dumping on him for? He already apologized. It's a rare man who can admit his mistakes."[6] Morris sold the Clintons on the almost-apology approach by comparing it to a smallpox vaccination: you get a little sick at first, but then you're immune.[7]

Still, from the very start of Clinton's presidential candidacy nearly every major news article introducing him to the country mentioned the rumors of womanizing that had dogged his footsteps throughout his career. The press carefully used the words "rumors," "alleged infidelities," and "unproven accusations" when broaching the topic. A typical article covering the Clinton campaign in the beginning included a statement like this: "Many analysts believe his campaign's major problem would be if anyone substantiates rumors, which have followed him for years, that he has had extramarital affairs."[8] In the thirteen months before candidate Clinton became President-elect Clinton, infidelity and draft-dodging emerged as issues that turned "Character!" into a political battle cry and left the mainstream media in fits of self-conscious psychoanalysis over its coverage of an official's private life.

Clinton initially tried to separate himself from his Democratic rivals by emphasizing the importance of character and good old-fashioned values. Democrats "should not be afraid to defend the values they were raised with," Clinton insisted early on in his campaign.[9] In the preseason of the campaign, Clinton aide George Stephanopoulos stated: "Specificity should be the character issue of 1992."[10] After his candidate's personal character had been under fire for months amidst classic-Clinton part-denial/part-admission evasiveness, Stephanopoulos admitted those words were "really going to come back to haunt me."[11] The campaign quickly turned from a "character counts" theme to "It's the economy, stupid."

In January 1992, a new name appeared on the pages of America's newspapers and opinion journals that would help change the debate over character. And what a name, too! Gennifer Flowers. With a "G," she insisted. (In the December 1992 issue of *Penthouse* Flowers said, "They can bury me upside down and kiss my a-- as long as they spell Gennifer with a G."[12] Classy.) Within weeks she would become a virtual synonym for "gold digger," "bimbo," and "white trash out for cash." When commentators cheered 1992 as The Year of the Woman, they probably didn't have this one in mind.

A New York tabloid, the *Star*, first published Gennifer Flowers's account of her affair with Bill Clinton—which had flickered on and off from 1977 through 1989—in January, at a point when the 1992 Democratic nomination was still up for grabs. The story (a *twelve-year* affair complete with pet names for each other's, umm, private parts), its heroine (a dark-roots blonde wannabe singer in her forties), and its medium (a supermarket tabloid, for crying out loud) together reeked of sensationalism, luring Clinton into a sense of security in denying it. Which he did. Sort of. At least until he was eventually compelled to testify about the matter.

Six years to the month after Gennifer Flowers had gone public and Clinton had repeatedly denied sexual involvement with her, Clinton vindicated Ms. Flowers. Never to her face, never in whole, and not willingly, but he admitted under oath that he had sexual relations with her. Gennifer Flowers was not the first woman to be put through the Clinton versus Women cycle of exposé-denial-smear; we saw that happen to Sally Perdue, and we'll see it happen again to Paula Jones and Kathleen Willey. But Gennifer Flowers was the first Clinton woman whose story garnered widespread media attention and attracted vicious public attacks from Clinton and his cadre. By the time the truth spilled forth from Clinton's mouth in a sworn deposition, Flowers was merely a footnote to the erupting scandal surrounding Monica Lewinsky. Even today, Flowers remains the only specific woman other than Lewinsky with whom Clinton has confessed to having an extramarital affair.

Revisiting the role Gennifer Flowers played in the 1992 presidential election isn't a glimpse into a particularly dignified era of American politics. However, her story, Clinton's reaction, the media's coverage of it, and her life after Bill, illustrate important aspects of how Clinton's liberal agenda impacted his treatment of women.

◊

Eura Gean Flowers grew up in Brinkley, Arkansas,[13] a town about seventy miles east of Little Rock. Brinkley's current mayor, Billy Clay, welcomes visitors to his town through its Web site by boasting of Brinkley's "most important asset—the great people that live and work in Brinkley."[14] This Web site advertises Brinkley as "surrounded by entertainment opportunities" including the Annual Fall Roundup Festival featuring "arts, crafts, duck-calling contests, chili cook-offs, softball tournaments, and the Miss Eastern Arkansas Beauty Pageant."[15] After graduating high school in this small town in 1968, young Geannie, as she was called, began using the name Gennifer in her singing career[16] and legally changed her name to Gennifer Flowers.[17]At age eleven she recorded an album under the name Geannie Flowers, and recorded another album under the nickname Little Scooter at age thirteen.[18] One of her favorite memories is performing "When the Saints Go Marching In" at Pete Fountain's Bourbon Street club on a trip to New Orleans with her parents in her teen years.[19] She sang in nightclubs around Arkansas, studied nursing for a while, and eventually took a college journalism class and started working for a Little Rock television station.

In 1977 Flowers was twenty-seven years old, with dark hair not yet dyed blonde, still dreaming of making it as a singer and reporting for the local TV station. After her connection to Clinton became headline news, Little Rock residents described her variously as a good local singer, a failed has-been, a "proverbial nice girl," and a woman who serially latched onto wealthy, powerful men. Perhaps the truth was somewhere in between, surmised one reporter, but it was going to be near-impossible to find it in Little Rock.[20]

Flowers interviewed Arkansas Attorney General Bill Clinton in 1977, and he began visiting her off and on for intimate encounters that spanned twelve years. His first words to her were "Where did they find you?"[21] They spent their first evening together talking, and he left with just a kiss on her cheek.[22] "It was wonderful…. I was hooked," she said. Clinton has "a lot of soul and emotion," she added. It wasn't the power that attracted her ("How much power do you think the attorney general of Arkansas had?"); she just thought he was "wonderful in general." He'd tell her he wanted to be president someday and she'd say "Honey that's nice" while thinking "how likely is that" to herself. But he always treated her with respect. He loved her ideas and goals and was proud of her for being an "independent, liberated woman." Well, at least as long as her independence and liberation didn't pose any threat to his objectives.

They continued their affair even when she moved out of the state in the late 1970s to pursue her singing. She lived at various times in Tulsa, Oklahoma; Branson, Missouri; and Dallas, Texas, but whenever she'd return to Arkansas, she and Bill would rendezvous at a variety of locations. When they first started seeing each other, Bill and Hillary had only been married eighteen months and didn't have a child; she and Bill even talked about the possibility of him leaving his wife, though she realized at some point that would never happen. She loved him, and believed he loved her.

When she returned to Little Rock in the mid-1980s, she moved into the Quapaw Tower at his request; he was now governor and told her he had aides living in that building so it would make it easier for him to pursue their relationship. [23] Per Bill's request, she communicated with him through government employees who could be trusted to keep everything discreet.[24] Two of those employees, former Arkansas state troopers Larry Patterson and Roger Perry, confirmed their facilitation of Flowers's affair with Clinton when they told the press in late 1993 that they assisted with arranging the trysts for half a dozen long-term affairs and innumerable random sexual encounters while assigned to the governor's mansion.[25]

She stayed in the affair for so many years because she was completely in love with him and believed even thirty minutes of "wonderful" with him was better than a lifetime of "OK" without him.[26] She also came to realize that they both seemed to be "addicted to the sexual excitement."[27] Bill was always a risk-taker; once, he wanted her to make love with him in a bathroom in the governor's mansion while his wife and fifty guests were just a few feet away out on the lawn.[28] In some ways she felt like she was more protective of his marriage and reputation than he was, since she'd be the one to nip those risky suggestions in the bud.[29] When she and Bill would appear at the same functions together, she'd discourage him from spending too much time next to her, out of respect for his family.[30] One night he jumped out of bed and put his back against the wall, crying.[31] He never explained, but she sensed he was feeling guilty.[32]

As Clinton's career escalated, so did the rumors of his extramarital dalliances. In her book, Flowers says she asked Bill about several women and believed most of his denials. When his former bodyguards went public with stories of countless liaisons, some with prostitutes, she began to wonder how safe it was to continue a relationship with Bill; after all, she had always trusted him enough never to insist on using condoms.[33] Flowers writes that from her personal experience with Bill, she knew he "felt an enormous sense of power from leading [her] into sexual adventures, so he very likely enjoyed using that power and influence he had as governor to conquer other women, too."[34] In her opinion, "I think Bill was addicted to the chase, not the sex act itself, but the actual conquering of all those women."[35] Her book *Passion and Betrayal* contains many similar insights into what makes Bill Clinton tick.

Flowers broke it off for good in 1989 when she had met someone else she cared for, a wealthy stockbroker named Finis Shelnutt. Bill was "sad" but "not surprised" and he wanted her to do well and have a good life.[36] Even after she got engaged, he kept in touch with her as a friend.[37]

One former friend would later say that Flowers had bragged about her affair with Clinton as her future ticket to fame and fortune years before the story broke.[38] Flowers's name first appeared publicly linked to his, however, not by her own disclosure but in a lawsuit filed against Clinton by disgruntled fired state employee Larry Nichols. After the Nichols lawsuit tossed her name out in 1990, Flowers's boyfriend, Finis Shelnutt, broke up with her.[39] He said she denied her affair with Clinton when he first confronted her, but when the rumors persisted he called it quits with Gennifer.[40] A local radio station had mentioned her name in connection with the Nichols lawsuit, and when she denied her affair to her boyfriend, she told Shelnutt she was going to sue the radio station for slandering her.[41] In January

1991 she even had a lawyer send a letter to the radio station threatening to sue for defamation, but she never filed a lawsuit.[42]

With no love and no money (her singing career wasn't doing so well), Flowers began calling on Clinton to find a state job. She contacted him requesting employment at least once by phone in September 1990, and at least once by letter in February 1991.[43] Clinton put an aide in charge of helping Flowers out, and she was finally offered a job as an administrative assistant with the state unemployment review agency, paying about $17,000 per year, in June 1991, just weeks before Clinton declared his presidential candidacy. Clinton appointee Don Barnes—head of the Arkansas Board of Review and Flowers's supervisor—said Flowers was hired based on merit pursuant to state guidelines.[44]

Even before the Nichols lawsuit cast the national spotlight on her, Flowers found herself in an uncomfortable position when an applicant for the job Clinton helped her get filed a complaint with the state grievance committee, alleging the only reason Flowers got the job was that she was having an affair with Governor Clinton.[45] When she learned she'd have to testify before the grievance committee, Flowers called Clinton, who told her to deny ever having an affair with him.[46] Appearing before the panel, Flowers was spared answering allegations about the affair because Don Barnes, who conveniently was also the head of the grievance committee, stopped the questioning.[47] Barnes had tried to avoid an investigation altogether but the other committee members outvoted him.[48] When asked under oath by the committee how she'd learned of the open position, she lied and said she'd see an opening in the newspaper; she made no reference to getting help from Governor Clinton.[49] The state grievance committee still ruled in favor of the complaining job applicant on the grounds that numerous state procedures had been violated in hiring Flowers and recommended compensating the rejected applicant, but Barnes refused to follow the committee's ruling.[50] When Flowers told Clinton all about this, and how she'd lied to the committee, he said "Good for you."[51] Good practice, too, for when she would be expected to lie publicly about her affair with him. She might have been willing to, but caught in a wave of confusion, emotion, and pressure from all angles, she turned out to be a woman Clinton couldn't count on when he needed her most.

◊

Gennifer Flowers's life hummed along as she bounced from gig to gig, struggling to make it as a singer, her days and nights punctuated by frequent rendezvous with Bill Clinton, until about a year after she had ended the affair and her involvement with him began to create complications. Because of the rumors flying around from the Nichols lawsuit, strange disturbances began cropping up and she was advised to tape record her conversations with Bill Clinton. She felt strange about doing it at first, but thought of the tapes as insurance in case something happened to her.[52] Her apartment had already been ransacked once, she and her mother had received phone calls threatening her physical safety, and she was afraid.[53] She once told him about her home being broken into and he said, "You think they were trying to look for something on us?" The tone in his voice made her suspect maybe it was Clinton who "had this done to [her]."[54] Maybe it was also the way he immediately asked her if phone records were among the items that were taken. A partial transcript of that conversation, courtesy of the Flowers Tapes, reads:[55]

> CLINTON: You think they were trying to look for something on us?
>
> FLOWERS: I think so. Well, I mean…why, why else? Um…
>
> CLINTON: You weren't missing any, any kind of papers or anything?
>
> FLOWERS: Well, like what kind of papers?
>
> CLINTON: Well I mean did…any kind of personal records or checkbooks or anything like that…? Phone records?
>
> FLOWERS: Do I have any?

CLINTON: Yeah…I wouldn't care if they…you know, I, I…They may have my phone records on this computer here, but I don't think it…That doesn't prove anything.

Another portion of the Flowers Tapes captures Clinton saying, "They [reporters] can't run a story like this unless somebody said, 'Yeah, I did it with him'" and then musing, "I wonder if I'm just going to be blown out of the water with this. I don't see how they can [garbled word] so far if they don't, if they don't have pictures."[56] Clinton had "an almost mystical faith in the absence of photographs," and as long as none turned up he felt invincible denying everything.[57] In typical Clinton fashion, he was partially correct. No pictures emerged, and Flowers's word was mud by the time Clinton and his gang finished trashing her. His word continued to carry some weight, even though on one tape from December 1990, just after he'd won re-election as governor, Clinton tells Flowers of a reporter questioning him about a list of women's names, including Flowers's; on tape Clinton says to Flowers, "God…I kinda hate to deny that!…I told you a couple of years ago, one time when I came to see you, that I had retired. And I'm now glad I have because they scoured the waterfront."[58]

In January 1992 the *Star* tabloid ran a piece about the Nichols lawsuit. Flowers had refused to talk to the *Star* but her name and picture appeared in the story anyway. Clinton immediately faced questions from the press about the article. He called the story "trash,"[59] "an absolute lie,"[60] and "totally bogus."[61] "You know the *Star* says Martians walk on earth and people have cow's heads," Clinton said smilingly during the opening round of the scandal that would follow him for the next eleven months.[62] *The Washington Post* published Clinton's denials and added that its reporters had been unable to substantiate any of the alleged affairs and had been told by some of the women named that they had not had trysts with Clinton.[63] London's *Sunday Times* reported that Clinton's aides privately admitted the governor had an affair a decade earlier but "has since been happily married."[64] In his autobiography Clinton arrogantly recounts the way he responded to press inquiries about the Gennifer Flowers story. When an Associated Press reporter hit him with a question about the women named in Larry Nichols's lawsuit, Clinton suggested the reporter contact the women Nichols had mentioned. Clinton writes, "He did, they all denied it, and the story basically died."[65] Even today Clinton apparently has no qualms about the fact that he denied an affair with Flowers even though he later confessed to it. Clinton elaborates on his reaction to the Flowers scandal:

> We [the campaign] didn't know what was on whatever tapes Flowers might have, but I remembered the conversations clearly, and I didn't think there could be anything damaging on them.
>
> Flowers, whom I'd known since 1977 and had recently helped get a state job, had called me to complain that the media were harassing her.... I commiserated with her, but I hadn't thought it was a big deal.
>
> The press reported that Flowers had been paid for the story, and that she had vigorously denied an affair a year earlier. The media, to their credit, exposed Flowers's false claims about her education and work history.[66]

On January 19, 1992, Clinton participated in a televised debate with his Democratic rivals and "took it on the chin" when Senator Tom Harkin accused Clinton of proposing "Reaganomics" (God forbid) and moderator Cokie Roberts questioned his political viability in light of the now-circulating rumors of marital infidelity.[67] The insinuations were a "pack of lies," Clinton protested, blaming Republicans for spreading rumors about him and assuring his audience that after running in seventeen elections there was nothing to fear from skeletons in his closet.[68] You have to wonder if he still "hated to deny it," and, for that matter, if he'd really "retired."

On January 23, 1992, *The New York Times* printed an op-ed by political science professors headlined "Has Clinton Said Enough?; A Yes or No Will Do."[69] The professors noted that Clinton had recently responded to a reporter's question ("Have you ever had an extramarital affair, governor?") by retorting "If I had, I wouldn't tell you."[70] The political scientists opined that voters deserved a straight answer because "a male politician's record of philandering says far more about his basic attitudes toward women than any number of policy papers or speeches on women's issues."[71] But Clinton continued in the vein of indignant denials coupled with vague admissions throughout the campaign.

Barely a week after the *Star* published its rehash of the Nichols lawsuit, Gennifer Flowers went public with her story—in the *Star* tabloid. Her appearance fed the fermenting interest into Clinton's "woman problem" for two reasons: she was the first woman to substantiate rumors of infidelity after he'd announced his candidacy, and she had audio tapes proving at least that Clinton knew her. Flowers had gone to New York with her lawyer to try to convince people to keep her name out of the public arena. When she arrived, she realized how out of control the situation was and that her name was going to be published with or without her acquiescence.[72] Only then did she agree to take money from the *Star* to come forward and tell her side of things. Hindsight being 20/20, she would have preferred her story come out in a more respectable way, but she's said, "I didn't have a master plan that I was accused of. I was a little girl from Arkansas [and] I was very scared at that point."[73] Once she decided to tell, she told it all, and she spent the next six years with her "dukes up" because "he denied our relationship and then he let loose his spin doctors to try to destroy me."[74]

No one knew quite what to make of this woman, bold as brass, proclaiming her love for Bill and how he broke her heart by denying their long, torrid affair. No one quite knew, either, what to make of her tapes—phone conversations between her and Bill recorded over the course of several months, the last in early January 1992. Clinton never expressly confirmed or denied that it was his voice on the tapes, but he acknowledged having talked to her on the phone, and implicitly admitted it was his voice on the tapes by protesting that some of the conversations took his words out of context and actually apologizing for at least one statement he made on those tapes. Clinton's defenders publicly accused Flowers of doctoring the tapes, leading her to initiate a years-long defamation lawsuit against James Carville and George Stephanopoulos, which has been dismissed and appealed several times and is still on-going. The Clinton team had private investigator Anthony Pellicano evaluate the tapes, and he determined they'd been doctored.[75] The same Pellicano was eventually caught hiring a thug to threaten to kill a *Los Angeles Times* reporter to get her to lay off a story about Hollywood ties to the Mafia; Pellicano was sentenced to two and a half years prison time on charges of illegal possession of firearms and explosives.[76]

In Flowers's interview in the *Star* she detailed the twelve-year affair, saying she had loved Clinton but was "sick of the deceit, of all the lies" and had come forward after hearing Clinton call the *Star*'s previously-published allegations about an affair with her "trash" and "bogus."[77] Flowers said, "For twelve years I was his girlfriend and now he tells me to deny it—to say it isn't true."[78] It was drama at its soap-opera best. The *Star* article claimed Flowers had tapes of fifteen phone conversations between Flowers and Clinton. One clip of a conversation printed by *Star* had Clinton telling Flowers: "If they [the press] ever hit you with it, just say no and go on. There's nothing they can do. I expected them to look into it and come interview you. But if everybody is on record denying it, no problem."[79] There would be no problems, Clinton assured Flowers on tape, "as long as everyone hangs tough."[80] Unfortunately for Clinton, Ms. Flowers didn't "hang tough" for long.

Clinton and his team responded immediately. For his part, Clinton repeatedly told the press, "The affair did not happen,"[81] "The story is not accurate"[82] and "The story is just not true."[83] But he also reminded everyone that he and his wife had been candid about the existence of past problems in their relationship and they had a strong marriage now. Denial on the one hand; some kind of admission on the other. No wonder the story wouldn't disappear. Hounded by one reporter shouting, "Can you prove your innocence?" Clinton replied, "I don't know if I can. The other charges I've always been able to actively, affirmatively disprove."[84] At this point in time this statement was generally true; he had managed to persuade some women, as we saw with Elizabeth Ward Gracen, to deny their affairs with him, and to discredit and silence others before their stories gained widespread publicity, like Sally Perdue the previous summer. After all, the campaign had for months been paying investigator Jack Palladino to collect affidavits from potential blabbermouth women; if they resisted, Palladino's assignment included taking other measures, like scraping up all the information he could to raise questions about their credibility or mental stability.[85]

Clinton admitted speaking with Flowers more than once over the phone, but insisted he'd only ever told her to tell the truth.[86] Just a few days into the uproar, Clinton decided to appear with Hillary on CBS's *60 Minutes* to try and put the story to bed (so to speak). On January 26, 1992, Super Bowl Sunday, Clinton told correspondent Steve Kroft and millions of Americans that the Gennifer Flowers story wasn't true, that she was only a "friendly acquaintance,"[87] but also said "I have acknowledged causing pain in my marriage."[88] Clinton refused to answer whether he'd ever committed adultery, appealing to everyone's desire for marital privacy. When Kroft told Clinton that the questions hadn't disappeared because Clinton's answers weren't clear-cut denials, Clinton responded, "Of course it is not, from your point of view, and that won't make it go away."[89] Huh?

Flowers had refused to talk to the press when her story came out in the *Star*. However, the day after the Clintons' unusual appearance on *60 Minutes*, Gennifer Flowers held a press conference with her attorney, complete with an opening statement and a dramatic "let the tapes speak for themselves" airing of some of her now-famous recordings. In her opening statement Flowers explained she was tired of lying for Bill and felt hurt by his denials of their relationship. She said calmly, but with emotion:

> Last night, I sat and watched Bill on *60 Minutes*. I felt disgusted, and I saw a side of Bill that I had never seen before. He is absolutely lying. I'm disappointed, but realistically I never thought he would come out and admit it.... The man on *60 Minutes* was not the man I fell in love with....I would like to think that after a twelve year relationship he would have the guts to say, "Yes, I had an affair with this woman, but it's over." And that's the truth....

> I will always have a place in my heart for Bill Clinton. He was twelve years of my life. I cared very, very deeply for him and shared very special things with him.[90]

Reporters threw all varieties of prurient questions at her (e.g. "Did he wear a condom?"), which she declined to answer.[91] A documentary released later that year entitled *Feed* showed behind-the-scenes clips of the presidential race, including off-camera footage of Flowers looking "bemused" at the zoo of a press conference she'd created.[92] Flowers and the *Star* held back giving the press full access to the tapes, playing only about fifteen minutes worth (she later sold them to the public through a Web site). CNN covered the press conference but refused to air the tapes because it had not verified them.

Legendary journalist Mary McGrory wrote the next day, "At least we know why she is doing what she is doing. The *Star* paid her an undisclosed amount of money for her story of snatched moments of bliss...."[93] *The Washington Post* and *Newsweek* reporter Michael Isikoff published a book in 1999 recounting how the *Post* got the tapes from Flowers in 1994 when looking into the Paula Jones allegations and an editor there found herself taken aback at the "other side of Clinton" revealed on the tapes: "arrogant, crude, and profane," and adamant about covering up his affair with Flowers.[94]

Obviously irked that Bill had called her just a friendly acquaintance, at her press conference Flowers stated, "When people hear my tapes I think they will realize that I am not a woman that he saw and spoke to infrequently."[95] Flowers had taken on Clinton and his cadre, and would find herself on the losing end of a smear campaign for the next six years. In his memoirs Clinton writes that Flowers's press conference didn't bother him because he and Hillary had "managed to put it in the right perspective on *60 Minutes*. The public understood that I hadn't been perfect and wasn't pretending to be, but people also knew there were many more important issues confronting the country."[96] He adds, "And a lot of people were repelled at the 'cash for trash' aspects of the coverage."[97] No need to mention that he and his gang coined "cash for trash" and other catchy phrases to discredit Flowers. In fact, in his book Clinton feigns supercilious sympathy for Flowers: "Gennifer Flowers struck me as a tough survivor who'd had a less-than-ideal childhood and disappointments in her career but kept going."[98] Actually, the same banal observation could be made of Clinton himself.

After receiving their candidate's assurances that Flowers's story was false, Clinton's insiders leaped into battle mode, amplifying their "cash for trash" smear and appearing on talk shows to denounce tabloid journalism in general and Gennifer Flowers in particular. When the first copy of Flowers's tabloid story reached the campaign, staffer Dee Dee Myers called Clinton media man Frank Greer, who said, "Our smoking bimbo has emerged."[99] After Flowers held her press conference, Clinton advisor James Carville declared "We're going to have to go to war," and appeared on the *Today* show the next morning to attack Flowers's credibility.[100] The campaign immediately released to the media a copy of the letter Gennifer Flowers's attorney had sent the Arkansas radio station in 1991 threatening to sue for defamation over the radio station's broadcast about the alleged affair.[101] That letter boosted Clinton's confidence in declaring, "She's obviously changed her story for money."[102] Palladino, the campaign's investigator, got busy and even went to the trouble of asking a former friend of Gennifer's "Do you think Gennifer is the sort of person who would commit suicide?"[103] Just curious, I suppose.

Palladino went "around the country talking to people who knew me," Flowers later said.[104] "I had calls from people—girl friends, guy friends, people I had known. It wasn't necessarily people I had known well."[105] If they had found any good dirt on her, they would have used it, Flowers felt sure. "They turned over every rock they could."[106] Good to know that Clinton campaign contributions (matched by federal tax dollars) were well spent.

Palladino returned my phone call to question him about his alleged activities. "I can't comment on investigations," he insisted, adding that most of what's been reported on the Internet is "science fiction." When I asked him if he could tell me whether he had ever engaged in intimidation or harassment tactics on behalf of a Clinton campaign, he dodged the question. Instead of denying that he'd ever done bad things, he told me about some good things he's done with his investigative career. He told me about high-profile investigative work he's done pro bono over the years, and said that this kind of charity work shows what kind of a person he really is. This guy is a lot like Clinton himself, I found myself thinking. In his mind the good works he does cancel out any abuses he may also have committed. But as with Clinton, the people he hurts count just as much as the people he helps. Women like Gennifer Flowers suffered greatly as a result of their tactics, and the fact that they do good things for others doesn't negate the real mistreatment they inflicted on her.

The media dug into Flowers's account half-heartedly, pointing out inconsistencies and weaknesses where they could, feeling oh-so-self-conscious writing about it at all. For instance, the *Star* had quoted Flowers as saying that when she moved to Tulsa in 1980, she and Clinton would sometimes hook up at the Little Rock Excelsior Hotel when she'd come back into town, but that hotel wasn't built until 1982. Flowers's attorney attributed confusion on that point to a misunderstanding on the part of the *Star* reporter.[107] At her press conference, her attorney also defended Flowers's claims that she'd sung back up for Roy Clark, appeared on television's *Hee Haw*, and had been a teenage beauty pageant winner; questions about the veracity of those claims had made the news as credibility problems for Ms. Flowers.[108] The *Washington Post* interviewed *Star* editor Richard Kaplan, who worked for *Newsweek*, *Ladies Home Journal*, and *US* magazine before managing the *Star*.[109] Kaplan said his paper had done everything a mainstream paper would have done to verify the Flowers story, including talking to Flowers's mother and a friend who corroborated her account and having the tapes analyzed by a New York lab.[110] More than that, said Kaplan, after decades in the news biz he knew the hallmarks of a true story, and he believed Flowers.[111] The press and public remained unconvinced.

One former friend, Lauren Kirk, freely offered her opinion of Flowers. In January when the story broke Kirk said she'd just heard from Flowers, who felt betrayed by Clinton's denials.[112] "People are trying to label her as being a trashy slut. That is so far from the truth."[113] In February Kirk was interviewed for *Hard Copy* and said that while she and Flowers roomed together for a couple of years in Arkansas in the mid-1980s, Flowers would ask Kirk to leave when Clinton was coming over.[114] "She loved to kiss and tell," Kirk recalled, adding Clinton "would tell her he planned to be president. Even then he had great aspirations and, god, such a big ego. They were actually made for each other, because she had a big ego, too....She is two-sided. Wonderful and witty, but also evil and cruel."[115] By November of the same year Kirk had dropped her ambivalence about Flowers's character, furnishing assessments like: "Gennifer is a wonderful liar, because there's always a kernel of truth in what she says."[116] Maybe her opinion of her friend took a nosedive when it became apparent over the course of 1992 that Flowers was making as much money as she could off her story.

Flowers's ex-boyfriend Finis Shelnutt spoke up for Flowers when the news broke. When he last talked with Gennifer a month before the *Star* article, he said, she was scared because reporters kept hounding her and she felt the story was about to break. "She said she did not want this to come out in the *Star*.... She wanted it to come out in a more credible publication."[117] Shelnutt had been seeing Flowers for about a year when he learned of the rumors through a press release issued by Larry Nichols about Nichols's lawsuit against Clinton. He was shocked, and confronted his girlfriend at her apartment. Flowers cried and said, "I knew you would hear this." She denied the affair and said "I'm filing suit against them." When rumors persisted he broke up with her. Shelnutt said, "I thought, well, maybe it's true, and my feelings just started dwindling, big-time. I guess I was pretty blind. I guess I was the last one to find out." Shelnutt called Flowers "an extremely intelligent person, very sharp," and added, "In my mind, in my heart, I'm a Christian person. And I believe her. I really do." He went on, "In a way I'm kind of proud of her for coming forward and admitting it, because the president of the United States is someone you're going to put your trust in. I have nothing against Clinton except, you'd say, his morals." There must have been "something about Gennifer" for Shelnutt; he married her in 1996 and they're living happily together today.

The Flowers Tapes caused Clinton some political embarrassment quite aside from the allegation that they proved marital infidelity. On one of the tapes, Clinton and Flowers are discussing New York's then-Governor Mario Cuomo. Clinton calls Cuomo "aggressive," and Flowers suggests maybe Cuomo has mafia connections.[118] "Well he acts like one," Clinton says on tape. [119] Near the end of January 1992 Clinton tried to apologize to Governor Cuomo for the remarks; Cuomo refused to accept the apology.[120] The tapes also had Clinton complaining that fellow Democratic contender Senator Bob Kerrey's bachelorhood kept Kerrey from undergoing the scrutiny Clinton had to face.

Because Kerrey is single, Clinton tells Flowers, "nobody cares who he's screwing." [121] Kerrey was offended.[122]

Though the Gennifer Flowers story broke barely a month before the New Hampshire primary, Clinton's almost-apology approach seemed to work; he finished second there. Clinton advisor James Carville boasted airily in mid-February, "It's like the story of the guy who takes the witness stand and when asked to tell the truth, the whole truth, and nothing but the truth, responds: 'I can do any of those, which do you want?'. . . Clinton told the truth, but he didn't have to tell the whole truth or nothing but the truth. People got it."[123] The "character issue" had emerged as a detraction, but his campaign continued gaining momentum, and in July 1992 he cinched the nomination. Along the way, Gennifer Flowers had a cameo in a cable soap opera, a book deal in the works, pushed her singing career overseas, and even appeared in a *Penthouse* issue that hit the stands the week of the November election. But she had long since been the butt of late-night jokes and no longer posed a serious threat to Clinton's dearest ambition. She voted for Ross Perot.[124]

◊

Flowers faded from the public glare after Clinton became president, but her day to day life remained difficult for years. She tried to rejuvenate her singing career but found everywhere she turned that FOB (Friends of Bill) and an unfriendly public shut her down.[125] She moved frequently, living in Little Rock, Dallas, and Las Vegas, unable to escape her reputation, and constantly found herself snubbed and excluded from local events and gigs.[126] Even local charities rebuffed her attempts to lend her services. "I was un-invited to help feed the homeless" in Las Vegas, she recalls.[127] She and Shelnutt later opened their own nightclub. In the interim she maintained her own Web site (now defunct) where she sold her book and maintained an advice column.

When word got out in 1998 that Clinton had admitted under oath to having "sexual relations" with her, her face and name appeared briefly in the press again and she felt vindicated at last. "I've been on the defense now for several years," she told reporter Lorraine Adams for *The Washington Post*. "Naturally I'm extremely pleased that the truth has finally come out."[128] She had always believed Clinton's denials and smear tactics had been about "protecting the power structure, and anyone would be sacrificed who got in the way of that."[129] *The Seattle Times* reported in September 1998 that Flowers, still in Las Vegas then, performed that week at the MGM Grand Hotel where she sang "Who's Got the Last Laugh Now" and "Why Haven't I Heard From You."[130] She even lectured at Oxford University in 1999 on "Surviving Sex, Power, and Propaganda."[131]

Flowers got phone calls from all kinds of people, including journalists, apologizing to her after the truth had finally come from Bill's own mouth.[132] While he never apologized directly to Flowers, Clinton's eventual admission to an affair with her seemed to impact his one-time "bimbo eruption" lieutenant Betsey Wright more than any other single episode of Clinton's life. Speaking from her quiet Arkansas orchid garden in January 2001, Wright, who hadn't spoken to the Clintons in years, expressed anger at Clinton. "How many times I asked him about Gennifer Flowers, and how many times he told me that they never had any kind of affair. And then I read in the newspaper that there was," mourned Wright.[133]

When reports of Clinton's surprising admission under oath began circulating in 1998, Clinton's press secretary Mike McCurry said "The president knows that he told the truth in 1992 when he was asked about that relationship and he knows that he testified truthfully on Saturday and he knows his answers are not at odds," but everyone had figured out by then, as Clinton aides privately confirmed, that this explanation meant that "the president may have found careful wording that allowed him to give technically accurate answers in both cases."[134] Maybe in

1992 Clinton was truthful in denying a twelve-year affair with Flowers. Maybe it had in fact lasted only eleven and a half years.

Journalist Lorraine Adams didn't "have the heart" to question Flowers about going public in a tabloid or posing for *Penthouse* after Flowers told her:

> I was one little girl without any kind of power structure behind me. I didn't have expert advisers. I just did the best I could without a book of instructions. I didn't have any women's groups coming to my aid. I was the vindictive bimbo, who was just out to hurt this man....
>
> My life will never be the same.... I've had people who wouldn't even consider hiring me, or who wanted to laugh at me, or make a joke about me. I didn't grow up that way. I grew up as the cheerleader and the popular girl that people liked. I wasn't used to being the bad girl. That's not something that came easy.[135]

After interviewing Flowers in August 1998 in the context of a long article looking at the women involved in the scandal then erupting around Kathleen Willey, Linda Tripp, and Monica Lewinsky, Lorraine Adams wrote, "She [Flowers] may have established a measure of normality in her life, but her past was indelible. Her willingness to sell her story—to participate in her own denigration—had assured that. And now, she'd lost all influence over the process."[136] Adams's article contemplating the way various women had been thrust into the "bimbo role" by association with Bill Clinton was one of the most thoughtful treatments of the subject by any journalist of the Clinton scandal epoch. Adams concluded:

> That's the thing about the bimbo role. No matter how a woman comes by it—whether she seeks it or resists it—the role will overwhelm her, imprison her, define her. It's the only role she's allowed, and there's no way she can reshape it. Betsey Wright may have been right in defining a true bimbo as a woman motivated by money, but implicit in that analysis is the fact that money equals power. And no woman's story will bring a high enough price to counter the powers that be.[137]

With the country reeling from Clinton's admission to a sexual relationship with Monica Lewinsky after months of public denials, and impeachment in the wings, Larry King asked Gennifer Flowers, "[D]oes it make you feel at all badly...that you started an American tragedy?"[138] She responded with considerable insight, "I may have started it, but I didn't perpetuate the problem. If there is a strategy as we sit here and talk it would be Bill Clinton's fault, and I think that he certainly should take responsibility for his actions, which at times he finds hard to do."[139]

Gennifer Flowers found a husband and a city that embraced her and her past. She and Mr. Shelnutt (who is, coincidentally, a former brother-in-law of Whitewater principal figure Web Hubbell) settled in New Orleans, where she performs in her own piano bar, the Gennifer Flowers Kelsto Club on St. Louis Street, just across from Bourbon Street.[140] Flowers feels at home in the Quarter, where no one hounds her about her status as a "national bimbo."[141] Friends of Bill may have stopped her from getting deals in Las Vegas and Dallas, but "Let 'em tell me I can't sing in my own club," she laughs now.[142]

She knew she could find a home in New Orleans when she visited once and saw a portrait of the infamous Madame X hanging in a friend's New Orleans antique shop.[143] When revealed to the world at a Paris exhibit in the late 1800s the portrait scandalized the international reputation of its subject and its painter on account of Madame X's plunging, suggestive neckline and palpable air of sensuality. Feeling a kinship of sorts ("I know all about scandal"),[144] Flowers came to regard New Orleans as a place of her own and has never regretted it. In January 2002 President George W. Bush came to New Orleans, stopping for a while at a restaurant not far from Gennifer's club. She didn't get to meet the president ("They wouldn't let me say 'hi' to George," she explained, "They thought I might cause some spectacle") but off-duty Secret Service agents stopped into her club to say hello and have a drink.[145] She loves George W. Bush. "I absolutely adore him. I am his No. 1 fan," she says earnestly, adding that it "meant a lot to know that I was just across the street from him."[146]

Now in her mid-fifties, singing to curious, appreciative audiences, living with a loving, faithful husband in a city that's happy to have her, she's made a pretty good life for herself.

◊

Without attempting an exhaustive chronicle of all women who fit into this pattern, we've highlighted the experiences of three women (Gracen, Perdue, Flowers) who (1) had consensual sexual affairs with Clinton, (2) kept quiet for some period of time at his request, (3) eventually went public, and (4) suffered retaliation for daring to speak out. No Clinton woman we've seen yet made herself more a spectacle than Gennifer Flowers. Then again, no woman we know about had more to feel betrayed about than Gennifer. (Except, perhaps, Dolly Kyle Browning, a childhood friend of Clinton's who claims the two had an intimate friendship spanning thirty years that included, at times, sexual intimacy.[147] Or perhaps Monica Lewinsky. All right, it's too difficult to say which Clinton woman has the most reason to feel betrayed by him.) Gennifer's story wasn't about a one-night stand or a brief affair; it was about a man who consumed her life for twelve years, from age twenty-seven to nearly forty, a man she thought remained a friend even after the sex had ended. Her best insight into Clinton probably came when she confessed that she should have realized that her feelings would not matter much to him compared with his desire to become president.

From her perspective, she fought him with all the strategy at her disposal. Compared to the tactics at his command, however, she didn't stand a chance. She lost the battle because the only channels open to her left her vulnerable to being dismissed as a money-hungry slut, even though she won the war when the (partial) truth eventually came out. As journalist Lorraine Adams contemplated, taking money in the process of seeking vindica-

87

tion inevitably labeled her a bimbo, but money and publicity were the only avenues open to someone like Flowers if she wanted to try to take on a man who had the political power structure behind him.

Didn't she bring the smear machine on herself? Shouldn't she just have kept quiet? Yes, she invited the public attacks by doing everything possible to make money off her story. But why should she have remained silent? Why should the man who made her feel special for twelve years get to breeze into the most powerful office in the land while publicly saying she was nothing special to him? Her name was in the game *before* she took money for her story. Clinton called her "trash" in public *before* she sold her tale. Why should her voice be silenced or denigrated while his would be heard from the seat of world power? Because she "used" her story to get money? Clinton used *her* to indulge his sexual and emotional needs for over a decade during his climb to the top. Why should she lie for him, or keep quiet while he lied about her? Demonstrated through action, Clinton's answer must be, "Because I'm more important than she is." She was a nobody, a wannabe-somebody, desperate to make it as a performer. He was *somebody*, a man who had already made it as a performer. How *dare* she try to expose him, embarrass him, make him answer to anyone for anything he'd done?

The course of action she chose over a twenty-five year span shows Gennifer Flowers as a multidimensional woman: independent, adventurous, tough, sometimes vulnerable, hardly coy about sex and her own sexuality, comfortable with locker room dialogue, casual about sleeping with married men. She was a woman with big dreams, a desire for material pleasures, and a hunger to be liked, loved, and adored. In a man, these characteristics wouldn't have set her apart in the slightest, and there would have been no bimbo label attached to her.

While there are dozens of synonyms for "bimbo" associated with females—slut, whore, tramp, hussy, jade, jezebel, wench, to name a few—the English language doesn't even have a good

word for the male equivalent. The closest is probably "philanderer," whose root you'll recall means "lover," a far cry from the
implications of "slut" or "whore." Clinton didn't think twice
before dismissing Gennifer Flowers as trash, even though her
actions were precisely reciprocal to his. They *both* participated in
an extramarital affair. Even if he had come clean from the start
and admitted sleeping with her, she would have been a bimbo;
he would have been an adulterer. She probably still would have
been ridiculed; he would have been forgiven as a wandering,
contrite husband. Clinton's mistreatment of Flowers consisted
chiefly in his use of her to perpetuate a double standard that
permeates even our enlightened, progressive society: cheating
men are wanderers; the women who help them cheat are slutty
seductresses. No matter what policies Clinton the politician ever
enacted promoting women's rights, Clinton the man showed
nothing but good old-fashioned misogyny toward Gennifer
Flowers.

In his January 17, 1998 deposition in the Paula Jones lawsuit,
Clinton admitted having sexual relations with Gennifer Flowers.[148] One time only, he said, in 1977.[149] His capitulation under
oath wasn't honesty for truth's sake; he'd found himself cornered
and knew a carefully planted gem of "honesty" about Flowers
could help him escape perjury charges, since in the same deposition he testified under oath that he never had "sexual relations"
with Monica Lewinsky. When forced to admit to sexual encounters with Lewinsky before a grand jury in August 1998 he was
able to point to his Flowers admission at the prior deposition to
help prove himself innocent of perjury.

In that grand jury testimony, Clinton's anger at Flowers
seeped into his words when he told the prosecutors how he'd
"rather have taken a whipping" than admit to an affair with
Flowers "after all the trouble I'd been through with Gennifer
Flowers, and the money I knew that she had made for the story
she told about this alleged twelve-year affair, which we had done
a great deal to disprove."[150] How *dare* she? After all his work

denouncing her as a slutty dollar-chaser he had to admit she'd been right and that just burned him. As we'll see in a moment, the interesting question is: What, precisely, did Clinton think he'd done to "disprove" Flowers's story?

It seemed to irritate Clinton that Flowers had made money off him. It seemed to agitate him even more that all his efforts to destroy her had come to nothing in the end. Unlike other accusations Clinton has fended off over the years, he seemed to take this one pretty personally. On the surface the two people seem an unlikely pair—an aspiring politician who ran the world for eight years, and an aspiring singer who ran around nightclubs most of her life. In other ways, though, perhaps Flowers's one-time friend had it about right when she said Bill Clinton and Gennifer Flowers were "made for each other." Each person exhibited a bold, strong personality, each seemed to crave attention, each showed tenderness and tawdriness at times, and each reacted with hostility at the thought of the other getting the better of them. Once she felt betrayed she did everything in her power to embarrass him; once he felt betrayed he did everything in his power to destroy her. Perhaps in too many ways Gennifer Flowers was Bill Clinton's female counterpart, a thought that may have fueled his personal anger at her—and a speculation that would help explain his behavior toward her. There's no clearer an example of misogyny than when a man strikes out at a women precisely *because* she's trying to prove herself his equal.

Feminist author Susan Faludi wrote in December 1992 that Hillary Clinton was already under attack by the "guardians of the rusting social order" for not behaving like a proper first lady *should*.[151] Faludi's point was that Hillary Clinton irked old-order folks not just because she was an independent woman, but because she *enjoyed* being an independent woman.[152] Faludi insisted, "She is doing something her predecessors didn't dare. She's abandoned the earnest, dutiful demeanor....And therein lies her sin: Hillary Clinton is visibly, tangibly having fun."[153] Faludi noted:

By combining equality with ecstasy, liberty with laughter, Hillary Clinton violated the cardinal trade-off rule of American womanhood. Women are told: O.K., gals, go ahead and do your liberated thing, but you must pay the price with personal happiness....

Sexuality for women comes with the same warning: If you have sex and enjoy it, prepare to face the consequences.[154]

But where was Susan Faludi, or other self-described advocates for women's liberation and independence, when Gennifer Flowers splashed across our TV screens and newspapers, declaring without remorse that she'd engaged in a long sexual affair with a powerful man and made no apologies for it? Flowers didn't come off as a contrite, dutiful woman who'd made a terrible mistake and begged forgiveness; she kicked up her heels and flaunted her "naughty" behavior. Flowers tried to keep up with Clinton, first playing his equal as a lover and then trying to play his equal in the town square face-off that followed. Along the way she smiled, she laughed, she made off-color jokes, she posed nude, and she made as much money as she could. Clinton made sure she paid the price for her "liberated thing," personalizing the social "rule of American womanhood" about which Faludi complains.

Flowers would later note that no women's rights organizations rushed to aid her in her public relations battle against Clinton, but it's hard to imagine feminists keeping quiet if Flowers had been sleeping with George H. W. Bush for twelve years and found herself in a he said, she said battle over it. Feminist groups like NOW certainly took the lead in calling for Republican senator Bob Packwood's political head when his decades-long harassment of female staffers came to light. Packwood, a liberal Republican, had long been a strong supporter of abortion rights, but with Clinton in office, feminists felt their reproductive rights agenda was in good hands, and could speak out against Packwood without risking political setbacks for their cause.

Maybe feminists were faintly embarrassed by Flowers. Maybe their time and money were tied up trying to make 1992 the "Year of the Woman" and Gennifer Flowers wasn't quite the right look for Poster Girl. Or maybe they'd gone so overboard equating women's rights with leftist policies that they had no interest in going to bat for Flowers if it meant risking another Republican administration—even if sitting on the bench revealed a double standard that left Flowers without team support from the supposed sisterhood while the man she'd slept with tore her to shreds.

◊

Clinton's outburst about Flowers during his grand jury testimony, combined with the dearth of support Flowers received from feminist groups, help reveal our third identification of a tenet of liberalism that can foster misogynistic attitudes and behavior in someone like Bill Clinton who is already prone to mistreat women.

In modern liberalism, the validity of the message is determined solely by the motives of the messenger. It cuts both ways. If a person has good motives, anything they're proposing must be a good thing. If a person has bad motives, nothing they say can be of any value. Moreover, determining a person's motive or intent is not a protracted process; it's usually enough to presume to know a person's intent and permit that presumption to dictate judgment of what they're saying.

To get an idea for how this tenet operates in the political left today, let's pick on modern politicized feminism again. The left's argument goes something like this: pro-lifers are wrong on the issue of reproductive rights because pro-lifers are misogynistic sexists who want to punish women. Differently stated, because pro-lifers' motives are bad (they want to punish women), nothing about their message is true or valid. Conversely, feminists are right on the issue of reproductive rights because feminists desire gender equality. In other words, because feminists' motives are pure (they want gender equality), their message is true and valid.

The way this plays out in current debate can be seen in how viciously feminists attack George W. Bush for being pro-life. They have determined Bush's motives to be pure evil—he is waging a war against women.[155] He desires a country where women's rights look like those in Saudi Arabia.[156] His pro-life message cannot possibly be valid because Bush's intent is to punish women. How do we know Bush's true intent? There is absolutely no reason to be pro-life other than misogynistic spite. With Bush's evil intent thus established, *nothing* he says or does is true, good, or valid. The circular reasoning is evident but apparently irrelevant.

It works in reverse, too. Hillary Rodham Clinton's motives are pure and good—she wants every American to be able to afford health care. Her mission to put the health care industry under government micromanagement is a superb idea because her motives are so admirable. Only people with despicable motives could possibly oppose her health care plan. Her good intentions established, everything she proposes is true, good, and valid.

There is a basic flaw in this approach. Ideas have validity and consequences quite apart from the motives of the person expounding them. Good people can have bad ideas, and bad people can have good ideas. People with bad intentions can speak true things, and people with good intentions can speak false things. For instance, the invalidity of the idea that the sun revolves around the earth did not depend on the motives of the world leaders who held on to that notion in the middle ages. Despite their good intentions (like wanting to preserve the belief that God made man the center of the universe), the idea was factually invalid and clinging to it had negative consequences (like impeding scientific knowledge and progress). Another example: the Framers of the Constitution intended to keep African-Americans in slavery, but their motives do not discount the validity and good consequences of the many brilliant constitutional ideas they proposed.

Under most criminal laws a person is judged based on her intent. For example, most criminal offenses require an element of *mens rea*, or guilty mind, on the part of the accused. To be convicted, the prosecution must prove the defendant *intended* to commit the crime. Let's say the facts of a case indicate that a baby died in his mother's arms because his mother held him very tightly causing the baby to suffocate. The mother, now our defendant charged with murder, stipulates to those facts. In general, what distinguishes murder from manslaughter is intent to kill. The prosecution has to prove the mother *intended* to cause the baby's death, as opposed to accidentally squeezing the baby to death. The law can hardly leave it up to each defendant to explain her own intent and leave it at that; human nature being what it is, only rarely would a person confess. So the prosecutor is allowed to prove the defendant's intent by circumstantial evidence. Was the baby bruised? If so, that indicates an intent to cause harm. Was the baby crying while being squeezed? If so, that indicates intent. Did our defendant tell her babysitter that morning that she sometimes wished she didn't have to take care of the baby anymore? And on and on for any particular case, looking at surrounding circumstances to try to determine what the defendant's intent was.

We go through this process under the law because given our purpose the alternatives are undesirable. We want to reserve our harshest punishment for people who intended to cause harm, yet the only beings who fully know a person's intentions are the person herself and God. We won't leave it up to a judge to consult God about a defendant's intent, and we're unwilling to rely solely on the defendant's own proclamation. That leaves the option the law has settled on: examining the circumstances surrounding the defendant's behavior and trying to infer intent.

Judgment under the law often turns solely on intent of the accused. Modern liberalism borrows the law's focus on intent and injects it into political debate, proceeding as though a political proposal or idea should be judged by the intent of its proponent. But the law's focus on intent consists of looking back in time, trying to establish in hindsight a person's state of mind with respect to a specific set of past actions, for the purpose of holding that person responsible for the consequences of those actions. The purpose of making judgments in political debate is completely different. In a legal proceeding the defendant herself is on trial. In a political setting, the message, not the messenger, should be on trial. In political debate the focus should be on the idea itself, not on the person advocating it. The purpose of political debate is to judge the validity and predict the consequences of alternative ideas, policies, plans, rules, laws. *Who* suggests the ideas, and their motive or intent in doing so, should take a back seat to the question of whether the ideas themselves have merit. In political debate, judging the message by the presumed motives of the messenger does the entire process a disservice by shifting focus away from principles and onto personalities.

Hallmarks of modern liberal ideology—equality for all, peace above all—and proposals purportedly made in support of those ideals simply cannot be challenged in today's political climate without facing a rush to judgment about the motives and intent behind such a challenge. For example, take the decades-old debate over whether the U.S. should sign the United Nations Treaty on Women's Rights (formal name: the Convention to Eliminate All Forms of Discrimination Against Women). Its very title overflows with a keystone of modern liberalism: gender equality. President Bush's reluctance to sign it has earned him vitriolic accusations of being in favor of worldwide, systematic subjugation of women. In June 2004, the *Chicago Tribune* ran an op-ed that quoted George W. Bush declaring eloquently, "The advance of women's rights and the advance of liberty are ultimately inseparable," followed by the writer's prescient inquiry: "But does he really believe that?"[157] The piece goes on to list foot-dragging on the UN Treaty on Women's Rights as a prime example of how George W. Bush in fact does not take women's rights seriously at all.[158] A feminist congresswoman cited Bush's reluctance to sign the treaty as proof of Bush's "global war on women's rights."[159] With that despicable motive ascribed to him, his position on why the U.S. might not want to sign is easily dismissed as further evidence of his intent for gender inequality to reign throughout the world. As Gennifer Flowers learned the hard way, maligning a person's motives can go a long way toward discrediting whatever they have to say.

How might this facet of liberal ideology encourage misogynistic behavior in a person predisposed to undervalue women? Well, what exactly did Clinton think he had done to "disprove" Flowers's story? He didn't attempt to use logic or evidence to disprove anything; he borrowed a page from his ideological book and encouraged everyone to judge her solely based on the evil motives he ascribed to her. He did everything he could to denigrate her message on the basis of her presumed motives. She was out for money and she was bent on destroying him. Therefore, nothing she said could possibly be true, valid, or of any consequence. The press and public largely reached the same conclusions for the same reasons. She's a bimbo out for money and notoriety; therefore she's lying. Or worse: she's a bimbo out for money and notoriety, therefore it doesn't even matter if she's telling the truth.

In March 1998, when President Clinton was still denying an improper relationship with Monica Lewinsky, Arianna Huffington (before she abandoned conservatism for populism) wrote an editorial denouncing the political elites' use of what logic textbooks call the "Fallacy of the Undistributed Middle."[160] The logical flaw, Huffington pointed out, goes like this: All oaks are trees. All elms are trees. Therefore, all oaks are elms. Huffington observed that the current political debate was applying the same fallacy evaluating whether Lewinsky's tales of fellatio were true, just as it had when discrediting Gennifer Flowers's claims:

According to the president's own deposition in the Jones case, it is now a matter of fact...that Gennifer Flowers told the truth and Clinton lied about whether they had had sex. Yet for the last six years, the American public has been bombarded by our oft-illustrated logical fallacy: Flowers says she had sex with Clinton. Flowers is a lounge singer, a bimbo and a gold digger who sold her story to a tabloid. Therefore, Flowers did not have sex with Clinton.[161]

Liberal politics alone does not a misogynist make. However, dedication to a political ideology that judges the messenger rather than the message may have made it easier for someone like Bill Clinton to mistreat Gennifer Flowers the way he did — destroying her not because her message was untrue, but because he believed her motives were suspect.

CHAPTER FIVE

OBJECT OF AFFECTION

O N MAY 6, 1991, in Cleveland, Ohio, Governor Bill Clinton gave arguably the most significant speech of his political life to that point. In a thirty minute speech delivered without notes or teleprompter to 800 delegates gathered for a national convention of the Democratic Leadership Council, Bill Clinton displayed sparks of promise to be the bearer of a message that could finally win back the White House for the Democratic Party. The Associated Press ran a headline "Clinton's Star Rises, As Does Cleveland's," quoting one listener saying Clinton's speech was "toe-tingling," and another who thought it was the best Democratic speech he'd heard in ten years.[1] Granted, even the AP insinuated that some might have thought the speech brilliant solely in contrast to Clinton's 1988 nomination speech for Dukakis at the Democratic National Convention in Atlanta. There, Clinton had been nationally mocked for droning on so long that delegates shouted at him from the floor. Hillary Rodham Clinton described that experience as "a humiliating introduction to the nation,"[2] even though Clinton's appearance a week later joking about it self-deprecatingly on *The Tonight Show* ameliorated any long-term tarnish on his status as a viable national leader. In Cleveland, there was general consensus that Clinton's opening speech fired up the troops and stood out as the highlight of the event.

The Democratic Leadership Council (DLC) had been founded by Democratic centrists in 1985 in an effort to build new coalitions that could spell victory for the Democratic Party and avoid another Reaganesque mandate. In his keynote address in Cleveland, Clinton, then chairman of the DLC, told his fellow partisans, "Too many of the people who used to vote for us, the very burdened middle class we're talking about, have not trusted us in national elections to defend our national interest abroad, to put their values in our social policy at home or to take their tax money and spend it with discipline. *We've got to turn these perceptions around* or we can't continue as a national party" (emphasis added).[3] Careful attention to the wording of Clinton's appeal yields a clue that he truly believed himself insulated from charges that the DLC was trying to go "Republican-lite." The word "perceptions" supports the notion that the essence of a Clintonian "New Democrat" is a traditional liberal Democrat who has learned how to appear moderate enough to avoid the negative connotations of the label "liberal" but has still found ways to accomplish the historical, ideological goals of liberalism. Senator Paul Tsongas of Massachusetts, who had already declared his candidacy in the 1992 race at the time of the DLC convention, was more explicit about the DLC's approach, urging his party to adopt pro-business policies while standing firm to traditional Democratic platform issues like civil rights, women's rights, and environmental protection.[4]

The two-day DLC event in 1991 was considered modestly successful at widening the selection of potential presidential candidates for the following year, despite inciting some bitterness between DLC members and more open liberals like Jesse Jackson who objected stridently to the DLC's proposal to backtrack on sensitive issues like racial quotas. In his memoirs Clinton says, "That speech was one of the most effective and important I ever made."[5]

Governor Clinton had recently promised his constituents in Arkansas, who had re-elected him just six months earlier in November 1990, that he would not seek the presidency in 1992; he would finish his term as governor.[6] (The law in Arkansas had changed in 1986, providing a four-year term instead of a two-year term.) Now that the political scene was buzzing over Clinton as a strong candidate, however, Clinton responded to questions with characteristic ambiguity. Even the AP couldn't resist opening its report on Clinton's rising-star speech by jesting, "Arkansas Gov. Bill Clinton wanted to say just one thing: he's not running for president. Well, two things. If he changes his mind, he'll first tell the people of Arkansas, [his] 'employers.'"[7] Faced with questions he'd rather not answer and inquiries where direct responses could lead to uncomfortable probing, Clinton's instinct always seemed to be the same—say a little of this, a little of that, kinda yes, sorta no; some truth, but rarely the whole truth. That pattern of hedging, always holding something back or leaving a loophole, would play itself out time and again whenever Clinton faced questions he feared could harm him.

It was almost paradoxical posturing from a politician who made his national reputation focusing on personal responsibility and family values. At the DLC convention Clinton told his colleagues that Democrats need to ensure that children are taught values at home. "Governments don't raise children, people do," he emphasized, "And it is time they were asked to assume their responsibilities and forced to do [it] if they refuse."[8] Every American must accept responsibility for his own actions, Clinton insisted, as well as for the actions of his family, community, and nation.[9] It was a well-developed theme that wrapped liberal ideological activism in a cloak of accountability. He promoted the concept of personal responsibility, but always connected it to *government's* responsibilities. He insisted that people were tired of hearing government promise to solve all their problems with new taxes and new programs, but refused to let his exhortation for everyone to behave properly rest with the bully pulpit; if you don't "assume your responsibilities," it's up to government to *force* you to do the right thing.

Clinton left Cleveland on May 7 knowing he had earned a realistic chance to lead his party to the White House. The next day in Little Rock, Clinton attended the Governor's Quality Management Conference at the Excelsior Hotel, sponsored by the Arkansas Industrial Development Commission (AIDC), a state agency.[10] Clinton gave a speech there in the morning, then stayed and listened to the afternoon speech by a management consultant for Ernst & Young. Afterward he milled about, chatting with people. What else Clinton did that afternoon became talk of the nation for most of Clinton's future presidency. That afternoon, Paula Corbin (soon to be Jones) told her AIDC co-worker that Bill Clinton had invited her upstairs to a hotel room where he proceeded to hold her hand, nibble her neck, pull down his trousers, touch himself, and ask her for a little favor. Later that evening, Paula Corbin drove to another friend's home and, very distressed, repeated the same account. She also described it to her two sisters and her mother, in varying degrees of detail, but she told her boyfriend merely that Clinton had made a pass at her.

With so much at stake, with an ultimate victory just on the horizon, Clinton chose the wrong object for his affections that day. On a day when he should have been content to bask in the glow of the success his Cleveland speech portended, Clinton instead tried to make a little magic with a woman he'd never before met. Within a few months, Bill Clinton was a household name by virtue of his success; Paula Corbin Jones joined him three years later by virtue of his failure. Among other things, their brief introduction that day led to a five and a half year court battle racking up millions of dollars in legal bills, a Supreme Court ruling that binds future presidencies, bitter family relations and the end of a marriage for Paula Jones, and compelled disclosure of incidents in Bill Clinton's "personal life" he'd rather have taken to his grave. Amidst the wreckage of legal and personal damage, one more facet of Clinton's liberal misogyny emerges.

◊

Somewhat ironically, as with Gennifer Flowers's story, it was men, not women, who dragged Jones's name into the spotlight. After her May 8, 1991, encounter with Bill Clinton, Paula Corbin married her boyfriend, Steve Jones. They had a little boy, Madison, and moved to southern California so Steve could pursue an acting career. On a visit home to Arkansas for Christmas in 1993, Jones's friend Debra called her after seeing an article in *The American Spectator*.[11] Jones had driven to Debra's workplace the afternoon of her encounter with Clinton in 1991 and had told Debra what had occurred. Over the phone, Debra read Jones part of the magazine article that mentioned "Paula."[12] Four Arkansas state troopers who used to be assigned to the governor's mansion during Bill Clinton's tenure there had spilled their guts in tawdry detail about helping Bill Clinton cover up several long-term affairs and facilitating countless one-time trysts for Clinton. One of the troopers had talked about approaching a woman, "Paula," at the Excelsior Hotel, asking her on Clinton's behalf to meet Clinton in a hotel room, escorting her up to the room, and waiting in the hallway. When "Paula" emerged from the room no more than an hour later, the trooper was quoted as telling his buddies that "Paula" had suggested she'd just had a satisfying sexual encounter and that she would be available to be the governor's girlfriend.

Paula Jones, listening to her friend read the story to her, was horrified and angry. "Oh my God, it's complete bullshit!" she exclaimed to Debra on the phone, "That's a complete lie!"[13] Paula had never heard of *The American Spectator*, but in her mind, this libelous version of her encounter with Clinton might be read and believed by all her friends and family. Her close friends and family, after all, knew Jones's version of her meeting with Clinton because she'd told them about it right after it happened in 1991. Now, a couple of years later, Arkansas state law enforcement officials were apparently telling the world a much different story. Would her family and friends believe her? She was twenty-seven years old, with a two year old son and a husband. She lived in California, thousands of miles away from her Arkansas crowd of family and friends. This mortifying story appeared in a national magazine. What would everyone think of her?

Her friend Debra put Jones in touch with a lawyer in Little Rock, Danny Traylor. Traylor talked to Jones about her options, and agreed with Jones that the best thing to shoot for would be a public apology from the White House to clear her name. As most of us would be, Traylor found himself a little bit stumped when he contemplated how to get a message to the White House. He decided to call a Little Rock businessman, George Cook, who was well-connected in the Democratic Party. Cook managed to communicate with Bruce Lindsey at the White House about Paula Jones.[14] The White House had already been fielding questions about "Troopergate," and polls showed the president's popularity wasn't jeopardized by the troopers' tell-all allegations. The message got back to Traylor: we're not worried about this story, so we have no interest in apologizing to Paula Jones.

Traylor's next move put him in touch with another Arkansas lawyer, Cliff Jackson,[15] a former Oxford classmate of Clinton's who had tried very hard over the years to stymie Clinton's career wherever possible.[16] Jackson had been the public relations force behind getting the Arkansas state troopers' allegations published. Jackson talked Traylor into piggybacking Jones's story with the troopers' tales by having Jones appear at a press conference with the troopers in February 1994 at a right-wing gathering of the Conservative Political Action Conference (CPAC).

Neither Traylor, nor Jones, seemed to realize the danger of aligning themselves so early on with the troopers and their Clinton-hating pushers, though at least two problems would soon emerge due to this alliance: first, Jones would be disparagingly dismissed by the media and feminist groups solely based on the perception that right-wing Clinton-haters were using her to attack Clinton for political reasons; second, Jones's version of May 8, 1991, events contradicted the troopers' version of what occurred, placing Jones and the troopers publicly and (later on) legally at odds. For her part, Jones followed her lawyer's lead. She wasn't a politically aware person.[17] She didn't even know the difference between a liberal and a conservative when she appeared at the CPAC conference.[18] She had registered to vote in 1992 just to vote against Clinton because of how he'd treated her.[19] Paula Jones's grievance against Clinton wasn't political; it was personal.

◊

When Troopergate broke in mid-December 1993, Clinton was wrapping up his first year as president. He hadn't faced a woman-related scandal since Gennifer Flowers during the campaign. He was, however, already limping through several embarrassing distractions. The firing of White House Travel Office employees, the inexplicable suicide of White House lawyer and friend Vince Foster, abandonment of his first nominee to head Civil Rights at the Justice Department (Lani Guinier), and a Justice Department investigation into a failed savings-and-loan endeavor in Arkansas that would soon lead to appointment of an independent counsel and become known as "Whitewater," had all taken their toll on the new administration.

In Clinton's memoirs, Troopergate takes up a mere two paragraphs and Clinton seems content to dismiss the state troopers' allegations by stating, "There were some allegations in the story that could be easily disproved, and the two [named] troopers had credibility problems of their own, unrelated to their allegations against me: they had been investigated for insurance fraud involving a state vehicle they wrecked in 1990."[20] Here, Clinton applies a standard to the troopers that he protested when it was applied to politicians. Clinton insisted that adultery doesn't reflect on presidential character, yet here he proposes that being investigated for insurance fraud means your character is so deviant that you can't be telling the truth about what your former boss was doing on his down time. Clinton would have been better off ignoring Troopergate completely than hypocritically trying to discredit the troopers this way.

A few days before Christmas, when Troopergate had just emerged, *USA Today* ran an article contemplating the impact of 1993 on Clinton and his presidency. "Though Clinton's friends, not surprisingly, paint the first year as a time of personal growth, not everyone close to Clinton would agree. His volcanic temper is still fierce, his penchant for disorganization and tardiness still worrisome and his almost instinctive need to talk an issue to consensus—sometimes by seeming to take both sides—remains."[21] The article continued, "The rumors of extramarital affairs continue to swirl...and Clinton's distaste for the Washington media has kept all but a few of those who cover him from having a sense of the real Clinton to balance against the caricature."[22] In the same article, DNC Chairman David Wilhelm surmised that Clinton "sees perhaps even more clearly his role as a moral leader, someone who is setting the tone for the whole country."[23] With the battle over government-run health care still looming, the last thing Clinton needed as 1994 began was a genuine sex scandal, but Paula Jones handed him one anyway. By the end of 1994, few people were trying to argue that Bill Clinton was on track to being a "moral leader" for the country; even his most loyal friends stuck to Clinton's policies rather than personal character as a rallying point.

Troopergate floundered around for about six weeks before Paula Jones came on the scene. On December 19, 1993, the Associated Press broke the Troopergate story in the mainstream press, reporting on the allegations published by notorious reporter David Brock in the January 1994 issue of *The American Spectator*, which had hit Washington in mid-December. The talkative troopers had also been interviewed extensively by the *Los Angeles Times*, which ran a lengthy story on December 21. *The American*

Spectator article penned by David Brock opened contentiously enough (emphasis added):

> While rumors of extramarital dalliances have surrounded many presidents in this century...the scale of Clinton's past indiscretions, if it has been sustained in the White House, as has been widely rumored, would appear to far exceed that of any of his predecessors, with the possible exception of John Kennedy. *If, as the troopers describe it, he is a sexual predator and exploiter of women, his behavior may be more egregious than that which destroyed the political careers and reputations of Gary Hart, John Tower and, most recently, Bob Packwood.*[24]

Brock's article withheld full names of all women talked about except Gennifer Flowers, since she'd already made her claims public knowledge.

The AP story on December 19 quoted White House advisor Bruce Lindsey: "The allegations are ridiculous."[25] When the AP asked Lindsey if Clinton has "denied having troopers assist sexual liaisons," Lindsey told the AP, "Yes, he has."[26] Lindsey continued, "Similar allegations were made, investigated and responded to during the campaign."[27] CNN cited a "top administration aide" the same day saying the charges were "scurrilous."[28] The story had legs in part because the White House admitted that Clinton had personally called troopers recently to find out what was going on; this didn't look good because some of the troopers had alleged Clinton had dangled offers of federal employment in exchange for their continued silence. A December 21 editorial in *The Washington Times*, drenched in skepticism, parsed Bruce Lindsey's initial denials:

> "These allegations are ridiculous." Yes, indeed, there is something more than a little ridiculous about the things done by the man described by bodyguards Larry Patterson and Roger Perry: sneaking off in the middle of the night to visit girlfriends, receiving oral sex in parking lots, and so on. There's no disputing that the allegations are ridiculous. Now, Mr. Lindsey, are they true?...

"Any suggestion that the president offered anyone a job in return for silence is a lie." This is a very specific statement indeed, Mr. Lindsey. No job offer in exchange for silence. No twelve year affair with Gennifer Flowers, either. OK, we'll bite. Eleven years and eleven months with Ms. Flowers? How about eleven years, ten months? Could you let us know when we're getting warm, at least?[29]

On December 21, Hillary Rodham Clinton came out swinging to defend her embattled husband and decried the troopers' allegations as "trash for cash."[30] Sound familiar? Pundits and press recalled going through the Gennifer Flowers saga, which seemed to have eroded sympathy for Clinton by the time Troopergate broke. By then, many had concluded that the Flowers tapes showed a close relationship between Flowers and Clinton, and now, former bodyguards were speaking out and confirming the essence of Flowers's claim to a long-term affair with Clinton. Still, in the early weeks of Troopergate, no women came forward to corroborate the troopers' allegations, prompting one Washington journalist to sneer, "Where are the women?" in a *Newsweek* article entitled "The Citizens of Bimboland."[31] As we've seen, many women had been contacted by Clinton and his cadre and then either refused comment or denied affairs when questioned by the press. One woman, however, had apparently never been contacted by Clinton's scandal team or the press, and she was about to tell her story.

◊

For all its steamy content, the troopers' first exposé didn't attribute to Clinton any interactions with women that involved *unwanted* sexual advances. The Clinton painted by his former bodyguards was sleazy, reckless, and disrespectful to women, but not rebuffed by any of them. Paula Jones had a problem with that. However charmed or seduced other women may have been by Clinton, she had been horrified by his crass advances and had adamantly refused to engage in any consensual fooling around with him.

Paula Jones appeared at a February 11, 1994, press conference surrounded by her lawyer, Cliff Jackson and his troopers, right-wing activists, and journalists, all hounding her for details of her encounter with Bill Clinton. Jones's lawyer, Danny Traylor, introduced her to the crowd: "Ladies and gentlemen, out of deference to the First Family [and] the presidency, I do not want to appeal to the prurient interests of us all....But let me assure you that what transpired in that room [between Jones and Clinton] is the legal equivalent of on-the-job sexual harassment."[32] Reporter Michael Isikoff was present for the press conference. In his 1999 book *Uncovering Clinton* he recalled his initial impression of Jones:

> Jones herself seemed a puzzle. Slight, somewhat mousy, with long dark hair, she had a high-pitched, squeaky voice. She was twenty-seven years old, the mother of a young boy.... When it was her turn to speak, she remained maddeningly circumspect. "It's just humiliating what he did to me," she said. What? reporters wanted to know. What had he done to you? "He treated me in a most unprofessional manner." Reporters hate nothing more than to be teased.[33]

She told the gathered crowd that on May 8, 1991, she'd been working at the registration desk for the AIDC at the Excelsior Hotel. A state trooper had escorted her to a hotel room and waited outside while Clinton asked her for a "type of sex." She also presented affidavits from two friends whom she'd told of this incident the day it happened. She gave few other details that day. Her lawyer, Danny Traylor, closed the saga with a "quaint entreaty," according to Isikoff: "We've got Bosnia. We've got a health care crisis.... Mr. President, this is something that shouldn't occupy your energy and your attention.... [T]ell the American people what the truth of this matter is. If you made a mistake, the American people will forgive you."[34] Clinton, of course, had no intention of doing such a forthright thing. The Jones versus Clinton battle had begun.

Another reporter who had attended Paula Jones's press conference described Paula as "a small, attractive, appropriately frightened-looking woman" and found her story credible; part of the reason he found Jones easier to believe now was that he had caught on to "the clever two-step scandal-avoidance strategy the White House has chosen.... The tactic can be summarized as: 'It's not true. It's not true. It's old news.'"[35] The same reporter explained why Paula Jones initially received such scanty news coverage:

> Clinton is also the best president we've had in a long time. That is the unspoken reason the sex charges haven't received as much play as you might expect. Reporters are patriots, too; it's their dirty little secret. So Jones didn't make it onto CNN. *The New York Times* buried a five-inch story on her charges, which featured Clinton's characteristic find-the-loophole denial. ("He does not recall meeting her. He was never alone in a hotel with her.") Few journalists want to see the president crippled now that he is making some progress cracking large, intractable domestic problems.[36]

Before Isikoff and his editors had decided when and how to cover Paula Jones's story for *The Washington Post*, the paper ran a biting, belittling story in its Style section writing off Paula Jones as another "eruption" of "Mount Bimbo."[37] The Paula Jones press conference received similar, spotty treatment in the mainstream press over the next couple of months. The story lingered in the background, put briefly into play again when Troopergate got a nudge in April 1994 after another trooper publicly backed the accounts of his colleagues.[38] This trooper, L.D. Brown, went public after the newly-appointed Independent Counsel Robert B. Fiske, Jr., subpoenaed him to testify about Whitewater events.[39] Trooper Brown said he had helped Clinton approach "at least one hundred" women over the years. "Certainly not all of those were successful, but in terms of making approaches, yeah, sure, at least one hundred," Brown claimed.[40] Most relevant to a revived interest in Paula Jones, Brown commented that some of the sexual encounters amounted to "just having a good time" but others bordered on sexual harassment.[41] "Truly it was taking advantage of a position of power over some of these women," Brown said.[42]

Meanwhile, after securing exclusive interviews with Paula Jones, her family, and friends over the course of a couple of months, *The Washington Post* had not yet run a piece on her claims, to Paula and her husband Steve's immense frustration. Right-wing Clinton bashers, eager not to let a political weapon slip away, approached Paula and Steve consistently, eventually persuading them to speak out in interviews for, among others, *National Review* and the documentary that later became *The Clinton Chronicles*, the bible for the I-Hate-Clinton crowd.[43] In April 1994, Paula told a writer for the *Orange County Register* that she wasn't in it this for the money; if she were, she'd have gone to the tabloids and talk shows that pay for interviews.[44] Steve told the same reporter, "But all we want is to get the truth out—that's why we gave the story to the *Post* and hoped they'd do something."[45] In the same interview, Paula said she waited to speak out because she felt "nervous and confused" and "dirty and humiliated."[46] Besides, who would she complain to—the police? "Remember, it was a state trooper who took me to Clinton's room."[47] She was coming forward now, after nearly three years, only because she had been labeled as a Clinton conquest in the Troopergate scandal and she wanted to clear her name.[48]

Jones's lawyer, Danny Traylor, was upset when he learned what channels Paula and Steve had been talking through, and when he called her from Little Rock she cried and apologized.[49] But the damage had already been done. Paula Jones would be branded a right-wing tool for the duration of her fight to hold Clinton responsible for his actions.

With no apology forthcoming from the White House, Paula and Steve were considering filing a lawsuit. The statute of limitations for filing a statutory sexual harassment claim under federal law had expired, but she could still file claims for deprivation of civil rights under federal law, and tort claims under Arkansas state law, up to three years after the incident. The deadline for filing her remaining legal claims expired on May 8, 1994. One reporter described Paula as feeling "edgy about becoming a high-profile focus of controversy" fearing "What if somebody wanted to hurt us?" but Steve's attitude was "Clinton is the scum of the Earth," prodding the couple to choose legal action over letting everything go.[50]

Even rumors of a possible lawsuit did little to publicize Paula Jones in the mainstream media. What finally got editors' attention and made it a story was Clinton's hiring of superlawyer Robert Bennett (older brother of conservative icon William Bennett) in anticipation of a lawsuit. "This event, plain and simple, didn't happen," the *Post* quoted Bennett saying in its long-time-coming, lengthy article delving into Jones's story.[51] Off the record, Bennett also began telling reporters there were "nude photographs" of Paula Jones floating around somewhere.[52] The president's lawyers immediately hired an investigative team to dig up the Joneses' finances, discovering they were carrying some credit card debt and had missed a rent payment for their Long Beach, California, apartment.[53] Betsey Wright had already dug into Paula Jones's reputation among her former co-workers at the AIDC, preparing to paint Jones as a gossipy slut.[54]

By May 4, 1994—just days before the deadline for filing a suit—the president's hiring of Bob Bennett to defend against possible litigation was the hook *The Washington Post* needed, prompting it to finally publish the results of the intense investigation Isikoff and two other *Post* reporters had been conducting for months into Paula Jones's allegations.[55] The *Post* article divulged many details it had gathered in its investigation, but the public would have to wait until Michael Isikoff published his book in 1999 to learn the behind-the-scenes details of the *Post's* in-depth inquiry into the plausibility of Paula Jones's story.

For example, the May 4 *Post* article quoted Wright using Clinton's reputation for womanizing as a reason *not* to believe Paula Jones. "What she [Jones] alleges is simply inconceivable as Clinton behavior," Wright told the *Post*.[56] What the *Post* story didn't include, though, was Isikoff's information through off the record interviews and conversations with women about their experiences with Clinton that lend support to the idea that Jones's allegations were perfectly consistent with "typical Clinton" behavior.

A fellow *Post* reporter told Isikoff that a Washington, D.C., school system official had no doubt Paula Jones was telling the truth, based on her own run-in with Clinton. When Isikoff spoke with this school official, Karen Hinton, Hinton said that she met Clinton in 1984 at a Mississippi restaurant.[57] Hinton, then twenty-four years old, was there with a group of people including Willie Morris, a former editor of *Harper's* magazine, of whom Clinton speaks highly in his memoirs. Clinton and his entourage showed up and sat with them for dinner. Hinton told Isikoff how, upon meeting her, "It's hard to describe, but the way he looked at me—nobody could have missed it—it was a direct flirtation. He made direct eye contact, he looked me up and down—it was very clear." As dinner ended, Clinton took out a napkin, scribbled something on it, and handed it to Hinton. It was Clinton's room number at the Holiday Inn, with a question mark. Hinton said he was looking at her as if expecting a response. She avoided his gaze and never went to his room that night. "I was offended," Hinton told Isikoff, "I felt a bit humiliated." Hinton remained a Democratic activist, working for the DNC from 1989 to 1991, where she said everyone joked about how indiscreet Clinton's womanizing was. Hinton didn't think it was funny. Her attitude was more along the lines of disgust, wondering how someone could call himself a supporter of women's rights and treat women that way.

Isikoff met with another woman, Cyd Dunlop, who opened up to him about her own experience with Bill Clinton.[58] Dunlop had been married to a Clinton campaign contributor in the 1980s, and Clinton often visited her husband and flirted with her. In November 1986, Dunlop and her husband spent the night in the Excelsior Hotel in Little Rock after attending Clinton's re-election celebration there. Well after midnight, Dunlop's hotel room phone rang. It was Bill Clinton. "I just wanted to hear your voice again," Clinton cooed. "Can you get out of your room?" Dunlop said she couldn't do that, but Clinton persisted, finally getting her to agree to meet him at the "old statehouse" the next morning. She said yes just to get him off the phone but never went to meet him. The next morning, she and her husband had breakfast with another couple, laughed about the phone incident, and let it go. Dunlop chuckled when she recounted her story to Isikoff. She hadn't felt "harassed" by Clinton, she said; she just "thought he was an idiot." Isikoff never reported these stories through the *Post* because, in his view, while they showed a side of Clinton not widely known, they didn't do enough to show out-and-out sexual harassment.

Perhaps not, but those women's stories (among others in Isikoff's book) provide a context for Paula Jones's allegations that diminishes the defense tossed out by Clinton loyalists—that sexual harassment wasn't "Clinton's style." Without the benefit of these or other women's stories, Paula Jones's lawyers filed *Jones v. Clinton* on May 6, 1994. Danny Traylor had sent an S.O.S. to experienced trial attorneys, and two Virginia lawyers responded to the call. For almost a week the two men, Gil Davis and Joe Cammarata, worked day and night drafting the complaint. After last-minute negotiations with Clinton's lawyers failed the evening of May 5, the lawsuit officially began on Friday, May 6.

In his memoirs Clinton brushes aside the Jones lawsuit as a nuisance, writing blithely that the first week of May 1994 was "another example of everything happening at once" in the White House.[59] Among other events that week, Clinton cheered passage of an assault weapons ban, "held a White House event to highlight the special problems of women without health insurance" and "got sued by Paula Jones. It was just another week at the office."[60] Clinton dismisses Jones by noting that she'd teamed up with his right-wing opponents like Cliff Jackson, and calls her husband a "conservative Clinton hater."[61] He then claims that she only filed the lawsuit after her lawyer attempted to extort a settlement from him. This is a severe mischaracterization of the pre-filing settlement talks.

The night before filing the lawsuit, attorneys for both sides felt the case might be settled out of court. Money wouldn't have been part of the settlement, and it wouldn't have included an express apology from Clinton. Clinton would just admit that he didn't challenge her claim that the two had met in a hotel room, state that Jones did not engage in any improper conduct, and express regret about any aspersions on her good name.

The settlement talks fell through, however, largely because Jones's oldest sister, Charlotte Brown, and her husband Mark Brown, started talking to the press and calling into question Jones's motives. Charlotte and Mark Brown told anyone who would listen that Paula was just out for money—and they were already communicating with the president's lawyers, giving them any dirt that could help discredit Jones.[62] Jones, watching an interview with her sister and brother-in-law, started crying. "Why is she saying that? Why?" she cried.[63] A White House aide the night of May 5 insinuated to CNN that Paula Jones wasn't going to file the lawsuit because she realized she had no case— her own family didn't believe her.[64] This inaccurate spin soured Paula and her lawyers on trying to settle, and they filed the next morning.

In a familiar turn, the Clinton cadre and media immediately branded Paula Jones "white trash out for cash" even though Paula had promised to donate any monetary award from the lawsuit to charity (after paying legal costs). Bob Bennett, Clinton's lawyer, told the press the lawsuit was "tabloid trash with a legal caption."[65] Clinton loyalist James Carville launched his most famous cheap shot at Jones by saying, "Drag a hundred dollars through a trailer park and there's no telling what you'll find."[66] Clinton was spared detailed responses to Jones's complaint in court for years because his lawyers immediately raised "presidential immunity" as a defense, arguing that a sitting president shouldn't have to face a lawsuit until out of office.

A flurry of news reports and commentary swept the media after the lawsuit was filed, but Paula Jones slid to the backburner over the summer as Whitewater investigations and the battle over health care reform intensified. She received splotches of coverage in the summer and fall of 1994 when she took to the interview circuits to give the public her point of view after suffering months of derision in the press as just another bimbo.[67] Nothing she said seemed to counter her image, already cemented in the press, as white trash. One journalist summarized the combined efforts of the White House and press to write off Jones's claims based on her presumed status as white trash:

> Jones must therefore be, in case you missed the point, a floozy, a tramp and a slut....
>
> Let us, for the sake of argument, say all these things are true. Does that mean that Bill Clinton did not proposition her in that hotel room? (Or might Clinton have propositioned her in so crude a manner because he thought her to be a tramp?)....
>
> But many stories suggest that a trashy woman like Jones either had to be asking for it from Clinton or is lying about it. Take your pick.[68]

That article quoted Paula Jones saying, "Just because I'm not a high official like a lawyer or somebody of high rank who's had a big degree or something, just because I'm from a little, small town, I'm not important. And because of who did this to me, I'm not important."[69] Journalist Roger Simon pointed out, "Clinton and Bennett are very important men. And they are automatically given a degree of courtesy, if not outright deference, by reporters who would never give it to 'white trash' like Paula Jones."[70]

Reporters traveled to Jones's hometown, Lonoke, Arkansas, and informed America this was "the land of big hair and tight jeans and girls whose dreams rarely soar further than a stint at hairdresser's school, an early marriage and a baby named Brittany or Tiffany or Brooke."[71] They talked about Jones's upbringing under the strict rules of her conservative, religious parents and how Jones and her two sisters eventually shed their parents' prim and proper ways. "In time," one article stated, "both of the older girls dropped out of high school, married and settled in trailers in nearby Cabot, raising babies. But Jones seemed to want more. By now, Jones had shed her prudish upbringing and was on her way to becoming a bubbly woman whose big eyes, wild hair and provocative clothes drew the attention she craved."[72] Similar pretentious assessments of Paula continued in the months and years following her lawsuit. Reports moved on to Jones's sister and brother-in-law, Charlotte and Mark Brown, interviewing them at length to get their "take" on Paula. "Charlotte speaks of love and hope for a sister gone astray. Mark focuses on money lust and what he says is Jones's cunning way of using men for cash," wrote *The Washington Post* in June 1994.[73] The battle was just beginning.

◊

The immunity issue took a long time to work its way through the court system. The federal district court judge Solomonically split the baby, ruling in December 1994 that Jones could conduct pretrial discovery but the trial itself should wait until Clinton left office, thus creating a kind of temporary, partial immunity for Clinton.[74] Neither side was pleased with this decision.

The November 1994 elections had brought Clinton enough bad news—for the first time in decades, Republicans won control of both houses of Congress. Hillary Rodham Clinton wrote that losing Congress in 1994 left her "[d]eflated and disappointed," and Bill was "miserable," feeling like he'd "let his party down."[75]

Clinton had to walk a tough political line. The defeat of Democrats in Congress had been so sudden and severe that he couldn't completely discount the conservative movement spreading through the Legislative Branch, yet he wasn't about to "go Republican" and endorse the GOP's "Contract with America" either. He told reporters in December 1994, "What I do not agree with them [Republicans] on is that somehow government is inherently the problem. There is a role for government in a modern society."[76] He insisted that government "cannot create opportunity but it can expand it."[77] Clinton made the most of his New Democrat stance, promising to work with the GOP on welfare reform and a line-item veto, while making his top priorities relatively conservative-sounding things like tax cuts for families, college education incentives, and tax breaks for retirement savings.[78] The only good thing about the Jones decision for Clinton was the promise that any trial would be held over until he left office, and appealing the district court's ruling could postpone pretrial discovery until after the 1996 election.

Both sides appealed the immunity ruling, and everyone waited. Finally, in January 1996 the federal court of appeals reversed the lower court's ruling and ordered the district court to let the matter go to trial.[79] This was not good news for Clinton, but he could still appeal to the Supreme Court. Also in the news that week: Whitewater documents long sought by the independent counsel magically turned up in the White House, and a memo detailing Hillary's involvement in Travelgate surfaced.[80] A few months later a federal jury convicted former Clinton business associates Jim and Susan McDougal, along with Clinton's successor to the governorship Jim Guy Tucker, of various criminal counts involving the failed savings-and-loan fiasco known by then as Whitewater.[81] Fortunately for Clinton, the Paula Jones lawsuit didn't heat up again until after the November 1996 election; he had enough trouble avoiding political damage from scandals like Whitewater without Jones's allegations making headlines during an election year.

Clinton appealed the *Jones v. Clinton* appellate decision to the U.S. Supreme Court, which agreed to take the case but didn't hear arguments for it until February 1997. In May 1997 the Supreme Court ruled nine to zero that a sitting president does not have immunity from civil suits concerning alleged conduct that occurred before he took office.[82] Clinton had avoided it until after his re-election, but by the summer of 1997 depositions and other pretrial discovery began in *Jones v. Clinton*.[83] For the first time in the whole drama, a new name surfaced: Kathleen Willey.[84] Jones's lawyers subpoenaed her to testify after being tipped off about an incident involving Ms. Willey and Clinton inside the White House. In September 1997, Jones's lawyers Gil Davis and Joseph Cammarata quit the case.[85] They had tried to convince Paula to settle in August 1997, but she insisted on an apology, which Clinton steadfastly refused. Soon after that round of settlement talks broke down, Paula and Steve found themselves on the receiving end of an IRS audit.[86]

In his memoirs, Clinton says that Jones refused to accept a settlement in 1997 "unless I also apologized for sexually harassing her," adding, "I couldn't do that because it wasn't true." [87] And we all know that Bill Clinton couldn't possibly say anything that wasn't absolutely, 100 percent true. The rejected settlement offer Clinton is probably referring to here would have included a $700,000 payment by Clinton's insurance companies plus a statement from Clinton that *Jones* never engaged in "any improper or sexual conduct" and that any implication to the contrary was regrettable.[88] Jones refused this offer—to her lawyers' consternation—because it didn't include an apology and she felt she had no need for absolution from Clinton.[89] The apology she wanted was for his boorish propositioning of her, not for "sexually harassing" her. Bill Clinton has made himself memorable for parsing words (it depends on what the meaning of "is" is) so it's not unfair to parse his own words. Sexual harassment has a specific, technical, legal definition, and that wasn't *specifically* the behavior for which Jones demanded an apology.

In August 1997 Judge Susan Webber Wright dismissed two of Jones's four claims, which knocked out the insurance carriers and left Clinton personally on the hook for any eventual payout to Jones. The two claims the federal judge dismissed were relatively unimportant sideshows to the sexual harassment issue: defamation and false imprisonment. In *My Life*, Clinton seizes on the dismissal of these two minor claims to make it sound as if Jones's whole case had fallen apart. Plus, Clinton goes on, after her lawyers quit in September 1997, her new attorneys were "closely associated with and funded by the Rutherford Institute, another right-wing legal foundation financed by my opponents."[90] He concludes smugly, "Now there was no longer even a pretense that Paula Jones was the real plaintiff in the case that bore her name."[91] Given that Jones had just refused to settle for big bucks without an apology, it seems odd to try to argue that her lawyers' connections to right-wing causes automatically discredit her. Clinton was able to hire top-notch bulldog attorneys (with substantial ties to Democratic causes) to defend him; if Paula Jones could find powerful attorneys only within the conservative camp to come to her aid, I'm not sure that goes quite as far as Clinton hopes toward discrediting Jones or her case.

In October and November 1997 depositions began in earnest. Jones, her sisters and mother, her two friends Pamela Blackard and Debra Ballantine, Dolly Kyle Browning, Gennifer Flowers, and others all testified under oath. In November 1997, as speculation once again heated up about Paula Jones's claim that she could identify "distinguishing features" of Clinton's genitals, Clinton's lawyer made the undignified protest on national television that a recent medical examination had revealed "In terms of size, shape, direction, whatever the devious mind wants to concoct, the president is a normal man. There are no blemishes, there are no moles, there are no growths."[92] The American public was doubtless relieved to hear that.

A few days before his own deposition, Clinton told reporters he expected the case to go to trial (it was set for May 1998) and that he dealt with the distraction by putting the unpleasantness "over in a little box" so he can "go on and do my work."[93] It was a coping mechanism he'd inherited from his mother Virginia Kelley, who once wrote: "I've always felt the past is irrelevant. I've always maintained that whatever's in someone's past is past, and I don't need to know about it....I've trained myself not to worry about what-ifs, either.... And when bad things do happen, I brainwash myself to put them out of my mind."[94]

On January 17, 1998, President Clinton became the first sitting president ever to be deposed as a defendant. (Coincidentally, the same week, Hillary gave sworn testimony about Whitewater to Kenneth Starr.[95]) Clinton testified that he could not recall with any specificity being at the governor's Quality Management Conference at the Excelsior Hotel on May 8, 1991, and that he never made sexual advances to Paula Jones. His own lawyer, cross-examining him, queried: "[H]ow can you be sure that you did not do these things which are alleged in Ms. Jones's complaint" given that you can't remember being at the hotel that day?[96] Clinton answered, "Because, Mr. Bennett, in my lifetime, I've never sexually harassed a woman, and I've never done what she accused me of doing. I didn't do it then, because I never have, and I wouldn't."[97] Maybe he just never thought of it as harassment. During his deposition Clinton admitted sleeping with Gennifer Flowers but denied sexual relations with Monica Lewinsky and others.

After his humiliation under oath, Clinton's lawyers filed a motion for summary judgment. The federal judge granted the motion on April 1, 1998, which meant the lawsuit was dismissed without a trial, on the ground that the judge determined that Paula Jones's evidence, even if believed, was not legally sufficient to prove sexual harassment.[98] (Clinton points out in his memoirs that the federal judge in the Jones lawsuit was once his law student. While on the campaign trail in 1974, Clinton lost a handful of law school exams he'd been grading. One of those exams belonged to a "good student" who, twenty years later, was the Honorable Susan Webber Wright overseeing the Jones case.[99] Clinton remarks, "I don't think she ever forgave me for losing the exam."[100])

Although Paula Jones's lawsuit was dismissed, damage had already been done. The same weekend as the president's deposition, *Newsweek* and other media sources began breaking the story that would culminate in impeachment proceedings: the Monica Lewinsky scandal.[101] Within a few days, names like Kathleen Willey, Linda Tripp, and Monica Lewinsky hit the headlines— and remained there for a year. By the time the lawsuit was dismissed by the lower court, Kenneth Starr was already investigating whether Clinton had obstructed justice by asking Monica Lewinsky to perjure herself in the Jones case.

Jones's lawyers filed an appeal with the Eighth Circuit Court of Appeals, and the two sides argued the case in October 1998.[102] By then, Clinton's seven months of denials concerning Monica Lewinsky had come to nothing, as he was forced to admit to a grand jury and a baited public in August that he'd been, well, less than completely honest.

Oral argument before the federal court of appeals seemed to favor Paula Jones, particularly since Clinton's public *mea culpa* suggested that his deposition for the Jones cases contained possibly perjurious statements.[103] Not wanting to risk the appellate court reinstating the Jones lawsuit, Clinton settled with Jones out of court on November 13, 1998.[104] She dropped her appeal, and he paid her $850,000 (more than she originally requested in her complaint). She never got what she set out for (an apology), and he ended up with more trouble than he'd ever bargained for from the five and a half year ordeal. A spokesperson for Jones pointed out in an interview after the settlement that even without an apology Paula had accomplished her goal: believability.[105] Especially after Clinton's public *mea culpa* in August, Jones's spokesperson said, Paula realized that nobody believed Clinton's denials anymore and became willing to settle the case even without an official apology from him.[106]

◊

The case took its toll on Jones's personal life. By March 1999, just a few months after settling the lawsuit, she and Steve were living separately. Jones moved back to her parent's home in Arkansas, publicly saying the plan was for Steve to rejoin his family soon. They filed for divorce later that year, partly due to the strain of the entire Clinton ordeal, and Paula stayed in Arkansas.[107] By the end of 2000, Jones was a single mother of two young boys, and she chose to pose for *Penthouse*, earning a tidy sum for her appearance and sparking harsh criticism from conservatives and others who had supported her through her battle with Clinton.[108]

(At the end of 1994, *Penthouse* shabbily purchased partially-nude photographs of Paula from an ex-boyfriend,[109] and printed them along with an article entitled "The Devil in Paula Jones" portraying Paula as a slut.[110] Paula sued to stop the magazine from publishing the photographs but the court permitted it.[111] She then sued her ex-boyfriend for appropriating her image that way but settled with him out of court when he apologized to her.[112] This incident, of course, made her decision six years later to voluntarily pose nude all the more controversial.)

Ann Coulter, a conservative tongue-lasher who helped use the Paula Jones suit as a political battering ram against Clinton, said after learning of Jones's display in *Penthouse*: "She used to have dignity and nobility and tremendous courage. Now she's just the trailer-park trash they said she was."[113] Her decision to go buff, Paula said candidly, was for the money, to help put her kids through college and get out from under her legal and tax debts.[114] She didn't actually see much of the $850,000 settlement payment after her old and new attorneys had hashed out entitlements to legal fees, and even by 2000 she still owed lawyers money.

Paula had said years earlier on a radio talk show that she would "never pose nude for any men's magazine," and when her voluntary appearance in the December 2000 *Penthouse* issue became public knowledge Larry King asked her, "What happened, Paula?"[115] She replied, "I meant it at the time, but I changed my mind." King pressed her: "You knew when doing it, though, that a lot of your friends, and supporters and people who stood by you would be outraged." Paula displayed a down-to-earth simplicity in her response: "None of my friends, first of all, Larry, are outraged...because you know what? If you have true friends in life, they will always be your friends no matter what decision that you make in life. They are going to love you, support you, they don't have to agree with it, but they can support you and love you and stick by with you, and I have not had a problem whatsoever with any of my true friends." Anyone who has struggled with their direction in life, taking heat from the outside world while finding solace among a few true friends knows what she meant.

When Larry King confronted her with another quote from Coulter—railing about how Paula is obviously not the Christian girl she'd held herself out to be and was no better than Monica Lewinsky—Jones said Coulter had a right to her opinion, and she was sorry Coulter felt that way. Coulter and other commentators, Jones explained, rallied around her during the lawsuit, but once it settled they all vanished from Jones's life, leaving her as a single parent, struggling financially. "And all of a sudden, I didn't hear from anybody after the lawsuit had been settled or whatever to say: 'Paula, how are you doing? Do you need some help or is anything going on in your life that we can help you out with? How's your day going?'" Paula told King that she had no regrets. And no, she doesn't feel any guilt about opening up the can of worms that became the Lewinsky scandal. "[T]hat's Bill Clinton's problem," she retorted. In March 2002, she caused more people to shake their heads in bemusement by appearing on Fox TV's *Celebrity Boxing* in the ring against former figure skater Tonya Harding.[116] (Paula lost.) By summer 2004 Paula Jones was happily remarried, living with her new husband and their child (her third son) in Arkansas.

During the five years of legal warfare, Paula Jones endured endless references as a white trash bimbo,[117] and the Clintons found themselves knee-deep in debt. Amusingly, in the beginning Paula Jones made money and gave it to charity; the Clintons, on the other hand, lost money and had to become a charity. In the summer of 1994, a clothing company paid Paula Jones $50,000 to be a spokesperson; she kept half of it for her legal defense fund and gave the other half to an Arkansas shelter for abused women.[118] (The shelter ended up refusing her donation.) The Clintons, around the same time, started an unprecedented legal defense fund and accepted contributions from the public.[119]

Paula and her husband Steve tried to live a relatively quiet life during those five years, giving interviews only sporadically, focusing on raising their children. After being told by Jones that she wanted to keep her life quiet, one reporter wrote in late 1996, "Neighbors say the thirty year old housewife passes hours with the TV blaring and rarely leaves the gated complex without Steve, her spouse. When she does venture out, strangers approach her in restaurants, shops and Von's Supermarket. Some hurl epithets, others compliment her spunk and perseverance."[120] Attempting to be balanced, the New York reporter wrote about how "Jones's detractors, including several anonymous White House aides" continued to dismiss Jones as "a big-haired trailer park queen" and a "money-grubbing opportunist determined to shake down and embarrass the president of the United States," while Jones's "defenders describe her as a somewhat naïve woman of simple values, motivated only by an obsession with clearing her name."[121] Jones told a friend, "I just want to tell my story. I deserve the chance to be heard."[122]

Paula Jones became a political football during the five years of her lawsuit, fumbled by conservatives who accused feminists of a double standard for not supporting Jones, and by feminists and left-wingers who used Jones to claim that conservatives never care about women until they have the opportunity to use one to attack a president they hate.

Paula herself once told reporters she felt nettled by feminists' refusal to come to her aid, speculating that maybe it was because of the hatchet job the press and Clinton defenders had done on her character. Comparing herself to Anita Hill, who received immediate, ardent support from feminists in 1992 Paula said, "You know, I'm not college-educated. And, I'm not a law professor. And they slammed me. They made me look like a—you know, some kind of a trash from Arkansas. And I think that people didn't believe me because of the bad things that—that they were saying about me."[123] Yet the cruelty continued. Journalist Andy Rooney snidely said after watching an interview with Paula Jones, he believed her—but his point was "what bad taste any man must have who was ever attracted to anyone so unattractive."[124] Rooney went on viciously:

> I went to a library that keeps copies of dirty magazines like *Penthouse* under lock and key. I was able to look at the issue featuring Ms. Jones. She may be the most unattractive woman ever to voluntarily take off her clothes in front of a camera. In her old age, Helen of Troy was said to have looked at herself in the mirror and wondered why ever she had been twice carried off. If Paula Jones looked at herself in *Penthouse* she must wonder if any jury is ever going to believe that Clinton was sexually attracted to her.[125]

It was certainly this sort of savage public humiliation that prompted Paula Jones to get a make-over[126] and eventually a nose job.[127] In its Style section, *The Washington Post* called Paula Jones's revamped image "one of the most jaw-dropping public make-overs ever," and condescendingly observed, "The new Jones is sleeker, softer and sexier than she was in 1994."[128]

About the time that the Supreme Court was preparing to decide the immunity issue in *Jones v. Clinton*, (but after the November 1996 election), Paula Jones began receiving markedly more generous analysis in the mainstream media, even before her amazing makeover. There seemed to be some regret for portraying her so quickly and ruthlessly as white trash. There also appeared to be more hesitation in swallowing every denial the White House issued. The turning point might have been a well-researched article, part legal analysis, part investigative journalism, by a respected (and liberal) lawyer, Stuart Taylor. He wrote a 15,000 word article for *American Lawyer* magazine's November 1996 issue that made the rounds among the Washington press corps and found wide reception there.

Taylor's article examined all the evidence available about the case, and concluded that you had to believe one of three things: Paula Jones made everything up and lied convincingly to friends and family about it; Paula Jones *and* her friends and family conspired to make the whole story up; or Paula Jones was essentially telling the truth. Drawing many comparisons and contrasts with Anita Hill's accusations against Clarence Thomas, Taylor thought Paula Jones's story had as much or more credibility than Anita Hill's, and chastised the liberal press for "class bias" for discounting Paula because of her lack of education and big hair while crediting Anita with her Ivy League education, style, and poise. Taylor's article even prompted *Newsweek* journalist Evan Thomas to recant his cruel depiction of Paula Jones as "some sleazy woman with big hair coming out of the trailer parks"[129] and feature Paula Jones and a reassessment of her case on the January 13, 1997, cover of *Newsweek*.[130] Other liberals took note of Taylor's article and began commenting on the hypocrisy of Clinton's public image and private conduct. Andrew Sullivan mentioned Taylor's article when writing in November 1996:

> Clinton has long been a public feminist, and constantly touts his concern and respect for women as his equals. Women, in general, have repaid the compliment by voting for him in disproportionate numbers. Indeed, women's groups have long been among his most vehement defenders. And yet Clinton is being sued for sexual harassment.[131]

Much of what was analyzed by Taylor remained the most telling evidence available throughout the remainder of the Jones lawsuit, since the case never actually went to trial; even the depositions ended up with more relevance for Kenneth Starr than Paula Jones.

◊

It's important to remember that Jones's lawsuit was eventually dismissed not on the basis that she couldn't sufficiently prove what happened in the hotel room, but on the judge's determination that even if things happened like Jones alleged, she couldn't demonstrate all the legal requirements of sexual harassment. Most importantly, it would have been difficult for Jones to prove she'd suffered on the job because of her encounter with Clinton. Records showed she'd received cost of living and merit wage increases, so it would have been mostly her own testimony about feeling uncomfortable at her job knowing that her boss was a friend and appointee of Clinton. Whether or not she could prove her legal case of sexual harassment is a separate question from whether she had credible evidence of being sexually mistreated during her fifteen minutes alone with Bill Clinton. Even granting that no witnesses were present in that hotel room, there were a lot of good reasons to believe she was essentially truthful in her account of what happened. Of course it came down to her word against his—yet another case of he says, she says. She told her version under oath, and he denied it under oath.

For our purposes, it's enough that Paula Jones's story possesses plausibility. No one was ever able to discredit her story, though many efforts were made to discredit her as a person. Although I summarized the encounter earlier in the chapter, here is a more detailed version (in more detail than I wish was necessary!) of Paula Jones's account of what happened, gleaned from her legal complaint[132] and from journalist Michael Isikoff's interviews.[133] The picture they paint is vivid and hauntingly plausible.

By May 8, 1991, Jones had been working for the AIDC for about two months. Pamela Blackard, a friend and co-worker, was working with Jones at the registration desk in the Excelsior Hotel that day for the AIDC-sponsored Quality Management Conference.

A man approached the registration desk and made small talk with Jones and Blackard, identifying himself as Danny Ferguson, Governor Clinton's bodyguard. He returned at about 2:30 p.m., told Paula the governor wanted to meet her and handed Jones a piece of paper with a room number written on it.

After talking it over with Blackard, Jones accompanied Trooper Ferguson upstairs. The bodyguard waited outside while Jones entered the room. Clinton shook her hand and they exchanged small talk for a few minutes. Clinton told Jones that her boss was a "good friend" of his. Jones asked him something about Hillary Clinton's work with children in the school system, and whether he was running for president.

After about five minutes, Clinton was standing near the window. He reached over and held her hand, pulling her close to him. Jones withdrew and tried to make conversation. Clinton was listening to her but his face was "beet red." He moved closer to her, leaning against the back of a chair, and put his hand under her culottes. She said "What are you doing?" and tried to retreat but he was now trying to kiss her neck.

She backed away and he said he'd been noticing her downstairs, how he loved her curves and the way her hair fell down her back. She sat down on a couch saying she really needed to be going. "Oh, you don't need to go right now," he said to her, and sat down beside her.

When she looked over, Clinton had his trousers and boxers down to his ankles and was sitting there, exposing himself. "I was literally just scared, shocked," Jones said. Clinton was "holding it ...fiddling it or whatever." Jones told Isikoff, "And he asked me to—I don't know his exact word—give him a blowjob or—I know you gotta know his exact words.... He asked me to do something, I know that. I'll tell you, I was so shocked. I think he wanted me to kiss it.... And he was saying it in a very disgusting way, just a horny-ass way that just scared me to death."

She jumped up and said she didn't want to, that she wasn't that kind of girl, and Clinton replied, "Well, I don't want to make you do something you don't want to do." As he pulled up his boxers he told her to call him if she got any trouble from her boss for being away from the registration desk. As she left, he told her, "You are smart. Let's keep this between ourselves."

A few weeks later, her job entailed delivering some documents to the governor's mansion. She ran into Clinton at the Capitol rotunda. He greeted her cheerfully, put his arms around her in a bear hug and said to his bodyguard, "Look at us, kind of like Beauty and the Beast, isn't it?"

For excellent analysis of evidence supporting these central allegations of Jones's story, there are two must-reads. First, Michael Isikoff's book *Uncovering Clinton*, and second, Stuart Taylor's article "Her Case Against Clinton" in the November 1996 issue of *American Lawyer*. Neither author appeared motivated by any political vendetta against Clinton; Taylor even wrote his article after writing two years earlier in the same publication that he thought Paula Jones was lying. The evidence, not politics, changed his mind. As someone who voted for Clinton, Taylor wrote, "I don't want to believe that the president is a reckless sexual harasser, and I'll never know for sure exactly what happened when Clinton was alone with Jones. But Jones's evidence is highly persuasive," leaving Taylor "all but convinced that whatever Clinton did was worse than anything [Clarence] Thomas was even accused of doing."[134] Since our purpose isn't to prove Paula Jones's case in a strict legal sense, we'll let readers interested enough to get their hands on Isikoff's book and Taylor's article decide for themselves how convincing Jones's case was. Meanwhile, let's explore what her story means in terms of Clinton's recurring mistreatment of women and his liberal beliefs.

◊

In the dry, stilted language of federal regulations, the federal Equal Employment Opportunity Commission defines sexual harassment this way:

> Unwelcome sexual advances, requests for sexual favors, and other verbal or physical conduct of a sexual nature constitutes sexual harassment when submission to or rejection of this conduct explicitly or implicitly affects an individual's employment, unreasonably interferes with an individual's work performance or creates an intimidating, hostile or offensive work environment.[135]

This definition of sexual harassment violates federal law, specifically, Title VII of the Civil Rights Act of 1964. Clearly, people can experience "unwelcome sexual advances, requests for sexual favors, and other verbal or physical conduct of a sexual nature" and feel violated, humiliated, embarrassed, and fearful in a variety of circumstances that would not meet this definition of sexual harassment because of a lack of impact on employment. For instance, how many creeps on the street or in clubs use obscene pick-up lines that make their targets feel uncomfortable, degraded, and even afraid for their safety? Legally, Paula Jones's sexual harassment claim hinged on her ability to connect what happened with Clinton in the hotel room to her job as a state employee. Personally, her encounter with Clinton amounted to real mistreatment regardless of whether it impacted her employment or whether her experience merited legal redress.

Because the phenomenon of legal bans on sexual harassment evolved in the context of workplace discrimination, sexual harassment has become a politicized issue polarizing the left and right on the ideological spectrum. The left pushed for legal prohibitions, while the right called attention to some of the excesses caused by such laws. Feminists and scholars in fields like sociology and psychology have theorized about the causes and impact of sexual harassment, but in political discourse the topic is usually reduced to generalizations thrown around by both sides. The left condemns any reluctance to enact or enforce anti-sexual harassment laws as attempts to stifle women's rights, while the right tends to view stronger anti-sexual harassment measures as attacks on free speech by man-hating feminists. What gets lost in this reductionist approach to the topic is the seriousness of the behavior that forms the crux of sexual harassment, and its impact on women who endure it. That behavior consists of unwanted sexual advances.

Whether inside or outside a workplace, unwanted sexual advances are almost always premised on a view of women as mere objects, and are usually more about power than sexual gratification. While both women and men can, and do, impose unwanted sexual advances on each other, women generally experience such advances in a different context than men do. One of the key reasons women are more sensitive about unwanted sexual advances than men are is that men are generally stronger than women. This means that in a situation where a man is verbally (let alone physically) pressing a woman for sex, a woman is more inclined to sense a threat behind suggestive requests. Even a one-time incident of unwanted sexual advances can leave a woman feeling afraid for her safety, fearing that her rejection of the man's advances will leave him frustrated enough to just take what he wanted.

This aspect of mistreatment through unwanted sexual advances is buttressed by realizing that such advances demonstrate a view of women as objects rather than whole, individual people. Having a man make uninvited—and, in Jones's case, completely unprovoked—sexual overtures toward a woman leaves her in serious doubt that he sees her as anything more than a useful device to fulfill some sexual desire. That impression can further a sense of fear that, when rejected, the man may not hesitate to use force to fulfill his desire, since it appears that he doesn't know her or care to know her except in a debased sexual way.

If this topic of discussion is leaving men a bit frustrated, I can't blame them. The line between *unwanted* sexual advances and flirtation based on mutual attraction is often fuzzy, complicated by basic differences in men's and women's perceptions and use of verbal and body language. Some men accused of sexual harassment no doubt feel greatly misunderstood, believing they were actually complimenting a woman or simply expressing a romantic interest in her. One of the contextual keys to identifying unwanted sexual advances, however, is whether a man's advances address themselves to a person, or just an object. Verbal communication and body language that bypass all aspects of a woman except her body, for instance, are likely to be perceived as objectification, triggering the sense of fear or intimidation that makes unwanted sexual advances disturbing rather than innocuous.

The difference between unwanted sexual advances that objectify and degrade women, leaving them humiliated, debased, and even frightened, on the one hand, and harmless flirtation and natural romantic interest, on the other hand, may not always be readily identifiable. However, some interactions fall clearly within the realm of unwanted sexual advances. Paula Jones's experience with Bill Clinton in that hotel room is one of the clear cases. The first aspect of her story that places her encounter with Clinton in the realm of unwanted sexual advances that left her feeling objectified and humiliated was the power differential between them. He was governor, she was a bottom-rung state worker. That dynamic factored into her ability to stand up for herself, since fending off the governor is likely to be mentally and psychologically much more difficult than fending off, say, an obnoxious bartender at the local pub. Using the police to arrange his meeting with her reinforced this power, enhancing her trepidation when he made sexual advances toward her.

The second aspect of Paula Jones's story that helps identify her interaction with Clinton as unwanted sexual advances is Clinton's physical overtures toward her after only a few minutes of small talk. That behavior sent a message that he had little or no interest in anything about Paula Jones except her body and its ability to please him. He held her hand, and when she protested, he slid his hand under her culottes. Stop right there. *After* she expressed reluctance, he made a physical grab for sex. At that point, he made two things clear to her: one, she existed to gratify his urges, and two, he might not take no for an answer.

She refused and backed away again. Partly because of the aforementioned power differential, she didn't leave the room at that point, not wanting to offend him too badly. She continued making small talk, and sat down on a couch away from him. He sat down beside her, sort of listening to her, and paid her what he perhaps thought were compliments about how he loved her curves and the way her hair fell down her back. Between lovers, these comments are complimentary, but between strangers, these comments only intensify the recipient's impression that this man knows what he wants and it's all about physical gratification.

The remainder of their interaction reinforces these two aspects: the power differential and his objectification of her. He sat on the couch next to her and pulled down his pants, exposing himself to her, asking her to perform oral sex on him. The unspoken thought that might zoom through a woman's mind in a moment like that may be, *Or what?* If she refuses, what happens then? His behavior has indicated a strong desire for her to service him; will he force her to do it? Jones refused and quickly got up to leave the room. His response? "Well, I don't want to make you do something you don't want to do." Reporter Michael Isikoff believed Jones's memory of that statement boosted her credibility. It's a "well, at least" kind of statement that a woman probably wouldn't include in her story if she were making it all up. Well, at least he wasn't going to force her to service him. Jones's reaction when Michael Isikoff pointed this out to her was: "Oh, wasn't that sweet of him? Asshole. That one little sayin' in there I guess will get him off the hook."[136] She's right. What a great guy, letting her know that he wasn't going to rape her. It doesn't get him off the hook, though.

Regardless of whether his actions fell short of sexual assault, Clinton's behavior falls squarely in the realm of degrading, humiliating, objectifying unwanted sexual advances. His behavior should be completely unacceptable from any man, particularly one who holds himself out to be a champion of women's rights. Women have fought for centuries to be treated with respect as individuals with souls and minds, who exist for their own purposes rather than as sexual toys for men. That kind of basic respect and appreciation for female autonomy is far more important than a slew of legal protections Clinton supported. Blatant refusal to accord this kind of respect and autonomy to women with whom he comes in personal contact amounts to a type of misogyny, as it demonstrates through action an assumption that women exist chiefly to fulfill his own whims and are not worthy of full personhood. One journalist queried during the Paula Jones lawsuit in 1995:

> How does a man who claims to hold women in high regard explain away what seem to be chauvinistic exploitations of women? Simple: Make the accusers out to be pitiable "bimbos" who, for reasons of politics or money, lie about their relations with the former governor of Arkansas. According to this strategy, conceived by [Betsey] Wright before the inner circle did her in, Clinton maintains his image among professional women by separating off the "bimbos" as spindle-heeled opportunists with big hair.[137]

Even before the 1996 election it was something of a problem for Clinton to maintain his grip on the women's vote while stories of his "private" mistreatment of women abounded.

The discrepancy between Clinton's public, official, political "treatment" of women and his personal mistreatment of them is more than "just" his personal weakness. Part of the discrepancy is due to his liberal political beliefs. Liberalism won't produce Clintonian misogyny in every adherent; it takes certain emotional, psychological predispositions to treat women the way Clinton does. But his politics does influence his behavior, and Paula Jones's experience helps illustrate a fourth aspect of liberal ideology that can breed misogyny.

Liberalism champions "groupism" rather than individualism. That is, liberalism classifies people into groups and focuses on policies to promote group welfare rather than individual welfare. People are only as important as their group membership makes them. Individuals' rights have little importance compared with so-called group rights. Thus, most policies and proposals from leftists concentrate on promoting the interests of certain groups rather than making rules that apply to all individuals as evenly as possible. Most of the groups liberals champion tend to consist of people who have historically been dominated by the powers that be. For example, liberals place much emphasis on helping minority racial groups and women. Under the guise of "equal rights for all," leftist policies usually end up calling for measures that in reality go far beyond removing actual barriers that have subjugated members of these groups and attempt to provide extra assistance or protection for such groups.

There are many problems with this core aspect of left-wing ideology. A glaring one is that human beings are much more than their physical, biological, or even sociological characteristics. Classifying people into groups according to those characteristics and then advocating policies with sole regard to those groups fails to account for people's individual interests. Not all people who belong to a group based on those kinds of characteristics possess identical interests or needs. Likewise, some people who do not belong to those groups have desires perfectly aligned with people in those groups. Giving pride of place to the welfare of groups overshadows the welfare of individuals who either do not belong to those groups, or belong to those groups but have their own individual needs or interests.

Leftism's elevation of group identity to center stage in policymaking necessarily pushes aside the value of each person's individuality. Group politics is a kind of short cut for trying to accomplish some good goals (like nondiscrimination) but like most short cuts it skips some important steps. One of those key steps is factoring in people's individual needs and interests. Black or white, people have an interest in acquiring employment when they want to work. Male or female, people often struggle paycheck to paycheck to support children. Gay or straight, people have an interest in an efficient, non-corrupt justice system. Instead of focusing the debate on solutions to common problems faced by individuals, liberal ideology centers the debate on promoting the welfare of certain groups, presuming to know the interests and needs of all members of those groups and discounting the needs and interests of those who don't belong.

Liberalism's focus on group politics also perpetuates the use of stereotypes that further degrade and undervalue people's individuality. When policies and proposals are constantly centered on so-called "minority rights" or "women's rights" it's inevitable that statements lumping all members of those groups together emerge in the debate. "Women want such-and-such," or "African-Americans need this-or-that," become part of the argument, as if the proponent actually believes herself competent to speak on behalf of every single member of those groups.

This perpetuation of group identity stunts the prospect of shaping laws and regulations that apply as generally and equally as possible to us all. Part of the value of law is to set up rules that people know to follow. Law tells each of us what society expects from us. Within the proscriptions and requirements of the law, our behavior is up to us; laws set a kind of boundary, warning us in advance what behaviors are unacceptable. If individual freedom of choice is truly valued, society will enact as few laws as possible and apply them as generally and fairly as possible. If values other than individual freedom of choice are paramount, laws and regulations quickly become complicated, nearly impossible to predict or follow to the letter, with some laws applying only to certain groups, other laws applying to everyone. Liberalism values group welfare much more than individual freedom of choice, so laws and regulations abound in their efforts to force "good" results for their target groups, at the expense of personal autonomy.

Let's return to the topic of sexual harassment to see this dynamic in action. It wasn't enough that women are not legally forbidden anymore from getting an education and entering the workforce. Feminists and other leftists thought the problem of workplace sexual harassment needed a legal remedy. Since sexual harassment is such a nebulous experience, defined so subjectively and turning on the perceptions of the people involved, laws banning it are difficult to articulate. But they have tried anyway, with the side result that many men self-censor themselves to avoid being accused of sexual harassment, and institutions remove valid expressions of art and learning to avoid even the appearance of sexual harassment. It's a classic example of leftism's emphasis on group identity over individualism. "Women need protection from sexual harassment in the workplace." This generalization pushes aside the fact that sexual assaults of all varieties were already punishable by law, and glosses over the reality that unwanted sexual advances are difficult to define and tend to be subjectively interpreted. Moreover, it's another political argument injecting stereotypes into the debate: "Women need ...." If you're a woman, you need this. By implication, if you're a man, you tend to engage in this negative behavior. Using those generalizations to shape law (which is always, fundamentally, the use of political force) discounts the individuality of many men and women whose needs and interests don't fit neatly into what liberals have deemed their respective gender groups' needs and interests and perpetuates the idea that conclusions about people can be drawn based on gender rather than individual behaviors.

Attached to a leftist ideology that treats people according to membership in groups, perhaps Clinton found it easier to rationalize treating Paula Jones with such disrespect and objectification. Liberalism calls for gender equality, but treats it strictly as a politicized group issue. Women's rights are equated solely with political initiatives like reproductive rights and tougher anti-sexual harassment measures. A person's individualism gets lost in this focus on groupism. Paula Jones is a member of the biologically-defined, politically important group "women." As such, Clinton took good care of her by the standards of liberal ideology: he advocated protecting her right to choose an abortion and her right to equal pay for equal work.

But Paula Jones standing alone as an individual person, unconnected to a political agenda for "women's rights," meant very little to Bill Clinton. In fact, as an individual he helped paint her as a member of yet another group, to be toyed with and mocked at will: white trash. That "group" gets scant attention from liberal activists, and her presumed membership in it far outweighed the importance of her membership in the group "women." Perhaps applying his ideological focus on groupism over individualism helped Clinton interact personally with individual women like Jones in a manner that demonstrated contempt, disrespect, and objectification, while maintaining his self-image as a promoter of women's rights; on balance, he was doing good things for women, and those women whose needs or interests weren't met by his policies didn't really "count."

Did Paula Jones's mistreatment by Clinton warrant the court battle she initiated? Probably not. Her case was weak by legal standards, mostly due to having to prove the unwanted sexual advances negatively impacted her work environment. Did Clinton's mistreatment of her justify doing all she could to call public attention to his behavior? Absolutely. There is no constitutional requirement that presidents treat women with respect. The public should, however, have information about their leaders' unofficial behavior when such information is available. Her efforts to embarrass him and wrangle an apology from him were, on a personal level, perfectly justifiable. While he racked up good marks for championing women's causes, she tried to point out that his personal behavior spelled misogynistic mistreatment of women. In that effort, she succeeded.

CHAPTER SIX

SHE ASKED FOR IT
REPEATEDLY

JUST A FEW WEEKS before Troopergate broke, and about ten weeks before Paula Jones's press conference, the White House arranged a meeting between President Clinton and a woman who had worked for several months as a volunteer in the White House Social Office. Kathleen Willey requested the appointment with intent to beg Clinton to help her find a paying job. Her husband Ed Willey was facing disgrace and financial ruin as a lawyer who had bilked clients out of substantial sums of money to cover his personal tax liens. Kathleen Willey was desperate. Strained by their financial quagmire, their future was on the rocks, and Kathleen believed her best hope was a full-time, salaried position. Clinton had always been friendly and approachable to the Willeys, so she pressed for an appointment with him. The White House scheduled her for a November 29, 1993, meeting with the president.

During that encounter in the Oval Office, Willey told Clinton she and Ed were in serious trouble and that she needed a job badly. He comforted her and expressed sympathy for what she was going through. He also kissed her, put his hand on her breast, and put her hand on his erect penis. She was shocked.

Her first reaction was to slap him, but "I don't think you can slap the president of the United States like that."[1] She left hurriedly and saw head of the U.S. Treasury Lloyd Bentsen,[2] chairman of the OMB Leon Panetta, and chairperson of the Council of Economic Advisors Laura Tyson outside the Oval Office waiting to meet with the president.[3] She couldn't believe what had just happened.

Kathleen and Ed Willey met Bill Clinton in 1989 at a political rally in Charlottesville, Virginia for Virginia Lieutenant Governor Douglas Wilder,[4] and again at a 1991 event for Clinton.[5] When Clinton announced his bid for the White House both Willeys were enthusiastic about his campaign. Virginia's first Clinton for President headquarters opened in Ed Willey's office in 1991.[6]

In October 1992, Kathleen Willey and a few other local Democrats greeted Bill Clinton at the airport as he arrived in Richmond, Virginia for a televised debate with George H. W. Bush and Ross Perot.[7] Clinton, suffering from laryngitis that day, whispered to Virginia Lieutenant Governor Donald S. Beyer, "I remember that woman from some fund-raising activity, but I can't remember her name."[8] Beyer replied, "That's Kathy Willey."[9] Video footage of this airport greeting depicts this conversation.[10] Nancy Hernreich, Clinton's Little Rock office manager who later became his director of Oval Office operations, approached Kathleen Willey that day and asked if the governor could have her phone number.[11] Willey obliged, and later that afternoon, Clinton called her at home.[12] Noting his raspy voice she commented, "It sounds like you need some chicken soup."[13] Clinton, ever the smooth operator, responded, "Would you bring me some?"[14] She hedged; Clinton said he'd have to call her back, and later that afternoon he did. Clinton asked again about the chicken soup but Willey told Clinton she'd see him that evening at a fundraiser after the debate; in her words, she was "starting to get the drift"[15] of Clinton's interest in her and "my instincts told me he wasn't interested in chicken soup."[16]

Despite sensing Clinton's inappropriate interest in Kathleen, the Willeys remained active supporters of Clinton's campaign and flew to Little Rock with their two college-age children on election night to celebrate Clinton's victory.[17] In April 1993, Kathleen Willey landed a volunteer position in the White House Social Office.[18] Still living in Richmond, she traveled by train to the White House a few days a week to help coordinate events like receptions and the White House Christmas party.[19]

Working in the White House wasn't an unfathomable leap in lifestyle for Willey. She and Ed had married in the early 1970s when she worked as a secretary in his real estate law practice.[20] One colleague of Ed's described him as "very prominent, very well-liked...an attractive guy," and said Kathleen was "involved in a number of charitable organizations."[21] The couple had two children, a son and a daughter.[22] Ed's practice succeeded wildly in the hey-day of the 1980s, but when the real estate market crashed they continued living an extravagant lifestyle even as their income dwindled.[23] They lived in what Willey called a "traditional Southern marriage" and her husband "took care of the finances."[24] They still found a way to donate money to Clinton's 1992 campaign and other Democratic causes,[25] but the trappings of a successful life were about to come crashing down around them.

By the fall of 1993, Ed Willey's embezzlement scheme had been exposed, and creditors hounded them.[26] One day, Kathleen Willey was driving to a Red Cross Meals-on-Wheels volunteer appointment when her husband called her.[27] He asked her to sign a note promising to repay $274,000 to help them escape legal trouble and criminal charges for his embezzlement.[28] She signed the note, which obligated the Willeys to come up with the money in just two weeks.[29] Over Thanksgiving, with that deadline only days away, Kathleen Willey told her family she intended to ask the president for help finding a job, to get herself and her husband out of their mess.[30]

Nancy Hernreich arranged the appointment for her, and on the afternoon of November 29 at about 3:00 p.m., Willey sat across the desk from Clinton in the Oval Office.[31] He asked her if she'd like a cup of coffee and escorted her through a hallway into a private kitchen, handing her a Starbucks mug of coffee. He showed her around the small hideaway office off the end of the hallway, pointing out his collection of political buttons. After a couple of minutes of small talk, she was near tears as she told Clinton about her husband's financial trouble. The bottom line, she told the president, is that she needed a job.[32]

She felt embarrassed and walked back down the hallway toward the Oval Office. When she reached the door that led to the Oval Office, Clinton caught up with her and hugged her. "I'm really sorry this has happened to you," he said. With her back against the door, coffee mug still in her hand, Clinton kissed her. "I was shocked," Willey told reporter Michael Isikoff almost five years later—off the record. "It was like an out-of-body experience."[33] She tried to push away but Clinton just said, "You have no idea how much I wanted you to come to Williamsburg and bring me that chicken soup." Willey asked if he was concerned about people waiting outside, but Clinton brushed it off, saying he had a meeting but he could be late. Clinton took the coffee mug out of Willey's hand and said, "I've wanted to do this ever since the first time I laid eyes on you." He began kissing her again, and his hands were "everywhere"—on her breast, up her skirt, in her hair.[34] He put one of her hands on his crotch. Willey told Michael Isikoff she knew Paula Jones was telling the truth because during this encounter Clinton's face was "beet red," just the way Paula later described him.[35] Someone knocked on the door, causing Willey to disentangle herself and say she had to go.

Willey was shaking as she walked out of the White House, trying not to look at anyone. When she spotted Linda Tripp, a former co-worker, Tripp said, "Where's your lipstick?" Willey took her aside and told her what had happened. Tripp shook her head and said to Willey, "I could always tell the president wanted you."[36] Indignant, Willey insisted that wasn't why she had gone to see Clinton that day. Years later, Linda Tripp would tell a much different version of this conversation. That evening, Willey drove over to her friend's house and recounted the story again. Two other friends later testified that Willey told them about the incident the day it happened.[37]

The day before, the stress of their financial situation had become too much for Ed, and he had left their home to stay at a friend's house for the night.[38] By the evening of November 29, Kathleen Willey was upset about her encounter with Clinton, but she was much more concerned with locating her husband.[39] She couldn't contact him. She found out the following morning that at about 5:00 p.m. the previous evening—a couple of hours after her encounter with Clinton—her husband, then sixty years old, had walked off into the woods and committed suicide by shooting himself in the head.[40]

◊

Without a doubt, November 29, 1993, was "absolutely" the worst day of Kathleen Willey's life.[41] In the midst of her grief, her desperation heightened. Clinton called her the next day. Though she was terribly upset and on sedatives she remembers him saying "You never saw this coming, did you?" and telling her he hoped she would return to work at the White House.[42] A friend had her hospitalized a few days after her husband's suicide.[43] Her legal troubles intensified; she was on the hook for the $274,000 note she'd signed at her husband's request. She was "sued the day after the funeral for half a million dollars."[44] An insurance policy on her husband's life provided some money but she renounced it, allowing it to go to her children to avoid its seizure by her creditors.[45] Clinton came through on a paid position for her (though he later denied any personal involvement getting her the job).[46] The White House hired her in the White House Counsel's office in March 1994,[47] but that only lasted six months.[48] In 1995 the White House sent her on at least two State Department trips at taxpayer expense, giving her the chance to visit locales like Copenhagen and Jakarta.[49] In September 1996 Clinton appointed Willey to an unpaid position with the United Service Organization,[50] which oversees the social needs of military service members.[51]

A friend told her the White House was just trying to keep her quiet, but Willey didn't seem to understand that, or care.[52] She needed help, and a connection to the president of the United States was more help than most widows find. She managed to "hold off a mountain of crushing debt" and "restore her family to financial security."[53] Even while taking full advantage of the White House jobs, one of Willey's friends told Michael Isikoff that the November 29, 1993, encounter left Clinton a "fallen hero" in Willey's eyes.[54] Willey genuinely looked up to Clinton and thought he was a wonderful president. Whatever betrayal she felt after his sexual advances in 1993 was nothing, however, to the betrayal she felt after her story hit the realm of public knowledge four years later.

As one reporter later put it, by 1997 Kathleen Willey "had, it appeared, emerged from a clouded past into the clear vista of the future," having survived her husband's wracking financial ruin and suicide.[55] She had "endured tragedy and scandal only to become a potential witness against the president of the United States."[56]

Kathleen Willey's name first appeared publicly as the target of a subpoena in the Paula Jones lawsuit in July 1997. The Supreme Court had just denied Clinton immunity from suit and the Jones lawyers busied themselves tracking down women as potential witnesses to Clinton's sexual predation. Willey came to their attention because of an anonymous phone call received by Jones lawyer Joe Cammarata in January 1997 while Cammarata was preparing for Supreme Court oral arguments.[57] The caller refused to give her name but gave enough detail about an incident of unwanted sexual advances inside the White House in

1993 to allow the Jones legal team later to identify the caller as Kathleen Willey. Willey denied she made that call but there existed so many similarities in the caller's and Willey's lives that the Jones team (and later a federal judge) thought it probable that Willey and the caller were one and the same. So, Willey was ordered to testify in the Paula Jones case.

Today, Willey still maintains that she did not make that call. She never intended to go public about her experience with Clinton. "I think it was either Linda [Tripp] or Julie [Steele]" who made the call to the Jones lawyers, Willey told me. Julie Steele was once a close friend—the friend to whose home Kathleen went the evening after her encounter with Clinton in the White House. But Steele was facing financial difficulties of her own and from the moment Willey confided in her about the harassment from Clinton, Steele constantly pressured Willey to sell her story. Long before Willey's name ever entered the public realm, Steele even went so far as to buy a stack of tabloids and sit down with Willey to talk about which tabloids to contact.

"I kept telling her I would *never* voluntarily tell my story," Willey recalls now, but Steele kept pressuring her to "just make it quick and dirty" by going for as much money as possible. "She eventually sold me out for $15,000," Willey says. Steele ran to the tabloids and sold them pictures of Willey and her children, traveling the country to get the highest price. The betrayal Willey still feels comes through in her voice as she confides to me, "That was the end of our friendship."

Before the May 1997 ruling by the Supreme Court in the Jones case, reporter Michael Isikoff spoke to Cammarata about the anonymous phone tip.[58] Isikoff thought Kathleen Willey was the caller and met with her in February and March 1997.[59] She denied she'd made the anonymous call, but eventually told Isikoff her story. She would speak only off the record, and hesitated to speak at all. She expressed concern for what her story would do to Chelsea Clinton, and she didn't want to hurt the president. She gave Isikoff the names of two friends whom she'd told of the November 29, 1993 incident immediately after it had happened. Isikoff now had two leads: Tripp and Steele.

Steele confirmed Willey's story to Isikoff in March 1997.[60] Tripp corroborated learning of a sexual encounter between Willey and Clinton on that fateful day in 1993, but told Isikoff it had been something Willey had been excited about.[61] Isikoff later wrote, "Sorting out the women's conflicting accounts is next to impossible. In Tripp's version, Willey was on a single-minded mission to ensnare Clinton. In Willey's, Tripp was consumed with the notion of a romantic attachment between the two [Willey and Clinton] and was constantly egging her on."[62]

Isikoff might not have been able to discern who was telling the truth at the time when he was writing his book, but by February 1999 Tripp herself told Larry King and his national audience that Kathleen Willey is "an honest person" who is "telling the truth."[63] Willey comments now that Tripp's "180 degree" turn-around was "bizarre," but chalks it up to the fact that Tripp felt "personally wronged" after being fired from the White House back in 1994. "Linda was very loyal to the Bush White House and hated the Clintons and their entourage," Willey tells me. The two women were friends while they worked together at the White House, but Tripp was so angry about being fired that their friendship ended bitterly.

When Lloyd Cutler moved in as the new White House Counsel in 1994, Willey was allowed to stay on while Tripp was shunted to the Pentagon. Willey tells me that when Tripp was told she was about to be fired, Tripp "went to [Bruce] Lindsey," a White House advisor and loyal Clinton confidant. Tripp told Lindsey that she knew "about something that happened in the Oval Office" and that he should think twice about firing her. This was no doubt a reference to Kathleen Willey's story. "Next thing you know," Willey sighs, "she's making $90,000 working at the Pentagon." Tripp was still furious over being fired from the White House though, and for some reason blamed Willey for it. On Tripp's last day in the White House in April 1994, she pointed at Willey and yelled "I'll get you for this!" And she did. By corroborating the essence of Willey's story—that Willey and Clinton had a sexual encounter in the Oval Office in November 1993—Tripp relentlessly dragged Willey into the Paula Jones case even though Tripp initially made it sound like the encounter was something Willey had wanted.

Ironically, Willey surmises now, by giving into Tripp's threats and transferring her to the Pentagon, Clinton inadvertently set himself up for the real trouble with Monica Lewinsky; when the White House sent Monica to the Pentagon to keep her away from Clinton, they sent her right into Linda Tripp's path— the one person with incentive and determination to get the president. "Linda Tripp was so devious; if there was anyone she could team up with to get at Clinton, she'd do it," Willey explains. "Of all the people in the world," Willey chuckles, for the White House to "put Monica in [Tripp's] vicinity—someone really messed up on that one. They could have put Monica anywhere, but they sent her to the Pentagon where Linda Tripp befriended her."

Tripp did her best to get back at Willey and Bill Clinton. Tripp's conversations with Isikoff helped get the story off the ground. After their victory in the Supreme Court on May 28, 1997, the Jones legal team hired investigators to track down Willey.[64] In July 1997 they were getting close, and Willey was getting nervous. She called Nancy Hernreich at the White House and warned her that a reporter had been asking her questions.[65] On July 4, 1997, Jones lawyer Joe Cammarata called Willey at her home.[66] She ignored the call and found an attorney for herself.

While Isikoff was talking to Kathleen Willey and others in an attempt to sniff out the Lewinsky scandal, Tripp called Willey one night. Willey hadn't spoke with Tripp in years. Tripp hinted that Clinton was having an affair with an intern and kept "trying to tantalize me with all these details," Willey recalls. Willey thought to herself, "Be careful," not wanting any part of whatever drama Tripp was cooking up. During the phone call, Tripp's call waiting beeped and she asked Willey to hold. When Tripp clicked back over to Willey she said, "Monica?" Willey answered, "No, it's me, Kathleen," and Tripp, sounding confused, hurriedly ended the conversation. Willey, of course, didn't make sense of that incident until months later when the Lewinsky scandal had broken. Recounting it to me years later she sounds bemused at the twisted set of circumstances she found herself embroiled in.

On July 25, 1997, Paula Jones issued a subpoena to Kathleen Willey[67] and the game was on. Willey's lawyer, Dan Gecker, had called Clinton's attorney Bob Bennett a couple of weeks earlier to try to find out what the White House's response might be if Willey was forced to testify.[68] Gecker's primary concern was his client's privacy; Willey did not want to open herself up to the Clinton spin machine by making her story public knowledge.[69] Receiving no definitive answers from the Clinton camp, Gecker objected to the subpoena, claiming Willey had no useful information for the Jones case. By the end of July, though, Willey's name began appearing in the news as an important potential witness. Other than a remark by Bill Bennett to *Newsweek*, the president and White House aides refused to comment on what Willey was expected to say. Spokesperson Mike McCurry even warned reporters to think twice about covering the Willey subpoena at all.[70]

When asked about Willey as a potential Paula Jones witness in early August, President Clinton "froze and glared at the reporter as he finished the question."[71] Clinton answered, "There was a request to be left alone and not harassed and we're just trying to honor it," (referring to Willey's attempt to quash the subpoena) and returned to listing his fall 1997 "priorities" including "education standards, entitlement reform, tobacco restrictions, campaign finance, expanded free trade treaty-making powers and limits on greenhouse gases blamed for global warming."[72] But the Kathleen Willey story was not going to disappear any time soon.

When the infamous Matt Drudge posted the bare outlines of Willey's probable testimony—being groped in the Oval Office—on the *Drudge Report* Web site on July 29, 1997, *Newsweek* decided to run a story, even though Isikoff could only quote Linda Tripp and Julie Steele, since Willey was fighting the subpoena and still refused to talk on the record.[73] Willey was horrified when the Drudge story hit; her lawyer called her that day and told her, "You've been sold out. The *Sun* [a tabloid] has the story and your picture's been sold for $15,000." Willey said, "It's Julie [Steele], right?" and her lawyer said it was. Willey was devastated at being dragged into the spotlight, particularly by a person she once considered a dear friend.

When Isikoff questioned Steele again, this time she told him she'd lied to him in March 1997 at Willey's request, and that no such incident like Willey described ever happened.[74] The way Steele talked to Isikoff, though, made it seem as if her retraction in August 1997 was her way of trying to avoid being named in the story.[75] (She paid dearly for this choice. In January 1999 the Office of Independent Counsel had her indicted by a federal grand jury for lying to federal officials when she repeated this retraction to them. Steele's trial ended in a mistrial in May 1999. Steele stuck to her revised story—that Willey never told her about a groping—even in the face of at least three friends who testified Steele had told them about Willey's sexual encounter with Clinton well before 1997.[76])

The August 11, 1997 issue of *Newsweek* carried a banner headline: "A Twist in the Paula Jones Case."[77] Isikoff quoted Clinton's lawyer Bob Bennett saying Clinton had "no specific recollection of meeting" Willey in the Oval Office, and while Clinton may have consoled Willey around the time of Ed Willey's death, it's "preposterous" to suggest that Clinton made a sexual advance in the turmoil of Kathleen Willey's distress.[78] The article quoted Linda Tripp on seeing Willey emerge from the White House that day "disheveled. Her face was red and her lipstick was off. She was flustered, happy and joyful" Tripp told *Newsweek*.[79] Bob

Bennett told America, "Linda Tripp is not to be believed."[80] This stung Tripp, who had been conversing with the White House (and Monica Lewinsky), trying to be a team player.[81] Julie Steele confirmed Willey's account of receiving a phone call from Clinton back in 1991 (the "chicken soup" conversation) but backtracked from her initial interview with Isikoff and said now that Willey had told her weeks after the alleged incident merely that Clinton had made a "pass" at her.[82]

A few days after the August 11 issue hit the stands, Isikoff received an anonymous phone call from a woman who told him that something similar to what happened to Willey had happened to her in the Oval Office, most likely *after* Willey's encounter.[83] She said after meeting Clinton many times at Democratic events, she would often be invited to the White House. On one such occasion, Clinton took her from the Oval Office through the same hallway into the private office. Clinton began kissing her and touching her breasts. She pushed herself away from him and Clinton turned away from her and "finished the job himself."[84] The woman said she'd been stunned; she'd never had a man take advantage of her like that. The woman refused to give Isikoff her name, citing her husband's on-going activity in Democratic politics, but wanted Isikoff to know "there are a lot of us out there who are not bimbos."[85]

Willey's attorney tied up the subpoena with legal objections until a court hearing in November 1997, when a judge gave Paula Jones permission to depose Willey.[86] The day before that hearing, Willey and her lawyer met with Bob Bennett, and Willey told Bennett that if forced to testify she'd have to admit that Clinton's advances on November 29, 1993 had been "unexpected" and "unwanted."[87] Willey said later that she had "felt pressured by Mr. Bennett," who had opened the meeting by telling her that the president "thought the world of [her]" and then said, "Now, this...was not sexual harassment, was it?"[88] When she remained silent Bennett pressed, "Well...it wasn't unwelcome, was it?"[89] After she said it was, Bennett suggested that she find herself a criminal lawyer, intimating that she'd face perjury charges if she dared tell her story under oath.[90] Bennett later told the press that "any suggestion that I threatened or intimidated her in any way is a bald-faced lie."[91] In Clinton-speak, it must depend on what the words "threaten" and "intimidate" really mean.

Before Willey was ordered to testify at her deposition, the Clinton team publicly kept quiet about her, hoping the subpoena would be quashed and she would keep silent. Strange, disturbing incidents occurred regularly, however, which left Willey feeling insecure and unsafe even before her deposition. She sensed she was being watched and followed, and her suspicions were confirmed by a number of people in her hometown informing her that strange men were asking about her. Before these things began to happen to her, Willey says, "It just never occurred to me that people would do things like this." But it wasn't difficult for her to guess who had the most motive to have her watched, followed, and intimidated. "I just know these people are so good, they are surrounded by layers and layers of people who will intimidate people like me," she told me, talking about the Clintons. "I was terrified. This is just the way these people do business."

A few months before her deposition Willey had three tires replaced on her car. "I remember standing at the tire place," she told me, "on a warm September day, waiting for them to fix my car." The mechanic approached her saying "It looks like someone has shot out all your tires with a nail gun; is there someone out there who doesn't like you?" I can hear the shiver in her voice as she says, "That really got my attention; that's when I started getting worried."

Just two days before her deposition, Willey disclosed later to the FBI[92] and in a lawsuit against the Clintons,[93] a man approached her while she was jogging.[94] The man, wearing sweat pants and a baseball cap, asked her questions.[95] He knew the names of her lawyer, her cat (Bullseye, her pet of thirteen years who had disappeared two months before), her kids, and about how her tires had been slashed recently.[96] "You're just not getting the message," the stranger said ominously.[97] "And you know, the message was to go into that deposition and lie," Willey said.[98] The threat left her "very, very, very frightened."[99]

Recounting the incident to me years later she says, "I can't tell you what it was like when this creep said 'Did you ever get those tires fixed on your car?' and told me what a 'nice cat' Bullseye had been. That's when I knew these people meant business." She remembers going home that day, shaken, sitting alone in her living room thinking "This is a whole new ballgame, and I am out of my league."

The harassment continued for months. Her mail carrier pulled her aside one day and warned her that a "creepy, scuzzy-looking" guy had shown up at the post office trying to get directions to Willey's home. A shopkeeper in her small hometown warned her that after Willey had come into the store recently, a man had come in asking questions about her. And on and on until Willey felt she was constantly looking over her shoulder. It was not the life she had worked so hard to build for herself. "I was a soccer mom," she says reminiscently. "A stay-at-home mom, and I loved every minute of it." She felt woefully unprepared to deal with this sort of intimidation.

◊

On January 10, 1998, Paula Jones's lawyers deposed Kathleen Willey.[100] President Clinton was scheduled for a deposition the following week. Willey was the consummate hostile witness, volunteering nothing, answering in tight-lipped monosyllables.[101] The Jones lawyers had to ask exactly the right questions to get Willey to testify about anything untoward that occurred on November 29, 1993. The depositions in the case were ordered to be kept secret by the court, but newspapers immediately reported from "sources" that Willey had indeed testified about an unwanted groping incident in the Oval Office.[102]

Parts of her deposition didn't square with how she'd told her story to reporter Michael Isikoff nearly a year earlier, but that's because with Isikoff she spoke freely, confident she was off the record. In her deposition she was forced to talk against her will as another victim of the Clinton version of the Cruel Trilemma. Her story implicated Clinton, not herself, yet she was understandably reluctant to testify and did so only under threat of being jailed for contempt of court. Her deposition evinces a genuine struggle on her part to walk a fine line between avoiding perjury and giving as little information as possible that might damage Clinton. But that couldn't possibly have anything to do with the string of intimidating incidents throughout the preceding months, Bennett's non-threats, non-intimidation five weeks earlier, nor with the terrifying verbal threat made against Willey and her children by a thug just two days earlier.

In deposition she described most of the conversation leading up to the sexual advance as occurring while she and Clinton were sitting across from each other at his desk in the Oval Office [103], though she had made it sound to Isikoff as if they went to the little kitchen and office almost immediately. She testified that when she got up to leave, Clinton walked over and hugged her. (She still hadn't testified about being led down the hallway into the private office.) Finally the Jones lawyer pried it out of her that she and Clinton had a cup of coffee in the private office. After more step-by-step questioning, she had to admit that the good-bye "hug" Clinton initiated as she was leaving the private office "just continued longer than I expected." The lawyer had to ask, "Was there any kissing involved during that hug" for Willey to answer, "There was an attempt." As easily as extracting a sliver from underneath a fingernail, Jones's attorney finally elicited the crux of Willey's testimony: "He put his hands—he put my hands on his genitals," but only in response to the very specific question "Did Mr. Clinton ever seek to take either of your hands and place it on his body anyplace?" Willey volunteered absolutely nothing else, and later in the questioning the lawyer thought to ask, "Did Mr. Clinton attempt to touch your breasts?" to which Willey answered reluctantly, "I think so." The lawyer patiently followed up: "And what's the basis for your thinking so?" Willey said shortly, "I have a recollection of that." Jones's attorney asked further, "Was he successful?" and Willey answered simply, "Yes." When the question had been in posed in every possible way Willey finally testified that after kissing her Clinton had said something about "always wanting to do that." Lawyers everywhere hope their clients will be as closed-mouthed as Willey under cross-examination.

Closed-mouthed, but truthful. Willey told me that one of the attorneys who represented the House of Representatives during the Clinton impeachment proceedings asked her why, after all the harassment, she had decided to go into that deposition and testify truthfully. As a law-abiding, upstanding citizen Willey told him "I had no choice," even though she desperately wanted to stay out of the deposition altogether. The House attorney told her, "If you had gone in there and lied, you would be dead today. Telling the truth was your life insurance policy." Willey says that the gravity of that statement still chills her blood.

Whether by instinct or design, many women whose stories we've revisited here have acted similarly, raising their public profiles in hopes that status as a newsworthy name would lessen the chance they would simply disappear under suspicious circumstances. Like Elizabeth Ward Gracen and Sally Perdue before her, Kathleen Willey suffered months of harassment and intimidation designed to keep her quiet.

The following Saturday, January 17, 1998, Clinton testified during his deposition[104] that he never attempted to kiss Willey, never attempted to touch her breasts, and never had any form of "sexual relations" with Willey. He "emphatically" denied Willey's claim that he ever put her hand on his genitals. Why, the lawyer asked, would she tell a story like that if it weren't true? Clinton responded long-windedly:

She'd been through a lot, and apparently the, the financial difficulties were even greater than she thought they were at the time
she talked to me. Her husband killed himself, she's been through
a terrible time. I have—I can't say. All I can tell you is, in the first
place, when she came to see me she was clearly upset. I did to her
what I have done to scores and scores of men and women who
have worked for me or been my friends over the years. I embraced her, I put my arms around her, I may have even kissed
her on the forehead. There was nothing sexual about it. I was trying to help calm her down and trying to reassure her. She was in
difficult condition. But I have no idea why she said what she did,
or whether she now believes that actually happened. She's been
through a terrible, terrible time in her life, and I have nothing else
to say. I don't want to speculate about it.

Clinton made a much worse witness than Willey, from the
defense lawyer's point of view; he talked too much and offered
too much information unrelated to the specific questions asked
of him. Clinton testified that he had casual conversations with
Willey sporadically during the campaign and when she volunteered in the White House, but the November 1993 meeting was
the first time he had ever talked with her one on one. In fact,
Clinton testified, he "vividly" remembered meeting with her that
one time in the Oval Office; it stuck out in his memory because
Willey was "so agitated and she seemed to be in very difficult
straits." Of course, when Willey's name first appeared in the
press back in August 1997, Clinton's lawyer had said Clinton had
"no specific recollection" of meeting with Willey.[105] Clinton
deigned to express sympathy for the distraught Kathleen Willey
even as his smear machine kicked into high gear.

◊

From the beginning of Willey's unwanted thrust into the
scandal spotlight, the White House and the press treated her
more gingerly than Paula Jones or Gennifer Flowers. Columnist
Arianna Huffington wrote just after Willey's name surfaced in
August 1997, when Willey had yet to say one word about what

happened to her and the only information available came from Linda Tripp: "The first lesson learned from Bill Clinton's latest bimbo eruption is that she [Willey] wasn't a bimbo."[106] The August 11 *Newsweek* article noted that Willey, then fifty-one years old, had suffered emotional distress over the financial devastation and death of her husband. It went on to describe her as a "former flight attendant" who had been "married to the son of an influential Virginia state legislator."[107] The couple "drove expensive cars, skied at Vail, and... contributed to the Democratic Party."[108] Not one word suggested Willey as another bump on the road to bimboland.

Within days of Clinton's January 17, 1998, deposition the Lewinsky scandal was bursting wide open. Willey was in the shadows of coverage and commentary compared to Linda Tripp and Monica Lewinsky. Articles discussing her testimony, however, continued to describe her in much more flattering terms than Paula or Gennifer ever drew. *The Washington Post* called her an "energetic woman in her early fifties" with "one of the most prominent political surnames in this politics-obsessed capital," referring to her late husband's father, powerful Virginia state senator Edward E. Willey.[109] After mentioning the difficult period Willey had suffered through over her husband's suicide, the *Post* concluded, "Today Willey lives in rural Powhatan County about thirty miles west of here, in a handsome house on a large, wooded lot at the end of a single-lane gravel road."[110] Patently, living in a "handsome house" rather than a trailer accorded Willey more respect than previous Clinton accusers. Another paper referred to Willey as a woman who had been dragged into "besieged celebrity," [111] painting her as a casualty rather than coquettes like Flowers and Jones.

At the end of January 1998, one article portrayed Willey as a virtual paradigm of virtue, observing that after her husband's untimely death her "life had come to revolve around her children and charity work."[112] For some reason (class bias? scandal fatigue?) the press treated Willey as a real person rather than writing her off as a slut or bimbo. Even when the White House got busy that spring and began another round of Clinton versus Women smearing, the press remained relatively reluctant to jump on the bandwagon.

Willey refused to speak out publicly for almost two months after Clinton's deposition and Kenneth Starr's sting operation using Linda Tripp to tape Monica Lewinsky erupted into the most tantalizing scandal to rock Washington in two decades. It may not sound like a lot of quiet time, but remaining taciturn for two months must have felt like two years to a woman caught in the middle of such a highly publicized political scandal. In January 1998 the *Los Angeles Times* stated after talking to Willey's lawyer that "Willey is not particularly interested in building Jones's case."[113] By late January, Monica Lewinsky's infamous "talking points" memo had been discovered as a "key piece of evidence" in Starr's investigation.[114] The talking points, a three-page memo that Lewinsky had given Linda Tripp, spelled out in detail what Tripp "should" say about the Kathleen Willey incident, with an obvious eye toward discrediting Willey's story. The talking points instructed Tripp to say things like:

> You and Kathleen were friends. At around the time of her husband's death (The president has claimed it was after her husband died. Do you really want to contradict him?), she came to you after she allegedly came out of the Oval and looked (however she looked), you don't recall her exact words, but she claimed at the time (whatever she claimed) and was very happy....

> [Y]ou now do not believe that what she claimed happened really happened. You now find it completely plausible that she herself smeared her lipstick, untucked her blouse, etc.... [115]

The relevance of the talking points to Starr's investigation concerned whether Lewinsky had been instructed by Clinton, Vernon Jordan, or anyone associated with Clinton to issue those talking points to Tripp, thereby encouraging Tripp to lie under oath in the Paula Jones civil suit. The relevance of the talking points to Kathleen Willy was that they possibly represented the White House's first attempt to discredit her.

Meanwhile, Clinton's deposition had not yet been unsealed for public viewing, so during January and February 1997 his version of their encounter was still left to speculation. In mid-February, Starr subpoenaed Willey.[116] The substantive veracity of her story could bear on Starr's ability to show that Clinton suborned perjury if he was behind the talking points attempting to influence Tripp's potential testimony about the Willey incident. It could also directly prove presidential perjury if Willey's story held up enough to contradict Clinton's (presumed) under-oath denial of it.

At the same time, Willey's former friend Julie Steele told Clinton's lawyers that Willey had asked Steele to lie the previous year to support her claim of an unwanted sexual advance, providing the Clinton scandal team with something to point to in an attempt to discredit Willey.[117] By early March, when Willey was still expected to testify before a federal grand jury in Starr's investigation, her story was, as one reporter wrote, "fraught with contradiction."[118] Another paper said "In the fifty months since [Willey's encounter with Clinton allegedly] occurred, there have been fragmentary and conflicting accounts of what happened, many leaked to the media by unidentified people with political or financial interests in the scandal."[119] With her name, reputation, and credibility being bandied about in the press, it should have surprised no one that by mid-March, Kathleen Willey steeled herself to suffer whatever fallout would come from publicly telling her story.

On March 15, 1998, a week after testifying to Starr's grand jury, Kathleen Willey appeared on CBS's *60 Minutes* with Ed Bradley. On March 13 significant portions of her deposition and Clinton's deposition had been publicly released, so Clinton's denials and Willey's stilted version of her story were public knowledge. The day the program was to air, *60 Minutes* executive producer Don Hewitt told the press that Willey's story was "very believable and very persuasive and leaves little doubt about what happened."[120] Willey agreed to appear on *60 Minutes* for one reason: the show's producers told her that a White House operative had been threatening her former friend, Julie Steele, about possibly revoking Steele's adoption of a child.[121] No matter what had gone wrong in her friendship with Steele, the idea that the Clinton White House dared threaten a mother with taking away her child infuriated Willey enough to tell her own story about what Clinton had done to her.[122]

One reporter surmised that unlike Gennifer Flowers or Paula Jones, Willey would be more difficult for the White House or press to dismiss because "[s]he has no known connection to the right-wing conspiracy cited by Hillary Clinton" and "there's been no talk of book or movie deals for Willey, or exclusive payola stories with supermarket tabloids."[123] The fact that her deposition showed how the Jones lawyers had to "pull the damaging testimony from a reluctant Willey" also "tends to enhance her credibility."[124] Hmmm. What would the Clinton spin machine come up with to smear *this* one? The nation wouldn't have to wait long to find out.

◊

On *60 Minutes* in March 1998 Willey said she was breaking her silence because "too many lies are being told, too many lives are being ruined."[125] Journalist Roger Simon evaluated her appearance and concluded: "Willey was calm during the *60 Minutes* interview. She was sometimes shy, sometimes a little hesitant, but she appeared credible."[126] The *Los Angeles Times* reported that "Willey appeared tense but resolute" in her interview.[127] "She spoke slowly and softly and paused frequently as she offered her account of the events of more than four years ago."[128] The story she told on *60 Minutes* tracks very closely with the account she'd given Michael Isikoff twelve months earlier, even though Isikoff never included her statements in any article since she had been refusing to speak on the record. As tens of millions of American households tuned in (making that *60 Minutes* show the most-watched program of the week)[129] Willey told the public what happened to her on November 29, 1993:[130]

> I went in, and the president was at his desk, and I sat down in the chair across from him, and I obviously looked very distraught. He asked me what was wrong. I told him I had a really serious problem and that I needed his help. And, he said, "Would you like a cup of coffee?" And I said, "Yes, I would."

> So he walked to…a door on the other side of the Oval Office, which led into a hallway, into his small galley kitchen, and there was a steward in there, I remember. And the president took a—a coffee cup down out of the pantry, and—a Starbucks coffee cup, I remember—and, he poured me a cup of coffee, poured himself a cup of coffee, and we started walking back down the hall towards the Oval Office and he said, "Why don't you come in here into my study? We can talk better in here."

> And, I stood and leaned—I was leaning against the doorjamb. He was in the office. We were standing facing each other, and I told him what had happened [to her family finances]. I didn't give him all the details. I just told him that my husband was in financial difficulty, and that things were at a crisis point, and….that I needed a—a regular paying job, and could he help me….

> He did seem sympathetic…. I had the feeling that he was somehow distracted when I was talking to him …he was not really listening, but I know that he did. I know he knows how distraught I was and how upset I was, because I…was very worried…about my husband, and—and—and what was going to happen….

> He said he would do everything that he could to help, and I turned around…out of the office, and he followed me to—I thought he was going to open the door to the—to the Oval Office, and right as we got to the door, he stopped and he gave me a big hug and said that he was very sorry that this was happening to me. And—I had—had no problem with that, because when I saw—every time I saw him, he would hug me.

> …And he took the coffee cup out of my hand and he put it on a bookshelf, and…this hug lasted a little longer than I thought nec-

essary, but at the same time—I mean, I was not concerned about it. And then he… kissed me on—on my mouth, and pulled me closer to him. And…I just remember thinking, "what in the world is he doing?"…And, I pushed back away from him, and—he—he—he—he—he's a big man. And he—he had his arms—they were tight around me, and he—he—he touched me.

[Q:] Touched you how?

Well, he—he—he touched my breasts with his hand, and, I—I…I was just startled…

[Q:] This—this wasn't an accidental grazing touch?

No. And—then he—whispered—he—he—said in—in my ears that, "I—I've wanted to do this ever since I laid eyes on you." And…I remember saying to him, "Aren't you afraid that somebody's going to walk in here?" …[He] said, "No. No, I'm—no, I'm not." And—and then…he took my hand, and he—and he put it on him. And, that's when I pushed away from him and—and decided it was time to get out of there.

[Q:] When you say he took your hand…and put it on him…Where on him?

On—on his genitals.

[Q:] Was he a—aroused?

Uh-huh.

Willey said she was "embarrassed for the president's behavior" but "decided not to file a complaint. Who do you file a complaint to anyway when it's the president?" [131] She felt that the president took advantage of her when she was so distraught over her financial woes.[132] She felt like slapping him, she said, but refrained because "I don't think you can slap the president of the United States like that."[133] She didn't feel "intimidated" but she did feel "overpowered."[134] As she left the Oval Office that day, Willey "just could not believe that that had happened in the office. I…I just could not believe the recklessness of that act."[135] Asked if Clinton was lying Willey replied simply, "Yes."[136] She also told America about the "chicken soup" phone call she'd received from Clinton in 1991.[137] She had considered the president a friend, and the incident in the Oval Office betrayed that friendship, particularly since her husband had also been a friend.[138] She'd let the cat out of the bag, and she paid heavily for it.

The Clinton defense squad opened fire immediately. Speaking directly about her story for the first time in public, Clinton declared "[N]othing improper happened," and said "As you know the story's been in three different incarnations."[139] He was counting Linda Tripp's version, of course, which couldn't really have helped him much since Tripp's account made it clear that *something* sexual had indeed occurred. Nevertheless he continued, "I have said that nothing improper happened. I have a very clear memory of the meeting. I told the truth then, I told the truth in the deposition.... I am mystified and disappointed by this turn of events."[140] Indubitably he was being honest there. He must have been genuinely "mystified" that his scare tactics (courtesy of his lawyer and possibly a thug) and generous job procurement efforts for Willey had not prevented her from refusing to commit perjury for him.

White House spokesperson Ann Lewis said on national television the next day that someone who claimed to be upset by something like this wouldn't go around asking to be involved in the 1996 campaign the way Willey did.[141] The drift: something is seriously wrong with this woman. As one columnist put it, Clinton couldn't come up with any good reason why Willey would be lying about him, "but if she's crazy, who needs a reason?"[142] Six years earlier, the same Ann Lewis lectured Pat Buchanan for questioning Anita Hill's veracity based on the fact that Hill followed Clarence Thomas from one job to another and continued to call him despite her claims of harassment. Concerning Hill, Lewis explained how and why a woman could act so friendly to a man who'd sexually harassed her: "You [Buchanan] don't know what it's like to be a young working woman, to have this really prestigious and powerful boss and think you have to stay on the right side of him for the rest of your working life or he could nix another job."[143] When Buchanan ridiculed Hill for not being able to "handle [a] fanny paddler[]" Lewis shot back:

> If you have trouble listening to women's voices, please listen to what I said again. I said, she was trying to stay on his right side because her economic career would be at stake. He was always going to be on her resume, this was her most prestigious, most powerful boss. It was in her interest, once she stopped working for him, to refashion that relationship so it would be friendly but distant and proper.[144]

But concerning Kathleen Willey, the very same Ann Lewis couldn't imagine how any sane woman could stay friendly toward her alleged harasser. Perhaps the Lewis of 1998 didn't dare cross her own "prestigious, most powerful boss?"

While disclaiming the move was motivated by any "animosity" toward Willey, the White House immediately released correspondence from Willey to the president dating from 1993 through 1997 that reflected Willey's friendly attitude toward Clinton.[145] The correspondence "shows that Willey made persistent requests of Clinton and the president took the time to deal with her entreaties personally," reported the Associated Press.[146] Willey explained later that she deliberately remained friendly toward Clinton on advice from her attorney.[147] Her letters to Clinton during the years after he groped her and before she was subpoenaed were her way of letting him know that she intended to keep quiet about what he'd done and that she needed paid work if he could find it for her.[148] For his part, Clinton super-lawyer Bob Bennett immediately spread the word that Willey was seeking a $300,000 book contract.[149] (Her lawyer handled offers from many publishers regarding book deals, but Willey never pursued any of them.[150])

◊

Public attacks on Willey's credibility weren't enough for the Clinton damage control team. They were also arranging other methods to discourage Willey from talking. A well-established, Maryland-based investigative firm, specializing in international security employing mostly former military and government agents, received an assignment to do "opposition research" on Kathleen Willey soon after her *60 Minutes* interview. Jared Stern, now owner of the firm, was the agent assigned to this project. When the news media began digging into this story after Ken Starr subpoenaed Stern, only speculation emerged as to who had hired Stern. CNN quoted an attorney representing Stern as saying "There was some indication from [Stern's] employer that this [assignment] had 'come from the White House,' but [Stern] had no independent knowledge of that."[151] Unidentified CNN "sources" asserted that prominent Clinton friend and Democratic fundraiser Nathan Landow was the client who hired Stern's investigative services, but Stern refuses to confirm this. It's not exactly a stretch to imagine that a Friend of Bill with money to spare—like Landow—might get a call from a wistful Clinton remarking, "It sure would be nice to dissuade this Willey woman from talking."

Stern and the other investigators involved with this assignment are understandably reluctant to disclose specifics, and Stern's grand jury testimony has not been released to the public. According to Kathleen Willey, Stern "called me and tried to warn me, using an anonymous name." To her understanding, Stern testified under oath that his orders came from the White House. When I spoke to him in early 2005, Stern refused to comment on the ultimate source of his assignment to do opposition research on Willey, but he didn't deny Willey's statements.

Stern confirms that he had "several conversations" with his boss and the clients involved in the Willey assignment, and some of those conversations "involved suggestions of strategies not appropriate or wholesome," but refuses to comment on the specifics of those suggestions or on whether such suggestions were actually carried out. Contrary to previously reported accounts, Stern says he did not "quit" the assignment, but he believes that the inquiries of Kenneth Star, law enforcement, and the media forced the opposition research efforts directed at Willey to "terminate…early." Careful not to say too much, Stern says he knows he was not the only person performing "opposition research" on Willey.

As to the telephone call he placed to Willey, Stern says that hypothetically, such a call by an agent in his position is often made "for more than one reason." Stern refused to elaborate, so I asked a private investigator who wished to remain nameless if he had ever confronted a similar situation and made such a phone call to a subject of an investigation. He told me that in his business, one purpose of such a call might be "to alert a subject of shady activities," while another might be "pretext to engage [a subject] in discussion to glean information about how much the person has talked" to authorities and so forth.

Stern expresses nothing but praise and sympathy for Willey for "taking the high road" throughout this ordeal. He couldn't help but believe her in her interview with *60 Minutes,* and opines of Clinton, "He's good-looking with some power; it's a joke to think he didn't do" what Willey and others claim he did. Stern met Willey at her home once for an interview with Chris Wallace, who then worked for ABC News. (This joint interview with Willey and Stern never aired. ABC News senior investigative producer Chris Vlasto told me it had been scheduled to air September 12, 2001, but it was preempted by coverage of the terrorist attacks of 9/11.) Stern says Willey's first comment to him when he entered the room was "I don't know whether to kiss him or smack him," which Stern found charming. "She's an attractive, smart, quality woman," he says, "but look at where she is," referring to her years of unemployment and scrutiny due to involvement in a Clinton scandal. Though his direct involvement with opposition research on Willey began after her deposition, he admits that based on his experience he has no trouble believing her accounts of being threatened by thugs and intimidated prior to her deposition.

Instead of gobbling up the White House's newest wave of spin, the press continued to render Willey in a relatively favorable light, consistently referring to her lack of ties to conservative groups, her well-to-do background and involvement with the Democratic Party, and her heroic struggles concerning her husband. Rather than reporting the Willey letters released by the White House as "new evidence that seriously calls into question Willey's story" the press typically began its reports with phrases like "The White House on Monday launched a counteroffensive against Kathleen Willey...."[152] Another report stated: "The release of the letters capped a day of damage control by the White House, as strategists tried to defuse the accusations made by someone they concede is the most credible accuser Clinton faces."[153]

One columnist surmised that Willey's better reception in the eyes of public and press was due to "popular prejudice and expectation about how a virtuous woman should look, behave and respond."[154] After all, Willey "is resolutely middle-class" (as opposed to Paula Jones?), "a respectable middle-aged widow" (as opposed to Monica Lewinsky?), "still pretty but not flashy" (as opposed to Gennifer Flowers?), "dignified, sensible and genteel" (as opposed to any of the women we've met so far?).[155]

After admitting that Willey was "clearly a supporter" of the president, thus making it difficult to "impute any motive to her," Clinton aide Paula Begala added, grasping at a straw, "But she has a friend who said she asked her to lie."[156] Jesse Jackson, who had been praying with Clinton in the midst of the Lewinsky scandal, chimed in with an excuse for Clinton rather than a defense: "Sex isn't the only string on the guitar," the Rev. Jackson said with a shrug, "There are nine more Commandments."[157]

Kathleen Willey's drama unfolded about a year after Paula Jones had begun receiving somewhat kinder treatment in the press, and with the Monica Lewinsky story percolating at the time, the media's willingness to believe Clintonian denials seemed to be eroding. Journalist Michael Kelly summed up this trend in two wickedly sardonic columns. Reading them yourself in their entirety would be an excellent and amusing use of a Saturday afternoon at the library. (Tragically, Mr. Kelly was killed in April 2003 while embedded with the Army's 3rd Infantry Division covering the Iraq war for *The New Republic*.[158] He was the first journalist to die in Iraq during Operation Iraqi Freedom.)

Kelly's column entitled "I Believe" was published February 4, 1998; its sequel, "I Still Believe," was published March 18 that year. Round one opened by declaring "I believe the president. I have always believed him."[159] Kelly continued with proclamations such as: "I believe Paula Jones is a cheap tramp who was asking for it. I believe Kathleen Willey is a cheap tramp who was asking for it. I believe Monica Lewinsky is a cheap tramp who was asking for it.... I believe the president has lived up to his promise to preside over the most ethical administration in American history."[160] In round two Kelly announced:

> I believe Ms. Willey is, like Paula Jones and Gennifer Flowers and Dolly Kyle Browning and Sally Purdue before her, and like the women who will come after her, a bald-faced liar. If Monica Lewinsky sticks to her affidavit that she never had sex with the president, I believe her. If she instead confirms the long hours of recorded conversation in which she detailed a sexual affair with the president and affirmed her intention to lie in the affidavit—well, then, I don't believe.
>
> I believe, as the White House whispering campaign already has it, that Ms. Willey is a bit nutty, and a bit slutty....
>
> I believe everyone is lying except my Bill.[161]

Even feminists seemed torn and divided about how to respond to Willey. Patricia Ireland, then president of NOW, said of Willey's story, "If it's true, it's sexual assault," not just sexual harassment.[162] "Now we're talking about, really, sexual predators and people who in positions of power use that power to take advantage of women," she elaborated.[163] Ms. Ireland cautioned that nothing had been proven but added, "Seeing the interview [on *60 Minutes*] was even more compelling than seeing the words on paper. I have to say she has a great deal of credibility."[164] Kate Michelman, then president of the National Abortion and Reproductive Rights Action League, said after Willey's *60 Minutes* interview, "I heard her story and this was a woman who sounded credible, who told a story that was compelling and believable."[165]

Not all left-wing feminists could agree. The bipartisan National Women's Political Caucus, the Women's Legal Defense Fund, and the National Women's Law Center all declined to comment.[166] Cynthia Friedman, then chairman of a Democratic group called the Women's Leadership Forum, gave a heartfelt version of Michael Kelly's "I Believe" sentiment by saying: "This is what I know: The president issued a very flat denial about Willey's accusation, and I really believe in the president."[167] California Senators Barbara Boxer and Dianne Feinstein, both of whom entered the Senate in the Year of the Woman (1992) in part due to the fallout from the Anita Hill/Clarence Thomas hearings, remained circumspect. Senator Feinstein even attempted to differentiate between Anita Hill and Kathleen Willey: "One involves the president of the United States, involves his word," she insisted.[168] "The word of the president is a very important thing."[169] As opposed to the word of a man who is "only" a Supreme Court Justice?

Anita Hill herself implied that Willey had no business coming forward at all: there was no comparison between her story and Willey's, since Clinton had been twice elected by a voting public who knew of allegations of sexual misconduct while Thomas was bound for a first-time lifetime appointment to the Supreme Court.[170] Apparently, unless your goal is to arrest the career of your accused harasser, you have no reason to tell your story. Hill added that since Clinton is "better on the bigger [women's] issues" nothing Willey had to say was "so bad" as to reject Clinton as a president.[171]

Feminist icon Gloria Steinem declared in a *New York Times Magazine* essay that Clinton's actions toward Willey might make him a candidate for sex-addiction therapy, but he didn't commit sexual harassment because he took no for an answer. This, Steinem insisted, was enough to make Clinton's troubles qualitatively different from those of Clarence Thomas or Bob Packwood, who were accused of *repeated* unwanted advances.[172] Apparently for Ms. Steinem there is no difference between talk and action. Clinton didn't even *ask* Willey for a sexual favor—he just went ahead and touched her all over and then guided her hand to his erect penis.

Elaborating on her position a few weeks later Steinem said, "The truth of the matter is that [Clinton's] behavior toward women is considerably better than any president I know of—at least as far as we know....We have to make clear that his behavior is not acceptable, and yet not keep him from being effective on issues of equality."[173] Which is it? His behavior is unacceptable, or he treats women better than any president in history? Steinem seems to be saying that it doesn't matter. What matters is that he supports reproductive rights and the Violence Against Women Act. His personal abuses pale in significance next to his righteous political agenda.

Steinem's tortured defense of Clinton prompted even the generally liberal *New York Times* to editorialize, "We doubt whether Ms. Steinem meant to advocate a new kind of 'no harm, no foul' mentality in the workplace. But that is the dangerous implication of her analysis."[174] Whether or not Willey's claims amounted *legally* to sexual harassment, argued the *Times*, "The Clinton case raises the very real possibility that if the president is seen as getting away with gross behavior, more bosses will feel free to behave abominably."[175]

Perhaps sensing the shift in the press and "[w]ary of a backlash if they hit too hard," the Clinton cadre kept its smear campaign "quiet," instead using whisper and innuendo. While Press Secretary Mike McCurry publicly denied that anyone was trying to besmirch Willey, White House advisers anonymously spoke to reporters about her background and suggested she was after a book deal, she was emotionally distraught, and/or she was under a lot of pressure.[176] In not so many words, this was a deranged, unbalanced woman who had mysteriously decided to attack the president. Even as the Clinton team continued to smear Paula Jones as "money-hungry and a tool of the Republican right" and denigrate Monica Lewinsky for wearing too-short skirts, "[i]n Willey's case, the spin has been more subtle."[177]

Clinton's tactics prompted *The Washington Post* to call the release of the Willey letters "perhaps the most vivid illustration so far of the White House's belief that information is a potent weapon."[178] The *Post* continued critically, "When facts are damaging, they are kept secret with few apologies" but when facts "are helpful...the White House becomes an advocate of public disclosure."[179] Once again, as we saw with Paula Jones, some Clinton defenders used his reputation for womanizing as a *defense* against Willey's story: "Clinton's not a coercive guy; he's very subtle," one advisor told the *Post* on condition of anonymity.[180] Maybe something sexual happened, the advisor conceded, but Willey was "lying about how she felt about it."[181] In case you missed it, Kathleen Willey was asking for it.

On August 17, 1998 Clinton testified before a federal grand jury in Kenneth Starr's expanded Whitewater investigation. Clinton continued to deny Willey's account and offered this helpful information to the grand jury [emphasis added]:

> I didn't do any of that, and the questions you're asking, I think, betray the bias of this operation that has troubled me for a long time. *You know what evidence was released after the 60 Minutes broadcast that I think pretty well shattered Kathleen Willey's credibility. You know what people down in Richmond said about her.* You know what she said about other people that wasn't true. I don't know if you've made all of this available to the grand jury or not. She was not telling the truth. She asked for the appointment with me. *She asked for it repeatedly.*[182]

Clinton was furious that his efforts to destroy Willey hadn't worked well enough. Perhaps the most chilling part of his tirade also expressed pellucidly his calloused attitude toward Willey: "She asked for it repeatedly." He was referring to her asking for an appointment with him, but the possibility of a maleficent dual meaning lingers hauntingly.

◊

Kathleen Willey got off easier than some of Clinton's women. She found much more support in the media, the public, and even from some feminists and left-wingers than Paula Jones or Gennifer Flowers had. Sure, she was threatened by a random thug and had trouble finding steady work (because of the controversy, she said in early 2001, "I don't think a lot of people are eager to hire me"), forcing her to declare bankruptcy and suffer several long years of unemployment before landing a permanent job.[183] She felt in enough danger that the day the Senate began deliberating Clinton's impeachment, Willey met privately with Senator Susan Collins (R-Maine). This meeting didn't become public knowledge until a year later. Willey approached her out of fear, caused by incidents including having her tires slashed and being approached while jogging by the nameless man who mentioned her children. "She wanted people to understand the harassment she had endured—not the crude come-on by the president," according to a review of a book about the impeachment trial written by journalist Peter Baker.[184] Collins, who eventually voted "not guilty" in the impeachment trial, believed Willey's story of harassment and found her accounts of being threatened "troubling."[185]

Overall, though, Willey has rebuilt a successful, fulfilling life for herself. She was forty-seven years old when Clinton advanced on her in the Oval Office, and she spent the following decade of her life recovering from the experience. After the spotlight had dimmed somewhat she "ran away" to the Florida Keys for a while.[186] An old acquaintance, Bill Schwicker, called her out of the blue and after many soothing hours sanding down his twenty-eight foot sailboat together, they married in 2000.[187] He has been a source of joy in her life ever since. "My husband and I have been through terrible times over this," she tells me. "He hung in there with me, but it hasn't been easy." She is also desperately proud of her grown children; her son is a boat captain and her daughter is a medical doctor.[188]

She largely stayed out of the spotlight from the summer of 1998 on, refusing a second interview requested by *60 Minutes* and speaking out only occasionally. In September 1998 she took two polygraph (lie detector) tests administered by the FBI.[189] The first results were inconclusive but the second test indicated she was telling the truth.[190] The House of Representatives avoided calling her as a witness in the impeachment proceedings, allowing her to continue trying to rebuild her life in peace.

In May 2001 she joined the conservative media outlet *World Net Daily* as a guest columnist and speaker.[191] Her occasional appearances on cable and radio talk shows concerned current events like former Congressman Gary Condit's involvement with Chandra Levy and feminism's politically-motivated hypocrisy.[192] In 2001, when the Clintons vacated the White House, their cat Socks went to live with Betty Currie, Bill Clinton's loyal secretary. Kathleen Willey wrote a cute mock letter to Socks,[193] with whom she had spent some time when she worked at the White House. Willey wished Socks well with his new owner, suggesting he was better off with Currie than the Clintons anyway. As proof of the Clintons' preference for dogs over cats, Willey reminded Socks that her *cat*, not her dog, had mysteriously disappeared allegedly at the hands of a Clinton-affiliated thug.

In March 2002, the Office of the Independent Counsel (OIC) released its "Final Report of the Independent Counsel In Re: Madison Guaranty Savings & Loan Association" (i.e., Whitewater and the expanded investigation into the Lewinsky affair and related suspected cover-ups). Appendix B of that Final Report detailed the independent counsel's findings regarding "Allegations Made by Kathleen E. Willey."[194] A surface glance at that appendix was all some Clinton loyalists needed to start crowing about Willey's lack of credibility.

However, a careful reading of Appendix B compels the understanding that the OIC decided it couldn't prosecute Clinton for perjury based on Willey's testimony not because her story lacked credibility but because of the he said, she said nature of her story. The OIC determined there was "insufficient evidence" to support criminal charges against any of the likely Clinton-related suspects for threatening and intimidating Willey before her deposition.[195] As to whether Clinton had committed perjury by denying Willey's version of their encounter the OIC concluded that "there was insufficient evidence to *prove to a jury beyond a reasonable doubt* that President Clinton's testimony regarding Kathleen Willey was false. Accordingly, the independent counsel declined prosecution and the investigation…was closed."[196] The OIC specifically cautioned that it was not "offering, and cannot offer, any opinion as to whose version of events is right, Willey's or President Clinton's" and "[i]n the narrow context of assessing whether to seek *criminal* charges against President Clinton for his denials" it therefore "concluded no more and no less than that charges could not be sustained against President Clinton concerning his testimony about Willey."[197] The biggest reason for the OIC's conclusion was that "Willey and President Clinton [were] the only two percipient witnesses to the alleged encounter"[198]—in other words, it was a he said, she said situation that would be nearly impossible for prosecutors to prove beyond a reasonable doubt. Without any supporting physical evidence the case would rest entirely on Willey's testimony, and her fear-motivated, reticent deposition testimony had caused her to look as though she'd elaborated on her story by the time she told it on *60 Minutes* and to the grand jury.

By the time Clinton left office, Willey considered herself politically a "Democrat in recovery."[199] After what Clinton did to the country and to her, she said, she was anxious for George W.

Bush's inauguration,[200] though initially she supported John McCain in the 2000 race.[201] She voted for Bush in the general election of 2000 because he is a "good and decent man."[202] Watching President Bush's first address to a joint session of Congress in 2001 made her feel "proud to be an American" for the first time in eight years, she said. Her experience with the Clintons "taught me a lot about politics," she told me. "My late husband and I had spent years donating time and money to Democrats, yet not one Democrat came to my defense."

Willey has publicly called Bill Clinton a "sexual predator" and predicted his behavior wouldn't stop.[203] In April 2002 she was briefly given her own radio talk show at a Richmond, Virginia station but it was canceled after only a month.[204] Around that time she was asked if she hated Clinton. "He's pathetic. I don't hate him. I just feel sorry for him. I just think he's a pathetic soul. I feel sorry for his whole family. I'm sorry for our country. You know, I really am, that we were put through what we were put through for eight long years."[205] With a note of weariness and only a hint of bitterness she tells me, "Everything he stood for amounted to nothing in my book after all that. You just can't have any respect for someone like that."

While she can't look at Bill and Hillary Clinton the same way she had when she first met them a decade earlier, she feels, and hopes, that she has "moved on."[206] If so, that's a remarkable accomplishment for a woman who once found herself in the crosshairs of the Clinton attack machine.

◊

Kathleen Willey turned to Bill Clinton in a time of distress, partly looking to him as a friend, but mostly looking to him as an accessible, powerful person who could help her. Almost all of us find ourselves in difficult straits at times; few of us can personally turn for help to the Leader of the Free World, but those who can probably do. Clinton occupied the most powerful position in the world. Implicit in the deal made between Clinton and the public who elected him was an understanding that he would use his official power for our benefit. Not every one of us benefits equally, of course. One of the understandable perks of holding an influential position is the ability to use it to help people you care about personally. In some way, I have no trouble believing that Bill Clinton genuinely enjoyed helping his friends when he could. But on November 29, 1993, when a friend approached him for help he took advantage of her instead. Clinton had no legal, official, ethical, or moral obligation to aid her. He did, however, have an obligation to refrain from harming her the way he did. Disregarding the responsibilities incumbent upon him as a public servant and as a human being, he swept her very real torment aside in the moment in order to gratify his own desires. Impeachable offense? Not even close. Despicable instance of mistreatment of yet another woman? Absolutely.

She remained his friend and political supporter even after the unwanted sexual advances. She allowed the incident to fade into the past. She sought no retribution from him and continued to call on him for help finding work. Through no fault of her own she found herself wrenched into telling her story. Less than a year after Clinton appointed her to a government post, he and his defense team began denigrating her character and integrity by denying she had anything "on" Clinton. They kept relatively quiet while she and her lawyer fought to kill the subpoena; if she had quashed it successfully, perhaps she would have remained on friendly terms with the Clintons. As late as January 1998 Willey's attorney was still claiming that Willey had a "continuing good relationship" with Clinton.[207] When she was forced to testify about the incident, which had been 100 percent of Clinton's own making and was politically damaging to him, he turned on her with a vengeance, doing all he could to depict her as an emotionally damaged, unstable, dishonest woman.

Clinton's uninvited pawing of Willey fits snugly into the category of unwanted sexual advances discussed in the previous chapter, and demonstrates yet again his objectification of women. Clinton's reaction to Kathleen Willey after she'd been forced to go public about that humiliating unwanted sexual advance illustrates yet another dimension of misogyny: patronization.

Clinton and his gang chose a different strategy to deal with Willey than with Paula Jones or Gennifer Flowers, at least publicly. They attacked her credibility not based on her motives (as with Flowers) or her lack of status (as with Jones), but on her presumed lack of emotional capacity. Poor Kathleen Willey. Left to deal with her husband's crimes and suicide, the poor little gal just snapped. She's even deluded herself into living in a fantasy world where Bill Clinton is some kind of pervert. In Bill Clinton's words, she was "upset," she was "in difficult condition," she's been "through a terrible, terrible time in her life," she'd "been through a lot," and all he did was try "to calm her down" and "reassure her." She was such a wreck, in fact, that she maybe "now believes that actually happened" but he has "no idea why she said what she did." That patronizing strategy designed to discredit Willey only highlights the misogyny lurking behind his mistreatment of her.

Some psychologists theorize that "sexism has a dual nature comprised of hostile as well as benevolent (i.e., subjectively positive) orientations toward women, both of which serve to justify and maintain women's subordinate status."[208] The existence of this dualized sexism, researchers maintain, is the result of two things: men's overall greater structural control than women, (i.e., "men are commonly in control of central economic, political, and social institutions") and the interdependence of men and women. In other words, men dominate, yet men and women need each other in intimate relationships. These societal conditions yield an "ambivalent" sexism with two faces: hostile sexism ("antipathy toward women"), and benevolent sexism ("subjectively favorable, yet patronizing beliefs about women").

Hostile sexism fosters the attitude that men properly have power over women, that women are inferior to men in competence-related fields like occupations and leadership roles, and that women's sexuality endangers men's status and power. Benevolent sexism is the flip side of the sexism coin and engenders beliefs like "protective paternalism (the belief that men should protect and provide for the women on whom they depend)," the belief that "women are the better gender, but only in ways that suit conventional gender roles," and the belief that "men can achieve true happiness in life only when involved in romantic relationships with women."

Hostile sexism views women as inferior; benevolent sexism views women as weak. Both provide justifications for treating women as less valuable, less worthy human beings than men. The benevolent variety is more palatable, to both men and women, because instead of expressing outright disdain for women, it expresses concern that women are incapable of handling autonomy; male dominance *benefits* women because it protects them. It's a softer way to enforce notions of gender inequality, utilizing patronizing condescension rather than forceful denunciations. It's a pat on the head with an intoning "Father knows best, dearie," instead of a violent beating or a ridiculing shout. It's softer, but no less damaging to women, and sometimes it's *more* successful than hostile sexism in maintaining gender discrimination and depriving women of a proper sense of autonomy, confidence, and competence.

For Bill Clinton, benevolent sexism provided a more acceptable vehicle for him to denounce, demean, and demoralize Kathleen Willey than outright hostility would have. After her story leaked, and especially after she dared tell it in her own words on national television, the Clinton team targeted her as a distraught, misguided soul whom Bill Clinton had done his best to rescue. Clinton posed himself as bewildered and disappointed by how she'd turned on him. Calling her a liar and a tramp might have backfired, since the press and public perceived

Willey as the "most credible accuser Clinton faces." So Clinton's sexism shifted gears. Abandoning open hostility, he instead tried to paint her as a helpless woman gone terribly wrong. His strategy with Willey may have found some inspiration in his leftist ideology and brings us to our fifth identification of a tenet of liberalism that seemingly contributed to Clinton's misogyny.

In modern liberalism, government bears a parental responsibility for the well-being of its citizens. From gun control to prosecution of tobacco companies, liberalism consistently calls for measures designed to save us from our own decisions. This kind of paternalism is beneficial for small children who have yet to acquire the life experience and maturity to make their own decisions, but such a parental approach is out of place with respect to the relationship between citizens and government. Perhaps many of the decisions liberals want to make for us would in fact be "good" decisions—don't smoke (or if you do, blame the tobacco companies), don't play with guns, don't hold prejudiced opinions of others, don't develop land that will displace the tree frog, and give your money to help the less fortunate. Perhaps liberals are right that the world would be a better place if we all made the "right" decisions. But perhaps that isn't really the point.

For all of liberalism's alleged emphasis on the importance of diversity, its government-as-parent approach eliminates diversity by denying people the opportunity to direct their lives according to their own priorities, moral principles, desires, and goals. Isn't that part of the "pursuit of happiness" promise in our nation's Declaration of Independence? Short of inflicting tangible harm on others, it's our God-given right to get to arrange our lives as we see fit. And some people, if they weren't prohibited by government, would choose to smoke cigarettes, own guns, hold irrational prejudices against others, develop their property even if it displaces a tree frog, and spend their money on their own family rather than give it away to strangers. Those decisions may be wrong by some standards of morality, but the choice should be ours to make, not our government's. Our parents have every right and reason to tell us when we're small children, "don't play with guns" and "don't smoke," but when we're adults, the level of risk or even self-destructiveness we engage in is a personal matter, and we should be expected to pay the price when our choices harm others. Even as adults, people and organizations with whom we associate often weigh in with their opinions and try to influence our behavior, but they have no business *forcing* their wishes on us. No matter how well-intentioned, liberalism's view of government as a superparent erodes the human experience of self-development and freedom of choice that forms a crucial part of living life as an authentic person.

Liberals typically defend their parental measures as necessary to prevent "harm" to others that flows from our "bad" decisions: smoking irritates non-smokers around us, owning guns risks accidental shootings, irrational prejudices unkindly demean those targeted by them, developing land that displaces tree frogs disrupts the delicate balance of the ecosystem, refusing to give your money to help the less fortunate is just selfish and perpetuates widespread problems of hunger and poverty. Only rarely do liberals identify a desire to protect people *from themselves* as the motivation for a law or program; they are more apt to point to "harm" done to third parties as the justification for paternalistic measures. But the condescension embedded in such measures shines through.

This is not to say that some ideologies on the right of the political spectrum don't advocate measures that step on the toes of individual autonomy. Social conservatives, for example, often support measures designed to curb activities they deem *immoral* (e.g., anti-sodomy laws, anti-prostitution laws). Social conservatives' impetus for such measures is not so much paternalism but a form of societal protectionism—shielding themselves and the rest of society from behaviors they find immoral and offensive. In this way, liberalism and social conservatism place government in a far different role than do libertarians. Libertarians focus on the *rights* of everyone involved; the outcome of respecting every-one's rights is not the business of government. For most libertarians, the only justification and role for government action is to facilitate protection of our rights to life and property.

However, only ideologies on the left advocate using political force to care for people's every need and eradicate every discom-fort known to human existence, from crime to poverty to poor education and health care. Only liberals pursue measures de-signed to save us from ourselves—measures that proceed from the assumption that most of us can't be trusted to do the right thing or make good decisions.

Take the current trend toward using government to cure the "social ill" of obesity. The libertarian magazine *Reason* displayed a cover article on a recent issue entitled, a bit crassly, "The War on Fat: Is the size of your butt the government's business?"[209] The idea of using all kinds of government-sponsored tactics to de-crease obesity has become a cause célèbre for liberals. Jacob Sullum writes, "[W]hile anti-fat activists treat 'freedom' as an empty corporate slogan, they seem to think the mantra 'public health' can justify any policy proposal."[210] By framing their desire to eliminate obesity as a "public health" issue, Sullum continues, these activists use a "rhetorical trick" to obscure "the fact that obesity is not a contagious disease; it does not spread from per-son to person in a way that justifies state action."[211] In fact, Sullum suggests, if it's okay for government to impose sin taxes on "bad" foods and use tax dollars to pay for advertisements and seminars designed to show people how to eat better and lose weight, there's no principled reason why government can't just *require* each of us to follow a certain diet and perform regular exercise. Is everyone ready for "mandatory calisthenics in the public square every morning?"[212]

No politician or activist is suggesting quite that level of gov-ernment intrusion into our lives (yet), but the point is that within an ideology that believes government bears responsibility for our general well-being, rather than simply protecting our right to control our own lives and property, there's no principled limit to how much government can step in and mandate our behaviors. Particularly with respect to issues like obesity, it's easy to discern that liberals' motivation stems from a desire to protect us from our own bad choices. They may demonize the big companies that sell us junk food instead of just wagging their fingers at us and imploring us to drive past the McDonald's, but the patronization remains. We are incapable of making good decisions for ourselves, and it's government's duty to make sure we make the right choices.

Outside a political context, on a personal level patronization and paternalism make useful tools for manipulating people to behave the way we'd like them to behave. When outright denunciation and ridicule (let alone force) might backfire, a good back-up strategy is to make people feel small, incompetent, and guilty. Look down at them, tilt your head a little, and say condescendingly, "You poor, misguided soul. You just aren't able to see clearly. It's not your fault; you just don't know any better. Take it from me—*this* is how you *ought* to behave. It's for your own good." Which is more or less the approach Bill Clinton took with Kathleen Willey when she was forced to testify against him and go public about the humiliation he put her through. Poor thing; she's just not able to see the truth through all her confusion and distress. Feel sorry for her, but for God's sake, don't *believe* her.

CHAPTER SEVEN

A REAL DON JUAN

THE FACT THAT MONICA Lewinsky's graphic descriptions of her consensual affair with President Clinton entered the public domain has to be one of the low points of American politics. I could have lived a perfectly fulfilling life without knowing the details of their sexual encounters in the Oval Office. For what my opinion is worth, the fact that prosecutors found this level of detail relevant and worthy of public dissemination constituted a breach of their responsibilities to conduct themselves and the public's business with a modicum of dignity and respect for the people involved. The subject matter of this book peremptorily kills the possibility of getting a "G" rating, but I will nevertheless spare readers the coarser parts of Ms. Lewinsky's fervid account of her affair with Clinton. In fact, since Monica Lewinsky far and away wins the prize for Most Loquacious Clinton Woman, her story appears here merely in abbreviated form. Prurient readers can find all the details in her grand jury testimony and her book. The acts Lewinsky and Clinton performed together are irrelevant to our analysis, but the way Clinton subsequently treated her does shed further light on how his liberal beliefs reinforced his misogynistic tendencies.

Months before the public knew about Monica Lewinsky, journalist Michael Isikoff had learned from Linda Tripp that

Tripp's "young friend" was having an on-going, consensual affair with the president.[1] In his 1999 book, *Uncovering Clinton,* Isikoff writes he wasn't sure at first that consensual affairs warranted further investigation. By the summer of 1997 so many "womanizing" scandals had plagued Clinton that Isikoff began thinking that the Lewinsky affair did justify unveiling it to the public:

> In the end, I thought, Clinton's serial indiscretions really did matter....They mattered because private misbehavior on Clinton's scale required routine, repetitive and reflexive lies to conceal itself....But lying, engaged in often enough, can have a corrosive effect....A culture of concealment had sprung up around Bill Clinton and, I came to believe that summer, it had affected his entire presidency.[2]

Isikoff argued, "Clinton's recklessness and arrogance deserved to be uncovered. But exposure—not impeachment—was the only remedy that interested me."[3] As we saw in the prior chapter, Kathleen Willey's story had done quite a lot to disintegrate the media's readiness to look the other way at Clinton's misdeeds. The press, considered so fundamental to a free society that protecting it from government control received pride of place in the very First Amendment to our Constitution, was doing its job, helping each of us form opinions about Bill Clinton as a person.

Arguably, the lies, deception, and consistent mistreatment of women could have been exposed without involvement of prosecutors, grand juries, or articles of impeachment. Those measures, perpetrated by people brandishing a political agenda as a sword sheathed in judgmental indignation, exacted punishments from Clinton that none of us had a right to demand. It would be the same if George W. Bush's political adversaries, who screeched that President Bush lied to Congress and the American people to get congressional permission and funding to go into Iraq, decided to push for an independent counsel to investigate the charge. The perspective of history, and information gleaned in hindsight, will help us judge President Bush's veracity concerning Operation Iraqi Freedom. Congress can hold all the hearings it wants, the press can investigate to its heart's content, Michael Moore can release as many sequels to *Fahrenheit 9/11* as the box office will support, and Ted Kennedy can bellow about frauds made up in Texas, but criminal prosecution and impeachment would be out of place.[4] The 70 million tax dollars expended by the Office of Independent Counsel (OIC) investigating potential crimes committed by Bill and Hillary during their tenure in the White House bought us little more than salacious details and a ready excuse for Clinton to maintain a posture of justified defiance when called to task for his misdeeds.

I realize the analogy isn't perfect; unlike President Bush, Clinton was accused of lying under oath in a civil suit and encouraging others to lie in the same lawsuit, and those actions might indeed be federal crimes. The reality of civil lawsuits, as any lawyer will tell you, is that people lie quite often in the course of a lawsuit, but it's hard to prove it. The burden of proof in a civil suit is proof by a preponderance of the evidence, which juries are told means anything more than 50/50. In other words, if a defendant in a civil suit says "I didn't do it" and the plaintiff says "he did it," a jury only has to believe that it's more probable than not that the plaintiff is credible to find in her favor. Does this mean the defendant lied under oath and committed perjury? Who knows, because the *crime* of perjury must be proved "beyond a reasonable doubt," and a civil jury's determination that the defendant was less credible than the plaintiff doesn't get you far toward proving a criminal offense.

Perjury is a serious crime because telling the truth under oath props up confidence in the judicial system. However, one element of perjury is that the lie under oath must concern a *material* fact that could influence the underlying lawsuit. If Clinton lied about having "sexual relations" or a "sexual affair" with Monica Lewinsky, it would be difficult to prove perjury because whether he engaged in consensual sex with Lewinsky has little or no relevance to Paula Jones's claims of sexual harassment. If Clinton lied about Kathleen Willey that gets closer to perjury because Willey's experience was closer to sexual harassment, but even so, the OIC determined there was insufficient evidence to even charge Clinton with perjury, let alone convict him. (As we noted in the prior chapter, that doesn't reflect at all on Kathleen Willey's credibility, it just means that proving the *crime* of perjury would have been too difficult.) If we spent millions of dollars trying to prove perjury every time the shadow of it appeared in our civil court system, we would soon find ourselves out of money.

The OIC's expensive, years-long attempt to pin criminal charges on Clinton seems unreasonable and appears to represent serious abuse of prosecutorial discretion: targeting someone for criminal investigation based on political or personal dislike. Charging people with "derivative crimes" like obstruction of justice, lying to a federal investigator, or perjury is a strategy too often used by prosecutors to nail a person for "something" when the prosecutor has been unable to prove any underlying crime.[5] The Martha Stewart prosecution was a good example of such a tactic; prosecutors couldn't pin any substantive crime (like insider trading) on her, so they charged her with lying to federal officials and obstruction of justice instead.[6]

The efforts of so many Republicans to bring Clinton to "justice" by way of criminal and impeachment sanctions backfired and even somewhat reversed the trend among the press and public to criticize Bill Clinton for his behavior. Because a majority of Americans saw the grand juries and impeachment proceedings as an ill-fitting punishment for what Clinton did, we fixated more on the overzealousness of Kenneth Starr than on the crux of Clinton's wrongdoing. Americans have a pretty reasonable view of justice, on the whole, and a keystone of our justice system is trying to make the punishment fit the crime. We recoil from disproportionate retribution, and we disapprove of punishment as vengeance. Family members of violent crime victims often fantasize about torturing the perpetrator, but we don't allow them that satisfaction. Overall, we do what we can to maintain a sense of proportionality and humanity even in the way we treat the criminals among us.

Whatever the nature of Clinton's offenses, this libertarian author believes that none merited the politicized assault he received by his adversaries. By contrast, the decision by the Arkansas Supreme Court to disbar Clinton[7] for his actions was a reasonable, justifiable consequence that the legal profession had every right to impose on one of its own. Clinton eventually admitted he'd intentionally misled the court in his Paula Jones deposition. Even as a witness/defendant in the Paula Jones case, he was still a lawyer bound by the ethics of his profession, and those ethical mandates do not smile with favor on intentionally deceiving the court. The legal profession's castigation of Clinton-as-lawyer demonstrated that Clinton did not escape consequences for his deceptive behavior.

We'll never know how Clinton's presidency might have unfolded if both sides of the aisle had contented themselves with denouncing Clinton's reprehensible behavior, discussing its significance in various contexts, and letting it go at that. I can't help thinking that Clinton's time in office would then have been crippled by a mounting perception of him as untrustworthy, deceptive, weak, and yes, misogynistic. Instead, his popularity rose in the aftermath of impeachment proceedings and Republicans allowed him to leave office with at least a relative moral upper hand because they appeared more vindictive than he did.

It's challenging to separate the political ramifications of Clinton's affair with Lewinsky from his behavior itself, but for our purposes it's possible and useful to differentiate between the two. "Clinton did what he did," writes Michael Isikoff, "quite apart from the...plotting of any right-wing cabals."[8] Clinton may have been unfairly targeted in a political vendetta but his adversaries would have fired empty cannons without the ammunition his own actions furnished.

◊

Just shy of her twenty-second birthday, Monica Samille Lewinsky arrived in Washington, D.C. in July 1995 to start an internship in the White House. Born July 23, 1973, Monica grew up in Beverly Hills, the daughter of writer/reporter Marcia Lewis and medical doctor Bernard Lewinsky, who divorced when Monica was fourteen. She graduated from a private, nonreligious prep school in 1991. Her headmaster remembers her as a quiet girl, except when singing in the school choir.[9] Monica took classes for two years at a junior college in Santa Monica, then transferred to Lewis and Clark College in Portland, Oregon, earning her Bachelor of Arts in psychology in 1995.

A Lewinsky family friend (and powerful Democratic contributor), Walter Kaye, advised Monica that she might enjoy working in the White House, and with Mr. Kaye's recommendation to give her an edge, she applied for an unpaid internship and set off for Washington, D.C. Living with her mom and younger brother Michael in the Watergate hotel, Monica interned for Leon Panetta, then Clinton's chief of staff, preparing correspondence. In just four and half months she acquired a paid staff position in Legislative Affairs at the White House, garnering a coveted "blue pass" that permitted access to the entire West Wing.

The first time she caught Clinton's eye was in August 1995 while she was still an intern with a less prestigious "pink pass" that restricted her access to parts of the West Wing. On August 9 at a ceremony on the South Lawn, Monica was in a rope line and as Clinton came by shaking hands they made "more intense eye contact" than they ever had.[10] Their flirtation continued from a distance the next day at a birthday celebration for Clinton to which interns were invited. For a few months they exchanged only brief greetings on a handful of occasions.

On November 15, 1995, they truly met for the first time. Monica was answering phones in Leon Panetta's West Wing office and Clinton came in several times that day. Everyone was working late because of the government shut-down resulting from the partisan stalemate on passing a budget that year. At about 8:00 p.m. Monica was walking to the restroom when Clinton approached her and invited her to accompany him to his study. After talking a bit, Clinton asked if he could kiss her.[11] She said yes. At about 10:00 p.m. the same evening Clinton found her again in Leon Panetta's office and told her it would be "fine" if she met him again in a few minutes.[12] This time their encounter was more intimate, including oral sex.

In *My Life* Bill Clinton writes that he celebrated his twentieth wedding anniversary in October 1995 by giving Hillary a diamond ring "to mark a milestone in our lives and to make up for the fact that when she agreed to marry me, I didn't have enough money to buy her an engagement ring."[13] Very romantic. Less romantic, and not mentioned by Clinton, is the fact that only weeks later he engaged in his first sexual encounter with Lewinsky.

Clinton's next intimate rendezvous with the young woman was two days later and the trysts continued sporadically for the next year and a half. Their relationship wasn't exclusively sexual. Lewinsky described their time together as "affectionate," with a lot of hugging, hand holding, and talk about all kinds of nonsexual things.[14] "We would tell jokes. We would talk about our childhoods. Talk about current events. I was always giving him my stupid ideas about what I thought should be done in the administration or different views on things. I think back on it and he always made me smile when I was with him. It was a lot of — he was sunshine."[15]

Bear in mind that Lewinsky could reminisce this fondly even though by the time she testified on August 6, 1998, Clinton had been telling *everyone* for seven months that she must be lying, that nothing "inappropriate" or sexual ever happened between them. But Monica was smitten. If she hadn't been forced to testify she wouldn't have; she didn't want to hurt Clinton. She dated other men during her eighteen-month affair with Clinton, and even used to tease him about having "competition,"[16] though she never told him about her fling with a high-ranking Pentagon official that led to her pregnancy and abortion in the fall of 1996, an unpleasant experience she didn't reveal publicly until she told her story in a book in 1999.[17]

Not that she kept all this to herself. She told two of her counselors, her mom, and a handful of trusted friends, in varying degrees of detail, about her relationship with President Clinton.[18] The recipient of the most detail of her relationship with Clinton was her friend and Pentagon co-worker Linda Tripp, with whom Monica spoke regularly about the affair from November 1996 through December 1997. Tripp eventually taped many of those conversations, unbeknownst to Lewinsky, and those tapes set in motion the chain of events that got the OIC involved and wound up forcing Lewinsky and Clinton to come clean about their affair.

While she worked in the White House, meetings between Lewinsky and Clinton would be set up by the president directly calling Lewinsky's office, usually on weekends, arranging for the pair to bump into each other in the halls and slip away to his private study.[19] Lewinsky was transferred from the White House to the Pentagon in April 1996 to be the Confidential Assistant to Ken Bacon, spokesman for the Pentagon. After that move her trysts with Clinton were arranged primarily by Betty Currie, Clinton's secretary.[20] When Monica told Bill she was being transferred he was upset and promised to bring her back to the White House after the 1996 election.[21] At that point, Clinton and Lewinsky agreed that Lewinsky should always say she was coming to visit Betty, so that nothing would look suspicious.[22] Though they shared the oral sex experience about nine times, they never had sexual intercourse; Clinton told her that at his age, "there was too much of a consequence in doing that."[23] Lewinsky "wasn't happy with that."

Neither was Lewinsky happy when the president told her he wanted to end their relationship. Lewinsky was able to provide the Office of Independent Counsel (OIC) remarkably specific dates for her meetings and conversations with Clinton because she had always "been a date-oriented person" and had a habit of circling dates she met or spoke with Clinton in her Filofax. According to her grand jury testimony, on President's Day 1997, and again on May 24, 1997, he told her that he just didn't feel right about the affair and wanted to do the right thing in God's eyes and for his family. The most intimate encounters after "D-Day" (Dump Day, as Monica calls that May 24) involved only kissing. Three days after Lewinsky's D-Day the U.S. Supreme Court ruled against Clinton and allowed the Paula Jones lawsuit to go forward.

Three months before D-Day, on February 27, 1997, she met with Clinton so the two could exchange (late) Christmas gifts. They hadn't seen each other much since the previous April. By that time Monica had been shunted over to the Pentagon, and a staffer didn't want Clinton alone with Monica anymore, so Betty Currie was the designated chaperone for that meeting. But Currie left the room and while alone, they engaged once more in oral sex. This time, Monica was wearing the now-notorious navy blue Gap dress that came into contact with "biological" proof of the tryst. She kept the dress not as a souvenir but because she wanted to wear it again.[24] But she told Linda Tripp about the dress and that she suspected some of Clinton's semen might be on it, and Tripp encouraged her to keep it and not have it cleaned.[25]

Monica desperately wanted to work in the White House again, and although Clinton assured her he had people trying to bring her back, no White House job ever materialized. By the summer of 1997 the Paula Jones case had heated up and Monica learned from Linda Tripp that reporter Michael Isikoff had been snooping about the Kathleen Willey story. In a July 4 meeting with Clinton, Monica warned him that Isikoff was on to Willey, but Clinton already knew, since Willey had tipped off the White House herself the previous week. That July 4 visit was not a pleasant one for Monica. She had written a letter to Clinton in which she made a veiled threat to tell her parents of their affair unless she got a job in the White House. Clinton began their meeting by lecturing her angrily, "First of all it's illegal to threaten the president of the United States."[26] She cried. He forgave her.

On July 14, 1997, Lewinsky had just returned from an overseas trip with the Pentagon when she received a call from Betty Currie asking her to meet with the president that evening.[27] Back in March, before Linda Tripp agreed to talk to Michael Isikoff about Kathleen Willey, Tripp tried to reach deputy White House counsel Bruce Lindsey at the White House. He never returned her page, which offended her, and when Isikoff approached her again she told him about learning of Kathleen Willey's encounter with Clinton. Now that Paula Jones's lawyers were on to Kathleen Willey, Clinton asked Lewinsky to please convince Tripp to call Bruce Lindsey, presumably to find out exactly what Tripp was prepared to say publicly about Willey. Lewinsky complied with Clinton's request.[28] In the same conversation Clinton asked Lewinsky if she had said anything to Tripp about her relationship with him.[29] Lying, Lewinsky said she hadn't.[30]

By October 1997 Lewinsky more or less gave up her efforts to secure a position in the White House, and redirected her energy to pressure Clinton to help her find a job in the private sector in New York. On October 9, 1997, she and Clinton had an argument about it over the phone, but they made up.[31] Two days later Clinton asked Lewinsky to prepare a list of companies she'd like to work for, with the idea that his influential lawyer friend Vernon Jordan could help her obtain a job with one of them. By early November Lewinsky had met with Jordan, who told her the president "highly recommended" her and assured her that finding a job from her list wouldn't be a problem. But all through November and December no job offer emerged.

On December 6, 1997, Lewinsky approached the White House gates trying to deliver Christmas presents for Clinton through Betty Currie. She couldn't reach Currie at first and when she did, she learned that the president was in the Oval Office with another woman. This upset Lewinsky, who fought with Currie over the phone and later that day received a phone call at her house from an angry Clinton, who told her it was none of her business who he was with and berated her for causing such a stir. He invited her over for a meeting that evening, though, and they had a "very nice" visit together. On December 11 Lewinsky met with Vernon Jordan again to discuss "contacts" to whom Lewinsky should send application letters for a job.

On December 17 Clinton again called Lewinsky at home and said he had two things to tell her: first, Betty Curie's brother had been killed in a car crash, and second, Lewinsky had been tapped by the Paula Jones legal team as a potential witness. Lewinsky was "upset and shocked." Clinton told her it "broke his heart." Clinton also suggested that before she got a subpoena maybe she could sign an affidavit. "You know, you can always say you were coming to see Currie or that you were bringing me letters." This strategy, obtaining preemptive affidavits from worrisome women, had served him well for over a decade. In the same phone conversation Lewinsky tried to persuade him to settle the Jones lawsuit. Clinton wasn't keen on that idea and changed the subject, saying he'd have Betty Currie bring Lewinsky's Christmas presents over to her. Monica flatly refused, insisting to Clinton that they needed to "let Betty be" since her brother had just been killed.

After talking with Clinton, Lewinsky called Linda Tripp. Tripp had been subpoenaed in the Jones case and Lewinsky had been pestering her to be a team player, to downplay the suggestion that anything sexual had ever happened between Clinton and Willey, and especially between Clinton and Lewinsky. That night, Lewinsky wanted Tripp to know that if Tripp lied about knowing anything concerning Lewinsky and Clinton, it would be okay because Lewinsky and others would make the same denials. Everyone could provide a "united front" and the problem might just disappear.

Two days later, on December 19, 1997, Monica Lewinsky received her subpoena in the Jones case. She "burst into tears" — calling it "sort of my worst nightmare." She said later she deeply resented being dragged into the Paula Jones case. "I lost my job because I was [Clinton's] girlfriend and the bottom line is that my affair with the president hampered, rather than helped, my job prospects. In fact, my experience ruined Paula Jones's arguments about sexual harassment."[32] Immediately she called Vernon Jordan, went to his office a couple of hours later, and showed him the subpoena. Jordan said there were two important questions: did she have sex with the president, and did the president ever ask her for sex?[33] She answered "no" to both of Jordan's questions that day, but testified later that she had assumed that Jordan knew she had a relationship with Clinton and was asking her those questions to find out what she was prepared to say under oath about it.[34]

After meeting with Lewinsky one more time on December 22, Jordan arranged for her to meet with a lawyer, Frank Carter.[35] Lewinsky told Carter there was no way she should have received this subpoena, that Paula Jones's case was "bunk," and that she would be willing to sign an affidavit denying a sexual relationship with Clinton and/or explaining away her frequent visits and correspondence to the White House by saying she was just over there visiting Betty Currie.[36] Lewinsky also asked Carter to convey all this to Bob Bennett, the president's lawyer, because in her mind, even a low-level political appointee like herself "work[s] for the administration and you're politically aligned with this administration and everything you do is in the best interest of the administration and, ultimately, the president. And that's where your goal and your focus should be."[37] Despite her many references to looking at Clinton as a man rather than as a president, Clinton's official status apparently played heavily into

Lewinsky's reluctance to do anything that might harm him politically.

On December 28, 1997, not even three weeks before his deposition in the Paula Jones case, Clinton invited Lewinsky over to the Oval Office where they played with Buddy the dog and he gave her Christmas gifts.[38] She had been struggling for a few days, wondering if she should tell Clinton that Linda Tripp knew about their relationship, but decided against it, wanting this visit to be a "nice" one since she was anticipating heading to a New York job soon and might not get to see Clinton much after that.[39] Maybe it should have seemed odd that Clinton would give her gifts when he knew she had already received a subpoena that required her to turn over all gifts from him, but at the time, she was "in love with him" and just "happy to be with him."[40] At her suggestion, Betty Currie soon stopped by her house to pick up a box full of the gifts Clinton had given Lewinsky.[41] (She kept some sentimental things out of that box but months later turned them over to the OIC.[42]) To Lewinsky, turning over her gifts to Currie was a way for her to reassure Clinton that she had no intention of getting him into trouble,[43] even if it meant hiding evidence and committing perjury.

On January 5, 1998, Lewinsky met with her attorney, Frank Carter, who prepared her for the probability of testifying in a deposition, since Carter wasn't sure an affidavit was going to satisfy Jones's attorneys. Carter said he'd draft an affidavit, and Lewinsky decided she wanted Vernon Jordan to look it over before she signed it, because Jordan was "the president's best friend" and she wanted the affidavit to be "blessed" by the president.[44] Later that day, Clinton called Lewinsky after she had told Betty Currie she didn't want to sign anything without talking first to Clinton. Monica was in a mood. She had seen a photo in the media of Bill and Hillary romantically intertwined on their vacation and felt "annoyed" and "jealous." She was short with him and told him she was worried about being asked in deposition how she'd gotten her job with the Pentagon. Clinton said she could always say that Legislative Affairs had arranged it for her; this would keep certain White House aides out of the discussion.

The next day, January 6, Frank Carter gave Lewinsky a draft affidavit. She showed a copy of it to Vernon Jordan, and the two agreed that some of the language was problematic because it mentioned that Lewinsky had been "alone" with the president once. With a few revisions, Lewinsky signed the affidavit under penalty of perjury the following day, January 7, including a paragraph stating she'd never had a sexual relationship with Clinton. She was more than ready and willing to do this because of her "love for and loyalty to" Clinton.[45] By signing the affidavit she felt like she was "putting on my team jersey" on the side of the president.[46]

Later that day Lewinsky flew to New York for a job interview with the parent company of Revlon.[47] The interview went poorly. She called Vernon Jordan to let him know she'd blown the interview. He said he'd call the chairman, and Revlon set up a second interview for Lewinsky and informally offered her a position.[48] On January 13, Revlon formally offered her a $40,000 salaried position in their public relations department and she accepted. She stopped by Vernon Jordan's office the same day, thanked him for the job, gave him a token gift, and showed him a copy of her finalized, signed affidavit.[49]

On January 14, 1998, Lewinsky typed out the "Talking Points" memo and gave it to Linda Tripp, directing Tripp to downplay and discredit Kathleen Willey's story.[50] Lewinsky drove Tripp that day to Tripp's lawyer's office so that Tripp could sign her own affidavit, and the two women discussed the talking points. Lewinsky maintains that no one associated with Clinton helped her write the talking points. In fact, in Lewinsky's opinion, the president never encouraged her to lie at all—she would have come up with the same excuses and means of covering up their affair whether or not he had ever suggested using Betty Currie as a cover. "For me, the best way to explain how I feel [about] what happened was, you know, no one asked or encouraged me to lie, but no one discouraged me either." They just shared a mutual understanding that they would both deny the affair. Somewhat reminiscent of Gennifer Flowers's observation that she sometimes felt more protective of Clinton's family than Clinton was, Lewinsky testified that she was sometimes the one to take extra care not to appear too close to Clinton publicly or take too many risks that might make people start wondering.[51] She would have continued to take steps to prevent the affair from disclosure with or without Clinton's encouragement.

Right up to the president's *mea culpa* admitting to their relationship on August 17, 1998, Lewinsky still "loved" Clinton.[52] After that little speech of his, she told the grand jury on August 20, she no longer knew how she felt about him.[53] She felt like he'd characterized their relationship as merely a service contract, and it was much more than that to her.[54] She had spent nearly three years doing everything she could not to hurt him, and in his public admission he didn't even directly mention her, and didn't acknowledge the pain the past seven months of denials had caused her and so many other people. After all their times together, talking and laughing, she just thought he had a "beautiful soul." Now, she couldn't know how she felt about him anymore, fearing that he had been an "actor" the whole time.

What she did know, she confessed to the grand jury, is that she didn't think it was "right to have an affair with a married man." She'd been through a similar love affair before she came to D.C. and she never expected to fall in love with Bill Clinton but she did. Trying to explain why she did what she did, Monica said in August 1998:

> There are obviously issues that—that—you know, a single young woman doesn't have an affair with a married man because she's normal, quote-unquote. But I think most people have issues and that's just how mine manifested themselves. It's something I need to work on....

Lewinsky didn't know until she had been apprehended by the FBI that Linda Tripp had been secretly taping their phone conversations, nor that Tripp had worn a wire in cooperation with authorities when the two women met for lunch on January 13, 1998, nor that her lunch date with Tripp on January 16 was the final set-up. On that day, Lewinsky was approached by the FBI (working with the OIC) as Tripp and Lewinsky arrived for their lunch meeting at the Ritz-Carlton.[55] "The agents flashed their badges, told Lewinsky they wanted to talk to her privately and took her to a room upstairs."[56] The agents told Lewinsky about Tripp's tape recordings, which contradicted Lewinsky's January 7 affidavit, exposing her to prosecution for perjury, and showed Lewinsky transcripts of the tapes and photographs of Lewinsky's wire-tapped lunch with Tripp earlier in the week.[57] "My life is ruined," Lewinsky told the agents.[58]

She spent the next few hours crying, refusing to talk without first speaking with her lawyer, Frank Carter, but she couldn't reach him. She had never felt so terrified. She thought about jumping from the ten story window.[59] She resisted cooperating — even though they threatened to prosecute her mother and told her if she called her lawyer they'd yank immunity off the table.[60] Monica insisted on calling her mom, who rushed down to the Ritz-Carlton and phoned her ex-husband, who in turn promptly contacted his friend, attorney William Ginsburg. [61] By the time Ginsburg spoke with Monica late that night, he said he couldn't advise her to sign an immunity deal because he hadn't heard the Tripp tapes yet.[62] Monica left the hotel that night frightened and devastated, but still unwilling to play ball with the OIC.[63] It took the OIC months of negotiating over immunity before Monica Lewinsky cooperated and told them everything.

At the end of Lewinsky's final appearance before the grand jury in August 1998 she was asked if she'd like to add to her testimony, so that she felt she'd had the fullest opportunity to tell her side of things. She answered: "I would. I think because of the public nature of how this investigation has been and what the charges aired, that I would just like to say that no one ever asked me to lie and I was never promised a job for my silence. And that I'm sorry. I'm really sorry for everything that's happened. [She begins to cry.] And I hate Linda Tripp."[64]

◊

But for seven strange, weary months, none of this was confirmed, except by the taped phone conversations courtesy of Linda Tripp, which didn't settle the question of how accurate Lewinsky's story was. Lewinsky's lawyers and the OIC negotiated over an immunity deal until the end of July 1998. Lewinsky refused to comment publicly during that period, neither recanting nor confirming her affidavit denying a sexual relationship with Clinton. Like Kathleen Willey, until Lewinsky found herself cornered by the legal system, she kept silent and did all she could to protect Clinton. Like Willey, Lewinsky found herself on the unpleasant end of a carefully executed smear campaign.

Lewinsky's had a different spin, though. Perhaps Clinton and his defense team held back out of fear they'd push Lewinsky into going public during those long months while she and her lawyers fought off the OIC. Perhaps Clinton personally felt reluctant to attack a young woman whose only mistake had been falling for him and blabbing to a girlfriend. Perhaps the Clinton spin machine once again sensed a backlash and knew they had to choose a less direct method of discrediting anything Lewinsky might say. Or perhaps they realized from the beginning of the Lewinsky story that certain circumstances didn't look good for Clinton, despite Clinton's denials of any improper relationship. After all, gifts, meetings, and phone calls could (and eventually would) be documented; those things would require explanation sooner or later.

Their solution was brilliant. Clinton and his defenders kept their angry denials and attacks off Lewinsky personally (with a few notable exceptions) and instead demonized the OIC and

Kenneth Starr. As Isikoff put it, "To prove his lies, Clinton knew, his foes would be forced into the gutter—or to go to such extraordinary lengths that, in the end, they would look worse than he."[65]

Just days after his January 17, 1998, deposition in the Paula Jones case, and less than a week before the State of the Union address, the Monica Lewinsky scandal hit the front pages. Working surreptitiously with Linda Tripp (to whom he quickly granted immunity), Kenneth Starr and the FBI "stung" Monica Lewinsky on Friday, January 16. They had Tripp's tapes and expanded authority to investigate accusations of obstruction of justice (and after Clinton's deposition, perjury). "Clinton Accused of Urging Aide to Lie; Starr Probes Whether President Told Woman to Deny Alleged Affair to Jones's Lawyers" rang the front page headline in *The Washington Post* on January 21, 1998.[66] On the same day, Revlon rescinded its offer of employment to Lewinsky, since Vernon Jordan, now facing investigation for possible obstruction of justice, had recommended Lewinsky to them.[67] "The president adamantly denies he ever had a relationship with Ms. Lewinsky and she has confirmed the truth of that," Clinton's lawyer Bob Bennett said. "This story seems ridiculous and I frankly smell a rat."[68] Lewinsky's attorney William Ginsburg said "If the president of the United States did this—and I'm not saying that he did—with this young lady, I think he's a misogynist," he said. "If he didn't, then I think Ken Starr and his crew have ravaged the life of a youngster."[69] Like Kathleen Willey and her lawyer, Lewinsky and hers attempted for months to stay on Clinton's good side.

Clinton's first public denials were terse. "There wasn't improper relations; I didn't ask anybody to lie."[70] Clinton said he was "furious" with the charges but would fully cooperate with Starr's investigation.[71] "The relationship was not sexual," Clinton insisted, as reporters continued asking for clarification of his relationship with Lewinsky.[72] Reporters seized on one of Clinton's initial statements: "There is not a sexual relationship; that is accurate."[73] Did his use of the present tense "is" convey that there was more to the story? Clinton also invoked his mother's coping mechanism of putting bad things aside: "I came here to try to change the country and to work to build the future of America and a new century. *And I just have to try to put this in a little box*, like I have every other thing that has been said and done, and go on and do my job."[74] This story, though, was bigger than any box Clinton could have used.

The first four days of Clinton's carefully worded denials prompted *The New York Times* to opine that Clinton's "cryptic, partial and insufficient" responses required complete explanation to a public that had not "prejudged the facts" but remained "troubled and mystified" by the facts known thus far.[75] "It is time for Mr. Clinton to tell the whole story in all its detail and context," *The New York Times* pleaded. But they would have to wait seven long months for Clinton to admit there had been any kind of sexual relationship, or to hear Lewinsky's version of events, and even longer—until Clinton wrote his memoirs—to hear any explanation from him about why he did what he did.

Hillary Rodham Clinton wasted no time in charging to her husband's defense, immediately declaring, "Certainly I believe [the allegations are] false. Absolutely."[76] She spent a lot of time "on the telephone rallying loyalists to come to her husband's defense" in the critical days just prior to the State of the Union address,[77] and on January 27 she told Matt Lauer on the *Today Show* that their political opponents were the true villains in unfolding drama: "[T]he great story here...is this vast right-wing conspiracy that has been conspiring against my husband since the day he announced for president."[78]

Despite the Clintons' heated denials and deflections, from day one of the scandal Republicans raised the specter of impeachment. Henry Hyde, then chairman of the House Judiciary Committee, assured the media "There will be great pressure to impeach the man."[79] In the beginning it wasn't just Republicans who threw out the "I" word. George Stephanopoulos, by then a former Clinton aide but still relatively loyal, said the seriousness of the charges, if proven, meant possible impeachment.[80] Clinton's former Press Secretary Dee Dee Meyers hinted at the same prospect. "If he's not telling the truth," she said, "I think the consequences are just astronomical."[81]

White House Press Secretary Mike McCurry offered only brief statements the day the scandal broke: Clinton was "outraged" and "never had any improper relationship with this woman."[82] Clinton told his Cabinet members the charges were untrue and they stood by him, many issuing public statements that they believed his denials.[83] Political consultant James Carville, usually Clinton's most vicious public relations attack dog, seemed rather subdued at first, saying only that he believed Clinton's denials and hoped everyone would "get to the bottom" of the charges as quickly as possible.[84] Administration aides, some of whom had defended Clinton since the 1992 campaign, told reporters on condition of anonymity that Clinton's initial denials had not been as clear as they'd hoped, and that if the charges turned out to be true Clinton should resign.[85] Clinton's person-on-the-street supporters of every stripe hoped the allegations were false, expressed anger at Ken Starr for "being prepared to pick up any available rock to throw at the president," but also immediately suspected that something indeed happened between Clinton and Lewinsky.[86] Why, many wondered angrily, would Clinton bring "aid and comfort" to his enemies by handing them a "lethal weapon"?[87]

Aside from attacking Starr, the media and administration officials also cast a few direct aspersions on Monica Lewinsky, mostly with an air of condescension, hinting that she'd been moved from the White House to the Pentagon because she had a "slight crush" on Clinton and made too many efforts to get close to him.[88] An official at the Pentagon described Lewinsky as a "sweet kid, a little flirtatious in a way that a lot of twenty-four year old women are," but others merely said she was a dedicated worker.[89] White House officials stated they'd transferred Lewinsky to the Pentagon in 1996 because she was "infatuated" with Clinton.[90] Not without reason, as it turned out.

One *Boston Herald* columnist expressed support for Lewinsky over Clinton, albeit in a patronizing way, by recasting the scandal as a boxing match.[91] In one corner, a fresh-faced former intern just twenty-four years old. In the other corner, "Slippery Bill, the aw-shucks, lip-biting serial philanderer with a 'pattern and practice,' as *Newsweek* put it, of using political office, power and perks for 'sexual predation.'"[92] Lewinsky's own lawyer helped create the patronizing image of her as a young, innocent pawn in a bigger game. Angling publicly for an immunity deal from Starr, Ginsburg proclaimed dramatically "She is at the vortex of a storm probably involving the three most powerful men in the United States — the president, Vernon Jordan and the independent prosecutor Kenneth Starr. She's devastated."[93] *The Washington Post* described Monica as "an enigma wrapped in conflicting images."[94] After noting that some White House aides derided Lewinsky for having a "conspicuous crush" on Clinton, the *Post* continued: "She is described by some as 'sweet,' 'polite' and 'intelligent'; by others as 'arrogant,' 'spoiled' and 'immature.'"[95] Ask enough friends, acquaintances, and co-workers of any of us and I'm sure you'd get a similar mixed bag of adjectives.

The most hurtful character assassination against Lewinsky came from Clinton himself and it became public because of a hardball tactic by Ken Starr. Under the guise of obtaining evidence that the Clinton cadre's public relations attacks on Starr and his prosecutors constituted actual "threats" that could impede prosecutors from doing their jobs,[96] Starr subpoenaed White House aide Sidney Blumenthal[97] and demanded that Blumenthal disclose the names of journalists he'd spoken with about the scandal and the substance of his conversations with them. Through Blumenthal's testimony, word leaked out that Clinton had told Blumenthal that Lewinsky was just a "stalker" who had come on to Clinton and been rejected by him.[98] Not only did Clinton fail to step up on a personal level and do anything to *help*

Lewinsky—paying her legal bills, for instance, would have been the least he could've done—but Clinton actually had the nerve to affirmatively *hurt* her.

Despite word from aides that Clinton would refuse any further comment or explanation on the scandal, on January 26 (just five days after the story broke in print, and the day before the State of the Union speech), Clinton addressed the American public for what he must have hoped would be his final word on the matter. At the tail end of a speech heralding a host of education reforms, "He put on his most determined face and punched the air with his finger to drive his point home," declaring firmly: "I want to say one thing to the American people. I want you to listen to me....*I did not have sexual relations with that woman, Ms. Lewinsky*. I never told anybody to lie. Not a single time. Never. These allegations are false, and I need to go back to work for the American people."[99] When Monica Lewinsky spoke freely about her reaction the following year she said Clinton's "that woman" phrase felt "very harsh" and hurt her.[100]

Speaking to Larry King the same day, Paul Begala said he believed Clinton, and believed the investigation would clear his friend and advisee. "You wait and see," Begala boasted to King.[101] If Begala ever felt betrayed by Clinton he didn't show it; he was Clinton's right-hand man editing the eventual confession speech the following August.[102] But most of us were far from convinced. Maybe because his "that woman, Ms. Lewinsky" denial came six years *to the day* after Bill and Hillary's joint appearance on *60 Minutes* to put the Gennifer Flowers story to rest during the 1992 campaign—and just days after he had reportedly admitted to an affair with Flowers at his deposition.

Fueled mainly by speculation and spin, the Lewinsky story continued to pound the public into disgust for the next several months. A federal judge dismissed Paula Jones's lawsuit in April, but the OIC investigation continued in full swing. Finally, at the end of July 1998, Lewinsky got an immunity deal from Starr and agreed to testify before the grand jury. In those intervening months, Clintonites fought fire with fire (in their view), hiring investigators to dig up dirt on Starr and his prosecutors, and threatening to go public with stories about the prosecutors' sex lives.[103] Carville ranted that Starr was obsessed with sex, Starr was out to "get" the president, Starr was an "out of control" partisan.[104] Carville had been waging war against Starr for years, and as the Starr-is-out-of-control mantra picked up steam throughout the Lewinsky scandal, Carville proudly claimed to have been a "prophet."[105] Baiting Starr into occasionally biting back and getting angry in public, says former Clinton political consultant Dick Morris, was referred to by the Clinton defense team as their "lift and loft" tactic—lifting Clinton "above the fight."[106] It worked especially well as the Lewinsky scandal intensified, but it didn't entirely diffuse the outrage and disappointment felt by many when Clinton finally confessed.

◊

Monica Lewinsky testified before the grand jury first on August 6, then again on August 20. In the intervening days, President Clinton testified on August 17. That concession on Clinton's part wasn't the result of a genuine desire to get to the bottom of things and clear up all misconceptions. Rather, it was the culmination of three events that summer. [107] Since January, Starr had been firing off subpoenas like they were going out of style to everyone who possibly had any connection to the scandal, methodically building a case against Clinton. By July 1998 Starr achieved three potent victories: first, he and Monica reached an immunity deal; second (because of the immunity deal) Starr now had his hands on the infamous "blue dress" and had it tested for Clinton's DNA; third, Starr subpoenaed Clinton, then withdrew the subpoena and arranged for Clinton's voluntary rather than coerced testimony[108] in exchange for a few conditions that favored Clinton (e.g., unlike other material witnesses or potential defendants Clinton was allowed to have attorneys present). This deal increased the probability that Starr would elicit relatively truthful testimony from Clinton for two reasons. First, if Clinton had been forced to talk under a subpoena, perhaps he would simply have invoked his Fifth Amendment right not to incriminate himself and said nothing. Second, Clinton could have tied up the process for months with legal challenges to Starr's right to force a sitting president to testify. Whether the decision to deal with Starr was legal, political, or (most probably) a combination, Clinton agreed to testify on August 17.

The videotaped testimony wasn't made public until the following month, but just after his testimony ended, Clinton addressed the nation. While some were still referring to Lewinsky as "hopelessly deluded" with a "90210 imagination"[109] Clinton issued yet another sort-of apology, this time in the form of a four-minute public address from the White House:[110]

> As you know, in a deposition in January, I was asked questions about my relationship with Monica Lewinsky. While my answers were legally accurate, I did not volunteer information. Indeed I did have a relationship with Miss Lewinsky that was not appropriate. In fact it was wrong.
>
> It constituted a critical lapse in judgment and a personal failure on my part for which I am solely and completely responsible.
>
> But I told the grand jury today, and I say to you now, that at no time did I ask anyone to lie, to hide or destroy evidence, or to take any other unlawful action.
>
> I know that my public comments and my silence about this matter gave a false impression. I misled people. Including even my wife. I deeply regret that....
>
> I had real and serious concerns about an independent counsel investigation that began with private business dealings twenty years ago—dealings, I might add, about which an independent federal agency found no evidence of any wrongdoing by me or my wife over two years ago....
>
> This has gone on too long, cost too much, and hurt too many innocent people.

> Now this matter is between me, the two people I love most, my wife and our daughter, and our God. I must put it right. And I am prepared to do whatever it takes to do so....

> And so tonight I ask you to turn away from the spectacle of the past seven months, to repair the fabric of our national discourse and to return our attention to all the challenges and all the promise of the next American century.

"Yep, I kinda misled y'all, but it's time to move on now—oh, and Ken Starr sucks" sums up the spirit of his so-called confession. But this was the most Clinton would say about his relationship with Lewinsky until he published his memoirs six years later. As for what actually happened between him and Lewinsky he explains: "During the government shutdown in late 1995, when very few people were allowed to come to work in the White House and those who were there were working late, I'd had an inappropriate encounter with Monica Lewinsky and would do so again on other occasions between November and April, when she left the White House for the Pentagon."[111] He continues, "For the next ten months I didn't see her, although we talked on the phone from time to time." Because of the blue dress he had to admit to seeing her at least once more, in February 1997, when "Monica was among the guests at an evening taping of my weekly radio address, after which I met with her alone again for about fifteen minutes." He adds, "I was disgusted with myself for doing it, and in the spring, when I saw her again, I told her that it was wrong for me, wrong for my family, and wrong for her, and I couldn't do it anymore." He also writes that he told her he "would try to be her friend and help her" but "nothing improper occurred" between them after that. What a stand-up guy.

He defends his testimony at his Paula Jones deposition, insisting that his denial under oath about ever having "sexual relations" with Monica was based on the legalistic definition of that term used by the lawyers that day.[112] The definition "seemed to require both a specific act and a certain state of mind on my part" and "did not include any act by another person," Clinton surmises.

As for the aftermath of his Lewinsky affair, Clinton admits, "What I had done with Monica Lewinsky was immoral and foolish" but he was "determined not to compound it by allowing Starr to drive me from office."[113] So, he continues, "I went along doing my job, and I stonewalled, denying what had happened to everyone: Hillary, Chelsea, my staff and cabinet, my friends in Congress, members of the press, and the American people." He regrets "having misled all of them." In the months before the scandal came to light he felt "[i]t was like living in a nightmare" particularly because he was understandably unwilling to "help Ken Starr criminalize my personal life...." Clinton's now-infamous explanation for *why* he engaged in his affair with Monica Lewinsky doesn't appear in his book. In a *60 Minutes* interview with Dan Rather in June 2004 promoting his memoirs he said that he did it for the most "morally indefensible" reason possible: "Just because I could."

The media didn't give Clinton a free pass. It was "no *mea culpa* speech," decided *The Washington Post* after Clinton's August 1998 public admission.[114] Agreed the inimitable Michael Kelly: "It was an everybody-else *culpa*."[115] The speech "seemed to have too much input from pollsters and lawyers, and not enough heartfelt contrition from Clinton," concluded another journalist.[116] *The New York Times* editorialized edgily that Clinton's time-tested strategy of "minimal confession and contained tantrum that got him elected twice" would "not make him a leader who will be missed once he leaves Washington."[117] When Clinton walked into the White House Map Room for his battle with prosecutors, delivered by live video feed to the grand jury, *The New York Times* opined that he faced a "force" more powerful and destructive than Ken Starr—his own "habit of stonewalling, of misleading by omission or concealment or fabrication or failure of memory, [that] has been the source of virtually all this administration's troubles."[118] There was no ringing endorsement for Clinton in the press that day. When Monica Lewinsky felt safe enough to talk about her reaction several months later, she said of Clinton's tepid apologies (which hadn't included her at all): "I felt like a piece of trash. I felt dirty and I felt used and I was disappointed."[119]

Former White House chief of staff Leon Panetta (Lewinsky's old boss) said Clinton staffers, aides, and advisers must be feeling "stab[bed] in the back."[120] Dee Dee Myers agreed that Clinton had "put them in an incredibly awkward position, completely by virtue of his own actions." Clinton, Myers said despairingly, "believes that character is an evolving thing." Consultant Dick Morris, who'd been kicked to the curb after a sex scandal of his own, scoffed at the idea of feeling sorry for Clinton's staffers. "[A]ny of them who were dumb enough to actually believe Clinton's stories deserve what happens to them," he said bluntly.[121]

Ann Lewis, one of Clinton's most ardent, vocal defenders, refused to talk to the press, saying she needed to think some things over. Her brother, Rep. Barney Frank (D-Mass.) said Lewis was in a tough spot because her close friend Hillary was in a difficult position. A handful of loyal Clintonistas immediately expressed unwavering support without a trace of bitterness. Media consultant Mandy Grunwald stated flatly, "He did it to protect his family. And it's none of our business."[122] Clinton must have thought it was the business of at least some of his close supporters. Without naming names, Clinton aides confirmed that Clinton had called them in one by one over the preceding weekend to tell them his seven-month string of denials had been false; he had, in fact, had an improper relationship with Lewinsky.[123] He expressed regret to some but not others.[124]

A CBS poll immediately after this speech showed that 63 percent of Americans believed the "matter should be dropped" now.[125] It wasn't dropped, of course, until after Starr released his report in September, the House of Representatives opened an inquiry into impeachment in October and passed two articles of impeachment in December, and the Senate acquitted Clinton in February 1999. *Then* it was over. *Then* Lewinsky's life could resume, though for months she remained fearful of losing her immunity if she spoke too freely. Commentary during the post-confession, pre-impeachment months focused mostly on whether Clinton's actions amounted to "high crimes and misdemeanors" warranting removal from office. Aside from her testimony during the Senate trial, the public didn't hear much from Monica Lewinsky until the following spring, when for the first time she spoke about her experience outside the frightening context of threatened criminal indictment.

◊

"I'm not going to pretend that it was always about something bigger than me," Lewinsky told *Time* magazine in March 1999.[126] "Because for me, it wasn't."[127] Her book, *Monica's Story*, hit the stands that month, and she had been interviewed by Barbara Walters on ABC's *20/20* ten days prior. She was living in New York with her mom and stepfather, worried about finding a job and getting her life back on track, unable to go out in public without wearing a disguise. As for Bill Clinton, she was finally over him. She hated him in some moments because she felt she didn't deserve from him "the way he characterized this relationship" and "[t]he way he allowed, if not orchestrated, the White House to say all those things about me."[128] Her ambivalence is understandable. "Sometimes I'm proud of him still, and sometimes I hate his guts," she told Barbara Walters. "And, um, he makes me sick."[129] She expressed no ambivalence with respect to Ken Starr and his investigation; his report to Congress, she said in her book, made her feel "raped and physically ill with myself,"[130] like the "world looked at me as a whore,"[131] and like "the most humiliated woman in the world."[132] Any regrets? On some days she regrets "ever having had this relationship begin" but on other days she just regrets "telling Linda Tripp."[133]

Her biggest mistake in the whole thing, she thought, was not being discreet enough, because she "betrayed the president in that way."[134] She felt sorry for causing pain to her family, to Chelsea and Hillary Clinton, and yes, to herself. "I was the one lying awake at night crying, scared I was going to go to jail," she said. "I was the one being followed. I was the one being torn apart in the press, and my family....But I don't know that the punishment fit the crime."[135] She doesn't consider herself a celebrity, and refuses to give out autographs when people ask: "I think that the root of the word [celebrity] is celebrated[,] someone society should celebrate.... I don't feel that I should be honored for what I'm known for."[136] She's right, of course, but our voyeuristic society still catapulted her into fame, illustrated by the fact that at her first major book signing in London, she sat in a chair at Harrods where the likes of Margaret Thatcher, Norman Schwarzkopf, and Mikhail Gorbachev sat signing their own memoirs in years past.[137]

The day that Lewinsky's two-hour interview with Barbara Walters aired in March 1999, Bill Clinton, Al Gore, and other prominent Democrats gathered to show a spirit of party unity and highlight their "Family First" party agenda for the year, focusing on Social Security and Medicare reform, health care and education initiatives, and raising the minimum wage.[138] With the impeachment ordeal only a few weeks behind him and less than two years remaining in his second term, Clinton finally found himself relatively scandal-free. After losing seats in the November 1998 election, Republicans ultimately got the point that the public didn't want to see Clinton kicked out of office for what he'd done and reoriented for the 2000 election. Hillary, riding a wave of public sympathy as the injured spouse who nonetheless loyally stood by her man, began testing the waters for a New York Senate bid.[139]

Over the next five years, Monica Lewinsky dabbled in a variety of activities that kept her name in the spotlight. She became a spokesperson for the Jenny Craig weight loss system, briefly hosted a Fox reality television show, designed and sold hand-bags, and devoted her spare time to studying Kabbalah (a Jewish mystical spiritual tradition), dating, flea-market shopping, and thinking about going to graduate school. It's probably not quite the way she imagined she'd spend her twenties, but she has proved herself to be resilient and determined to make something of her life.

◊

In popular culture, Don Juan remains a synonym for a man who charms and seduces women, a real ladies' man, portrayed by Johnny Depp in the 1995 film, *Don Juan de Marco*, (whose title character boasts of having 1,500 lovers by age twenty-one) and borrowed for the name of a popular "how to get women" Web site for men.[140] The fictional character first entered literature in a Spanish play, *The Seducer of Seville* by Tirso de Molina, in 1630. Additional artists transported the Don Juan legend into other countries throughout the seventeenth and eighteenth centuries, and by the 1800s he had been memorialized in several famous musical and literary renderings, including Lord Byron's satiric poem "Don Juan," (1819-1824), Mozart's opera "Don Giovanni" (1787), and George Bernard Shaw's "Man and Superman" with its famous Act III titled "Don Juan in Hell" (1907). These later works "portray Juan as a tragicomic hero, destroyed by his obsessive search for the ideal woman."[141] Don Juan, along with Casanova, Romeo, lady killer, stud, gigolo, playboy, etc., has become a name for a sexually active, intriguing, charming man who "eats women for breakfast—and lunch, and dinner."[142]

The tag "Don Juan" has evolved over the years until the point where it has been watered down by popular culture and now applied to any charming ladies' man. This popular interpretation of the term is not appropriate in the case of Bill Clinton, especially since it might imply that he and Monica were equally responsible for the fallout from their affair. Because of this, perhaps a less common but more forcefully descriptive word needs to be used. A real Don Juan is what some authors have caustically termed a "femivore:"

> The femivore's essential nature is that he infatuates and seduces women and leaves them bereft of spiritual and often physical life.... Most often, in literature and mythology, he escapes consequences and responsibilities and is allowed to remain a memorable and ephemeral treasure whose supernatural prowess defies mere mortals....In all cases, he is unbearably independent...and does not linger to concern himself with the futures of the ravished females he leaves behind. Such a creature, of course, makes any sense of love and *eros* inconsequential. The femivore's concerns are immediate and lustful. He doesn't nurture. Thus, he debilitates any sense of past or future.[143]

The same author observes it "would be easy enough to label the femivore as misogynist and wastrel: indifferent to humanity in women, insensitive and irresponsible to all but himself," but the fascinating question is how and why such a man, who should be "anathema to all women," is continually viewed by female conquests and male idolizers as merely "mischievous" and "boyish," a "lovable bastard," a model of a healthy, if overactive and sometimes reckless, male libido.[144]

The cause of the femivore's vitality is clear: society has mistaken him for some kind of hero, enticing women to fawn before him even as he leaves "broken hearts (and devastated psyches and self-concepts) scattered behind" him. A real Don Juan—a femivore—is a hero who "may be a subtle, likable, socially enviable, and glamorous rapist, for whom beguilement replaces force." The success of the femivore, unlike a rapist, "requires a conspiracy and mutual acquiescence from both sexes" whereby both "seek individually and mutually destructive power" and both "denigrate what it means to be human."

It doesn't seem much of a stretch to label Bill Clinton a Don Juan or femivore in the context of his very mutual, very consensual affair with Monica Lewinsky, particularly when she talks about how he confided to her that his romantic affairs "multiplied" after he married Hillary Rodham, and he continued to work through his marriage even though he had to circle on his calendar the days when he'd been "good."[145] Monica was just one of many, though he made her feel special and unique. Once Clinton's fun was over, he took no action to help her pick up the pieces of her life.

Given Lewinsky's own feelings that Kenneth Starr caused her perhaps more trauma than Bill Clinton ever did, some have argued that Starr was a bigger misogynist than Clinton, claiming that he willingly ruined the lives of women like Lewinsky, her mother, Betty Currie, and others in order to build his case against the president. This isn't accurate; comparing Starr and Clinton with respect to mistreatment of women is apples and oranges. It's true that Starr's actions had devastating impacts on women like Lewinsky. But his actions were motivated not by a desire to hurt women *per se*, but by a willingness to aggressively prosecute Bill Clinton. Clinton's mistreatment of Monica Lewinsky begins and ends with yet another demonstration of his belief that women in his life exist to serve at his pleasure and deserve little or no respect "in the morning," so to speak.

Clinton didn't take advantage of Lewinsky; she was an equal participant every step of the way, from initial flirtation to repeated sexual encounters. There was never a time when Clinton pressured her to do something and she felt offended or trapped the way Paula Jones or Kathleen Willey must have. She loved him and believed he loved her. She caught the eye of a femivore, and responded the way women have throughout history. She got caught up in the excitement, the flattery, the fantasy, of receiving sensualized attention from one of our "heroes." Clinton played his part flawlessly, too. He captivated her with charm and flattery, empathizing with her and holding her tenderly. He also berated her whenever she threatened to cause too much of a scene, and left her brokenhearted but strung along in the months between "D-Day" and when the scandal reached public ears.

After it did, she was "that woman, Ms. Lewinsky" to him, and finally an "improper," meaningless encounter who didn't deserve a public apology from him or concern for her reputation or internal well-being.

What might any of this have to do with Clinton's leftist ideology? Could liberal politics have any influence on Don Juan de Clinton? The essential characteristics of a real Don Juan apply by analogy to help identify our sixth tenet of liberalism that may have made it easier for Clinton to behave the way he did.

Modern liberalism seduces citizens by portraying government as charming, benign, and all-powerful. I have argued in previous chapters that liberalism views government as a useful, efficient tool for *forcing* us to behave the way we *should* behave. But an equally prominent, effective aspect of modern liberalism involves presentation of government not as brute force, but as a seductive answer to all our problems. Like the femivore's conquests who work with him for their own debasement, many of us regularly support the vision of government as a powerful, effective, win-win way to improve our lives. Overall, Americans have come to expect government to "manage the economy, address social problems, protect the environment,"[146] and of course, rid the world of terrorism. Liberalism never fails to champion government action as an appropriate way to help us better our lot in life. From Social Security, Medicare, welfare, and other entitlement programs, to subsidized college loans, rent control, and minimum wages, liberalism encourages us to seek help from our fellows through confiscation of their money (taxes) and control over their choices (laws and regulations).

The fact that progressive policymakers have consistently won elections and garnered support throughout the decades shows that many of us don't look at widespread government activism as an imposition, but rather as a favor. Even when we protest government-sponsored entitlement programs we do so usually on grounds of efficiency or pragmatism, not philosophical objections. For example, the recent push for prescription drug benefits for senior citizens met with tremendous public support. Those who opposed it raised concerns like "how are we going to pay for it" rather than "why must the federal government be responsible for this problem." Although a Republican administration backed the idea, it probably supported the idea not on principle but in response to the idea's popularity, and didn't go far enough to escape criticism from liberal Democrats.

The popularity of a measure like government-funded prescription drug benefits exemplifies a prevalent attitude of acceptance among the public to embracing government action to tackle any problem that appears intractable. In the New Deal era, the seemingly intractable problem was finding enough work for able-bodied people who needed jobs. In our day, senior citizens too often find their fixed incomes inadequate to provide for their medical needs. Emotionally, those problems feel intolerable, and the left has seduced us to turn to government as our protector and provider. What we never count on, and what liberalism refuses to acknowledge, is that the government is rarely capable of making good on all it promises.

Government cannot possibly come through as the hero that liberalism promises. Looking to government to solve all the problems liberals insist it can solve requires assumptions that contradict reality. To truly believe that government can come to our aid as a heroic power, we have to fall prey to a version of the "Illusion of Omnipossibility." Psychotherapists use this term to describe a reluctance to commit to a particular path for fear that making one choice forecloses all other options. Liberalism pushes us to accept a twist on this Illusion by encouraging us to forget the reality of the world in which we live—a world characterized at a basic level by finite, scarce resources. Liberalism ignores this basic reality and instead encourages us to believe that with government, all things are possible. The spiritual maxim "With God all things are possible" rings true for most of us precisely because it is *untrue* within this world. Within the confines of our earthly reality, all things are *not* possible, and promises to the contrary will always be proved false.

Just as no one of us can produce and distribute *all* things for *all* people, we cannot accomplish that goal through heavy-handed governmental action, either. When we talk about government providing Social Security and subsidized housing, eradicating terrorism and corporate fraud, we have been seduced into the Illusion of Omnipossibility, the assumption that all things are possible with enough political will. Assuming away the reality that we are working with limited resources — money, time, energy, innovation, natural materials, etc. — we engage in political debates over what problems government *should* solve as if all problems *can* be solved by government. Most of us avoid the Illusion of Omnipossibility in our personal affairs; we recognize that our paychecks can't stretch to cover *all* our desires. But liberalism has costumed government as a superhero who exists above petty restraints like scarce resources, who can and will accomplish all the goals we wish.

In a post-9/11 world, the political version of the Illusion of Omnipossibility is more dangerous than ever. The very real danger of further attacks on American soil and interests abroad should give us all pause when thinking about the role of government. The imminent threat of terrorism should remind us of government's fundamental purpose: protecting us from foreign aggression. If our resources are limited, and if eradicating terrorism should be our primary goal, then it's time to give up the illusion that government can pursue all possibilities. September 11 should wake us up to the importance of prioritizing our goals and respecting the limits of the world in which we live. Government can't do everything for us, but it should at least devote itself to the one activity we originally entrusted to it: providing for our national security.

Even today we still hear liberals subscribing to the Illusion of Omnipossibility. President George W. Bush may have interpreted his re-election as an opportunity to reform the "third rail" of American politics, but as soon as he began to suggest ways to salvage the collapsing Social Security program he attracted a torrent of liberal attacks. Left-wingers such as House Minority Leader Nancy Pelosi assailed Bush's suggestion that privatized retirement accounts be incorporated into the system as a way of transitioning from the current bankruptcy-bound Ponzi scheme. This liberal defense of Social Security comes in spite of the fact that members of Generation X don't even count on the program to be there for them when they retire, or else they view it as a bonus to whatever they manage to save for themselves. Baby boomers are approaching their time to cash in on Social Security, but have also realized from their parents' experiences that the average monthly check of $874 isn't going to get them far.[147] This disappointing situation facing millions of Americans is what remains of FDR's promise to provide secure golden years for every average American. No one bankrupted Social Security on purpose; it's the inevitable result of an entitlement program that promises more than it can ever deliver. But try telling that to liberals like Pelosi.

The underlying approach to progressive "great experiments" like Social Security and every other massive scheme entailing redistribution of wealth is this: spot a problem, convince people they can't solve it without you, and promise them too-good-to-be-true returns on their trusting hand-over of higher shares of their incomes and autonomy. Like women on the receiving end of some Don Juan's charm, we buy it time and again, to our eventual disappointment and detriment. Why? We're enticed by the seductive attention, the link to power unfathomable to most of us as individuals, and the promise of being cared for without the personal risk we'd face if we were left to fend for ourselves with "only" our families and communities for support. We need a hero, and liberalism has dressed up government to meet that need—a power ready, willing, and able to rescue us from any and all of life's discomforts. When it fails, we rarely blame the hero. So we'll try again and again to "save Social Security" rather than admit it's failed and challenge ourselves to retain some of our money we've thrown into it and create safety nets of our own design.

Bill Clinton as a politician embodied this aspect of liberalism. He sincerely believed in government's ability and responsibility to help us. His personal charm and optimism seduced us into giving him the chance to prove that government can rescue us from the challenges of life: expensive health care, costly college educations, monthly bills that outstrip menial labor wages. What gets lost in those promises is the vision of what we could accomplish if we kept our hands on our own paychecks, made our own investments, teamed up with each other in our own ways to tackle those challenges. You can't blame Bill Clinton when the results fall short of the promises. In search of a hero, enough of us are willing, over and over, to turn our lives over to the care of government.

As a man, Bill Clinton used the personalized version of this approach to seduce a young woman and leave her in the dust. You can't entirely blame Bill Clinton for the disappointment and despair Monica Lewinsky experienced when the results of their affair fell short of the promises. In search of a hero, she was willing to turn herself over to the care of a femivore who ensnared her—and the rest of the republic—in a painful web of deceit and denials. He apologized to us, but never to her. He'd like you to remember his affair with Monica Lewinsky as just a mistake made by a mortal man. He'd like you to forget that his behavior painted him as a femivore who preyed on a vulnerable young woman whom he seduced into participating in her own entrapment.

CHAPTER EIGHT

SOUNDS LIKE OUR GUY

U P TO THIS POINT, I have carefully avoided using the word "victim" to describe any of Clinton's women. I made that conscious effort in tribute to the maxim that overuse of a word dilutes its meaning. As comedian Ellen DeGeneres once put it, when *everything* is "the worst thing" then people run around saying "Oh, paper cuts—they're the *worst thing*," as if a paper cut is a "worst thing" in the same way as the death of a loved one is the "worst thing." While Gracen, Perdue, Flowers, Jones, Willey, and Lewinsky suffered undeserved mistreatment at Clinton's hands, none of those women found themselves victimized by Clinton in the most extreme, brutal sense of the word. Four of those women engaged in consensual affairs; the other two suffered the humiliation of unwanted sexual advances, including unwanted touching, but neither suffered forced sexual intercourse—rape.

In this final profile, the "V" word appears at last, and I hope that by reserving it for Juanita Broaddrick, its meaning will remain robust, for there is no more appropriate place for it than in her story.

◊

In March 1976, Bill Clinton took a leave of absence from his professorship at the University of Arkansas, Fayetteville law school to run for Arkansas state attorney general. Calling the post "the principal protector of the people,"[1] Clinton faced off in the Democratic primary against the secretary of state and the deputy attorney general. Rebounding from his November 1974 loss in his first political race (popular Republican incumbent congressman John Paul Hammerschmidt narrowly beat him), Clinton poured more energy and networking zeal into his attorney general campaign than the other two primary candidates combined. It paid off. He garnered more than 50 percent of the primary vote, thereby avoiding a run-off, and faced no Republican challenge in the general election, leaving him free to campaign around Arkansas for Jimmy Carter until he began his career as a public servant in November 1976, at age thirty.

Already, supporters knew that Clinton was their "governor-in-waiting," and sure enough, by 1977 he began contemplating his bid for the chief executive spot.[2] His only question was whether he should skip this step and go directly to the U.S. Senate. His first campaign call was to Dick Morris, to help him decide whether to run for governor or senator. Once he'd decided on the governorship, he spent the spring of 1978 running two campaigns. Publicly, he had his own primary election to deal with, though he was far and away the strongest Democratic candidate. Privately, he spent hours plotting with Dick Morris to improve the then-governor's chances of beating his Democratic rival in the U.S. Senate race—in hopes of neutralizing that rival's status as Clinton's main competition as rising Democratic star in Arkansas politics.[3] In the general election that fall, Clinton won with 63 percent of the vote to become governor at age thirty-two.[4]

In 1978, thirty-five year old Juanita Hickey worked as a registered nurse. She was married to her first husband, Gary Hickey, but having an affair with her future second husband, David Broaddrick. She had started her own nursing home in Van Buren, Arkansas, a successful endeavor that eventually grew into two residential facilities—one for the elderly, and one for severely handicapped children. The young, charismatic Clinton was in the midst of his gubernatorial race and had made a campaign stop at her nursing home that spring.[5] While glad-handing there, Clinton told her to be sure to stop by campaign headquarters if she was ever in Little Rock.[6] She was so impressed with him that for the first time in her life she volunteered to help a political campaign, agreeing to hand out bumper stickers and signs.[7] She thought he had "bright ideas"[8] for the state and felt eager to pay a visit to his Little Rock headquarters, excited about picking up T-shirts and buttons to hand out.[9]

Not long after that, she attended a seminar of the American College of Nursing Home Administrators[10] at the Camelot Hotel in Little Rock. She stayed in a hotel room with her friend, Norma Kelsey. After they checked in to their room, Broaddrick called Clinton campaign headquarters and was told to call Clinton at his apartment.[11] She did, and asked Clinton if he was going to be at his headquarters that day. He said no, but suggested they meet for coffee in the hotel coffee shop. A bit later the same morning, Clinton called her and asked if they could meet in her hotel room because there were reporters crawling around the coffee shop. She agreed.

She felt "a little bit uneasy" meeting him in her hotel room, but felt a "real friendship toward this man" and didn't feel any "danger" in him coming to her room. When Clinton arrived she had coffee ready on a little table under a window overlooking a river. Then "he came around me and sort of put his arm over my shoulder to point to this little building and he said he was real interested if he became governor to restore that little building and then all of a sudden, he turned me around and started kissing me. And that was a real shock." Broaddrick pushed him away and said, "No, please don't do that" and told Clinton she was married. But he tried to kiss her again. This time he bit her upper lip. She tried to pull away from him but he forced her onto the bed. "And I just was very frightened, and I tried to get away from him and I told him 'No,' that I didn't want this to happen but he wouldn't listen to me." But he "was such a different person at that moment, he was just a vicious awful person." At some point she stopped resisting. She explained, "It was a real panicky, panicky situation. I was even to the point where I was getting very noisy, you know, yelling to 'Please stop.' And that's when he pressed down on my right shoulder and he would bite my lip."

Clinton didn't linger long afterward. "When everything was over with, he got up and straightened himself, and I was crying at the moment and he walks to the door, and calmly puts on his sunglasses. And before he goes out the door he says 'You better get some ice on that.' And he turned and went out the door." The whole encounter lasted less than thirty minutes, but it changed Juanita Broaddrick's life forever.

When questioned by an interviewer, "Is there any way at all that Bill Clinton could have thought that this was consensual?" Juanita Broaddrick answered, "No. Not with what I told him, and with how I tried to push him away. It was not consensual." The interviewer, NBC's Lisa Myers, pressed for specificity. "You're saying that Bill Clinton sexually assaulted you, that he raped you?" Broaddrick answered, "Yes."

Broaddrick's friend Norma said that when she left their shared hotel room that morning, Broaddrick had told her that she planned to meet with Clinton. When Norma called around lunchtime, however, Broaddrick sounded so upset that Norma returned to the room to find Broaddrick's lip and mouth badly swollen and her pantyhose ripped off. Broaddrick told Norma that Clinton had sexually assaulted her.

Broaddrick was too upset to stay for the nursing home meeting, so she and Norma drove the two hours back to Van Buren immediately, stopping for more ice to apply to Broaddrick's swollen mouth.[12] On the drive back, Norma says, Broaddrick was in shock, and very upset, blaming herself for letting Clinton into her room.[13] "But who, for heaven's sake, would have imagined anything like this?" Broaddrick said years later. "This was the attorney general—and it just never entered my mind."[14] In her NBC interview, Broaddrick said she didn't tell her then-husband, Gary Hickey, who says now that he doesn't remember her lip being swollen (she says she explained that to him as an accident). Broaddrick did tell her now-husband, David Broaddrick, soon after she returned home, that she had been assaulted by Clinton. David Broaddrick recalls that her lip was "black" and "mentally she was in bad shape." Broaddrick told three other friends soon after the attack, all of whom vouch for her story.

About three weeks after the rape, Broaddrick told Lisa Myers, and her first husband attended a Clinton fundraiser together. She still "felt in denial" and "very guilty" and at that time still felt like she should "just shut up and accept [her] punishment" for letting Clinton into her room, since that must have given him "the wrong idea" about what she had wanted to happen. After that, Clinton called her half a dozen times at her nursing home. Once he got through to her and asked when she was coming to Little Rock again. She just said, "I'm not," and left it at that.

In 1979, Broaddrick accepted a non-paying position on a state advisory board relating to nursing homes—a position to which Governor Clinton appointed her. For over a decade she dealt with the governor's office on occasion but not Clinton personally, except for a 1984 letter Clinton sent her after her nursing home was named one of the best in the state. At the bottom is a handwritten note, "I admire you very much." She interpreted it as a "thank you" for her silence.[15]

In 1991 she attended another nursing home meeting in Little Rock, with two friends. In person, Bill Clinton called her out of the meeting; one friend confirms seeing the pair talking. Immediately, Broaddrick says, Clinton "began this profuse apology," saying to her, "Juanita, I'm so sorry for what I did. I'm not the man that I used to be, can you ever forgive me? What can I do to make this up to you?" Feeling "absolute shock," she told him to go to hell and walked away. "In that moment," Broaddrick tells me, "I let go of my guilt and put it where it should have been all those years: on him." She continues, "It was a relief not to blame myself anymore." When she went to lunch with two of her friends who were also nurses just after the freak encounter with Clinton, the three women "actually began to discuss the possibilities that Bill Clinton might be remorseful." However, "that faded as soon as he announced his candidacy for President about three weeks later." Broaddrick and her friends were all at work when the news broke, "and we just looked at each other and shook our heads in disgust."

As early as the 1992 presidential race, Juanita Broaddrick's story entered the realm of rumors that swirled around Bill Clinton. Though her own account didn't appear in the news until one week after the Senate acquitted President Clinton in February 1999, her name had been circulating among the media, Clinton's political opponents, and later, Paula Jones's legal team. Broaddrick's "phone rang incessantly with requests for interviews, all of them refused" until January 1999.[16]

In November 1997, investigators for Paula Jones confronted Juanita Broaddrick—and tape recorded the encounter—but she slammed the door in their faces saying she didn't want to relive the "horrible thing" that had happened.[17] When Jones's attorneys subpoenaed Broaddrick, she signed an affidavit saying she'd never experienced unwanted sexual advances from Bill Clinton. Paula Jones's lawyers used Broaddrick's story, disguised as "Jane Doe #5" in a court filing based largely on a 1992 letter to Broaddrick from a friend of hers, Philip Yoakum. In that letter, Mr. Yoakum wrote that he was "particularly distraught when you told me of your brutal rape by Bill Clinton, how he bit your lip until you gave into his forcing sex upon you."[18] When this letter and the Jones court filing hit the news in March 1998, Mr. Yoakum told reporters he'd tried to get Broaddrick to go public during the 1992 campaign, but she'd said to him, "Who would believe me, little old Juanita from Van Buren?"[19]

Some people would. Reporting in March 1998 on the Yoakum letter, NBC's Lisa Myers called Broaddrick's story "potentially the most explosive allegation out there."[20] Myers pointed out that "Juanita Broaddrick has never tried to sell any story. She has never gone after the president. She is a nurse who built a nursing home business. She is a respected member of her community in a little town in Arkansas."[21] Through lawyers, the White House called Broaddrick's story (as represented in the Paula Jones court papers) "outrageous" and smugly pointed journalists toward Broaddrick's affidavit denying it.[22]

Ken Starr provided the impetus forcing Juanita Broaddrick's story into public view when he subpoenaed Paula Jones's lawyers for records relating to Broaddrick and three other specific women (in addition to Kathleen Willey and Monica Lewinsky) in March 1998.[23] In April 1998 Broaddrick admitted to the OIC that she'd lied in her affidavit, but Starr didn't pursue her story because she insisted she'd never been threatened or bribed into silence—hence there was no obstruction of justice angle for Starr to use in his investigation. [24] To the public eye, Juanita Broaddrick's story remained a mere footnote to the Paula Jones lawsuit and the Monica Lewinsky scandal engulfing the Clinton administration throughout 1998. She spoke with *The Washington Post* in April 1998 but insisted on staying off the record.

Even though she'd signed the affidavit and had consistently refused to discuss her story on the record, "Jane Doe #5" appeared in materials turned over to Congress during impeachment hearings and reportedly influenced several wavering Republicans to vote in favor of impeachment,[25] although House of Representatives prosecutors declined to include her story in their case against Clinton at the Senate trial.[26]

Rumors about her story wouldn't disappear. Some of them offended Broaddrick, and one in particular pushed her over the edge into public disclosure: on New Year's Eve 1998 a friend handed her a tabloid story stating that Clinton had bribed David Broaddrick to suppress his wife's account.[27] By January 1999, NBC correspondent Lisa Myers had been trying to persuade Broaddrick to tell her story publicly for months. Kathleen Willey tells me, "Lisa Myers called me and asked me if I would talk with Juanita." Willey talked with Broaddrick "many times… I told her what I went through" going public with her story. "Juanita would tell me, 'I'm just so afraid that I'm finally getting this off my chest and then people won't believe me,'" Willey tells me sadly. "She kept saying, 'I don't want it to be for naught.'"

After everything Willey had been through herself, she didn't feel like she could offer Broaddrick much comfort. "I had to tell her there are no guarantees; look who you're dealing with," Willey says, before adding quietly, "All of us involved in this Clinton thing, we really have not fared well." Willey stopped short of giving Broaddrick any specific advice. "I wouldn't tell her what to do," she says.

Broaddrick was in her mid-fifties in January 1999 when she finally relented and taped an interview with NBC. NBC had the scoop, but held off airing the interview for a month, citing the need for further investigation into the details of Broaddrick's account.[28] The delay frustrated Broaddrick, who said NBC had been investigating for nearly a year already, even combing through "old papers about the case we settled with two employees fired for theft twenty years ago."[29] During the delay, NBC interviewer Lisa Myers told Broaddrick, "The good news is you're credible. The bad news is that you're very credible."[30] The story looked explosive, and NBC wanted to make sure it was "rock solid" before airing it.[31]

Broaddrick wound up giving *The Wall Street Journal*'s Dorothy Rabinowitz a heart-to-heart chat, which the *WSJ* published on February 19, 1999,[32] a week after the Senate acquitted President Clinton. NBC aired its interview with Broaddrick on *Dateline* on February 24, 1999.[33] *WSJ* editorial writer Dorothy Rabinowitz described Broaddrick as "a woman of accomplishment, prosperous, successful in her field, serious; a woman seeking no profit, no book, no lawsuit." Ms. Rabinowitz continued:

> [She is a] woman of a kind people like and warm to. To meet Juanita Broaddrick at her house in Van Buren is to encounter a woman of sunny disposition.... She sits talking in the peaceful house on a hilltop overlooking the Broaddricks' forty acres, where thirty cows, five horses and a mule roam..... It's a good life all right.[34]

By the time it finally aired its interview with Juanita Broaddrick, NBC had done the thing properly. Lisa Myers reported that NBC had talked to four friends who corroborated Broaddrick's story, and had even tracked down a detail that would be often used to challenge it: Broaddrick could not remember the month or date of the rape. Springtime of 1978 was as close as she could recall, though she recalls with clarity many other details, like what she was wearing, the hotel room furnishings, the view from the window. NBC checked all of Juanita Broaddrick's personal and business records, public records, nursing home records, and convention schedules, and learned that there was a nursing home meeting at the Camelot Hotel in Little Rock on April 25, 1978.[35] State records even show that Broaddrick received credit for a seminar that day. The White House refused to answer NBC's requests for information, and NBC could find no evidence about Clinton's whereabouts that day which contradicted Willey's claims; he had no "public appearances on the morning in question," and newspaper articles "suggest he was in Little Rock that day."[36]

Other details checked out, too. The "little building" visible from the hotel room window that Broaddrick says Clinton pointed to was the Pulaski County jail. Though it was torn down later, in April 1978 it was visible from river-facing rooms in the Camelot Hotel.[37] Local law enforcement officials told NBC that Broaddrick was a solid citizen with no criminal record, and that they took her allegations very seriously; of course, there was nothing that law enforcement could do, since the statute of limitations for the crime of rape had run out more than a decade earlier.

Why did she refuse to report it when it occurred, or come forward when Clinton ran for president? "[Given the] mentality of the '70s," she said, "There I was, I was married, I was also in a relationship with another man, and...I was there alone in a hotel room with the attorney general and I didn't think anyone would possibly believe me."[38] As for coming forward during the 1992 campaign, she and her second husband, David Broaddrick, talked about it in 1992, but "[it] brought up a lot of hurt, and a lot of things that I'd buried years ago. And then we just decided it wouldn't be in our interest to do it. So we decided not to."[39] Lisa Myers asked, "Did you receive any payoff to stay silent," to which Broaddrick responded, "Oh goodness, no. I mean how could anyone be bribed or paid-off for, for something that, to not say anything about something that horrible?" No one ever threatened her, either; staying silent for so many years was strictly her choice. Why did she sign a false affidavit? "I didn't want to be forced to testify about one of the most horrific events in my life," she told Lisa Myers. "I didn't want to go through it again." But signing the affidavit hadn't called off the hounds and there she was, reliving it all over again on national TV.

When Kathleen Willey finally came forward with her story of unwanted sexual advances in March 1998, Broaddrick told Myers that she struggled again over whether to tell her side of things. "I would get up in the morning and I would think: it's the thing to do. Then by nighttime I would think that could bring no good whatsoever to my life. And I'm sorry for these women. I'm sorry for what they went through, but I just wasn't brave enough to do it. There's nothing else to say." She talked to Ken Starr in April 1998 only because he granted her immunity and she was afraid of lying to federal prosecutors. By the time she bared her soul in public in January 1999, she "just couldn't hold it in any longer." Although she had "buried this a long time ago," she now felt compelled to "clear up all these stories" floating around about her. Time had not healed all her wounds, however. When asked how she felt about Bill Clinton, she replied, "I couldn't say it on the air. My hatred for him is overwhelming."

As difficult as it was for Broaddrick to come forward, she expresses sympathy for the trouble her *Dateline* interview caused Lisa Myers. "I feel that Lisa suffered during this time," Broaddrick confides to me. While NBC postponed the airing of the *Dateline* interview, some people created buttons that read "Free Lisa Myers" that were worn by Brit Hume and others on Fox News Network. Despite Myers's painstaking research and reporting, airing Broaddrick's story still carried a professional and political price. "Lisa and I remain good friends," Broaddrick tells me. Clearly, Lisa Myers remains one of the few journalists with the courage to stand by Broaddrick through this ordeal, and Broaddrick must deeply appreciate her professional integrity and personal support.

Broaddrick is also tremendously proud of her son, attorney Kevin Hickey, who appeared on *Larry King Live* in March 1999 defending his mother against guests Dee Dee Myers and David Gergen, former Clinton advisors.[40] Kevin was only nine years old when the rape happened, and his mother didn't burden him with her ordeal until rumors began surfacing during the 1992 campaign. Then, she sat down with Kevin and told him what Bill Clinton had done to her. He was shocked, and angry at then-candidate Clinton. "I couldn't believe what was happening," Kevin told Larry King. "But I could tell, just by the look in her face, that this was just a terrible, terrible experience." When Larry King asked Kevin what his feelings were toward Clinton, Kevin replied, "Disgust. The guy has got into a high office—a lot of people think he's a very good politician and that may be true, but I think he leaves a lot to be desired as a person and that's pretty much my feelings of him." Dee Dee Myers and David Gergen were left fumbling for words, admitting that they found Kevin and his mother quite believable. Gergen said that Kevin's interview gave him pause because "what mother would tell her son that she had been raped if it hadn't happened?" Broaddrick says of her son's interview, "He was awesome.... Dee Dee Myers and David Gergen were speechless after Kevin's interview."

After Broaddrick's interview with the *WSJ*, the White House issued its first direct statement mentioning Juanita Broaddrick by name. "Any allegation that the president assaulted Ms. Broaddrick more than twenty years ago is absolutely false," read a statement from the president's personal attorney, David E. Kendall.[41] That was it. No attempt to argue that Clinton wasn't even in Little Rock on the day in question, or that he had never been alone with her, or even that they hadn't had sexual relations. The denial was immediately parsed by some in the press and public wary of Clinton's overly-technical, legalistic use of the English language. Broaddrick wasn't known as "Ms. Broaddrick" in 1978, some noted—at that time she was "Mrs. Hickey."[42] She alleged *rape*, not "assault."[43] The denial even seemed to leave intact a possible loophole—Clinton could retort that *consensual* sex had occurred, just not rape. Clinton never addressed the charges; when questioned he answered, "Well, my counsel has made a statement about the...issue and I have nothing to add to it."[44]

An initial smattering of coverage followed the February 20 *Wall Street Journal* interview, but the story faded quickly. On February 23, 1999, journalist Richard Cohen wrote of the Clintons:

> None of the rules of political gravity apply to them. They just float above everything.
> Take the rape charge. It is that—get it? I feel I have to emphasize it: The president of the United States is accused of raping a woman back when he was attorney general of Arkansas. An account of this alleged rape ran on Page 1 of *The Washington Post*. Get it? Page One! *The Washington Post*! Do you want to know what happened next? Nothing.[45]

A second wave of commentary and coverage washed up after NBC aired its interview on February 24, 1999. Much of it focused on the perceived weaknesses in Juanita Broaddrick's account—particularly, that she could not recall the month or date of the rape, and that she attended a Clinton fundraiser just weeks after it happened.[46] Coverage focused on her story's import to the media industry more than on the impact of her story as such. The *Chicago Tribune* wrapped up its article with a tone weary with scandal fatigue: "The Broaddrick allegation—a devastatingly serious but old and unproven charge against the president of the United States—presented every newsroom in the country with a difficult decision."[47] Columnist Mary McGrory wrote that Broaddrick's allegations were treated more as a "press mystery"[48] than as a bombshell. Michael Kelly spotted the problem: no one cares. Clinton's lawyer, Kelly observed, declared the allegation "absolutely false." But the lawyer couldn't know for certain the charge was false. "At best, he can know that Clinton says the accusation is false," Kelly wrote. "And what is that worth?" Kelly concluded, "But [Clinton's lawyer] of course doesn't really care whether Broaddrick's story is true or not. He doesn't really care whether the president is a rapist or not. He doesn't really care, because he figures you don't really care either—at least, not enough to do anything about it."[49]

Richard Cohen, a columnist for *The Washington Post* since 1976 who is no friend of conservatives (in a column after President Reagan's death Cohen refused to give Reagan credit for ending the Cold War, saying flippantly that the Soviet empire "would have collapsed sooner or later"[50]) remained troubled by Juanita Broaddrick's story. "Is it possible the president's a rapist? Am I supposed not to care?" Cohen wondered. "Who is this guy?" Cohen wrote, and answered himself: "At one time, I thought I knew. He was a somewhat left of center southern governor—progressive, a policy wonk, a product of the antiwar movement, and, of course, a womanizer. This much I knew, and none of it, including the last, bothered me much."[51] But Gennifer

Flowers, Paula Jones, and Monica Lewinsky were not what Cohen expected from Clinton. Now, with Juanita Broaddrick, "A woman has cried rape. She sounds credible. . . . The White House denies the charge, but so what? I would expect nothing less. Anyway, we're not talking George Washington here. With Clinton, if there's a cherry tree down, we know who did it."[52] You can almost see him shaking his head in dismay as he closed by repeating, "Who is this guy?"

But Bill Clinton's constellation of previous denials-turned-admissions had at least somewhat caught up with him. Donna Shalala, Clinton's Secretary of Health and Human Services, had firmly and publicly expressed complete belief in Clinton's denial of the Monica Lewinsky affair in 1998.[53] A year later, when asked whether she believed Juanita Broaddrick, Ms. Shalala would only say that she took the charges seriously, hadn't reached a conclusion about whether she believed Broaddrick, but didn't need to decide that in order to be "a patriot and a professional" and do her job in the Clinton Administration.[54] A senior White House official, speaking only on condition of anonymity, said: "Bill Clinton has got a problem. If he weren't president he would be in counseling.... But I don't think because he's got a sickness, that corrupts everything about him.... He is a great president."[55] A sickness? Perhaps, but sexual addiction is just one part of the mix of influences shaping Bill Clinton's mistreatment of women.

Former Clinton loyalist George Stephanopoulos, whose book about life in the Clinton White House, *All Too Human*, came out less than a month after Broaddrick's charges aired, said it "rips my stomach" to think of being in the White House and trying to duck her story.[56] He thought Clinton's lawyer's denial was worded to give cover to the idea that there might have been a consensual sexual encounter. The man he knew and worked for from 1991 until 1996, he said, wasn't capable of such an assault, but "I did not know Bill Clinton in 1978." Hardly a ringing endorsement from someone who used to consider Bill a friend as well as a boss.

One newspaper editor wrote, "[W]ho can say Broaddrick's charges are preposterous, outrageous, unthinkable? Who can say with certainty we don't have a rapist in the White House? Indeed, her story is so credible that NBC News—nobody's right-wing conspirator—aired it after weeks of double-checking the details. Major networks don't run such stories every day."[57] The editor continued, "Jones, Willey and Broaddrick—there's something about Bill and sexual assault. He's either the most victimized man in America or our most famous victimizer.... Alas, his own may not have been the only lip Bill Clinton's ever bitten."

The media didn't give Clinton a free pass on the Broaddrick story, but there did exist an overall lack of direction; "where do we go with it from here," summed up the sentiments of many journalists. With no legal, criminal, or impeachment machinery pushing the story along it petered out quickly, with most commentators' final words centered on the sad thought that no one will ever know for sure whether we twice elected a rapist to the highest office in the land. Noting that *Newsweek's* only coverage of the Broaddrick story had been a pithy remark in its "Conventional Wisdom" item-of-the-week box (she got a sideways arrow for not coming forward sooner but, opined *Newsweek*, her charges "sound like our guy"), one columnist summed up the reaction to Broaddrick this way: "He raped you, Juanita? Yeah, sounds like our guy. But what's your point?"[58]

Refusing to comment directly on Broaddrick's credibility, *The New York Times* editorialized that Clinton's "talk to my lawyer" statements were insufficient responses: "There is no legal or constitutional remedy for the [Broaddrick] situation," wrote the *Times*. "But surely there is a limit to how long Mr. Clinton can speak through his lawyer on these matters.... [I]t would be nice to hear Mr. Clinton himself address the matter and provide his version of what transpired, if in fact the two did meet in a Little Rock hotel room in 1978."[59] Professor Susan Estrich called *The New York Times* "deeply out of touch with the people of this country"[60] for making such an unreasonable request of Clinton. *The Washington Post* also disagreed with *The New York Times*—but for a different reason. Hearing Clinton speak directly to the matter wouldn't help us figure out Broaddrick's story one bit, editorialized the *Post*: "Mr. Clinton's word in this realm by now has no value. That leaves us with an accusation that cannot be reasonably accepted, nor easily ignored. It is a mark of where Mr. Clinton has brought us as a country that he cannot begin to ameliorate that fact."[61]

On an episode of NBC's *Today*, Dorothy Rabinowitz, the journalist whose *Wall Street Journal* interview with Broaddrick brought the story into the mainstream, defended her assessment of Broaddrick's credibility. She said that Broaddrick's twenty-one year delay may mean the legal system offered no recourse, but history still had a right to know her story in order to evaluate the person of Bill Clinton.[62]. Rabinowitz, who had earned respect among her peers for her investigative reporting about false claims of child sexual abuse in the mid-1990s, added that talking face to face with Juanita Broaddrick is to "find yourself in the presence of someone you suspect is telling something that happened."[63] The show's other guest for the segment, Alan Dershowitz, dismissed Broaddrick's story as "gossip," though he admitted that Clinton's word wasn't any better than Broaddrick's when it came to matters of sex.[64]

Attacks on Juanita Broaddrick's character were kept to a minimum, but some pundits took their shots. Bill Press, co-host of CNN's *Crossfire*, wrote for the *Los Angeles Times* that he didn't believe Juanita Broaddrick for the following reasons: (1) she couldn't remember the date of the rape ("If she was scarred for life, wouldn't she remember the date?"); (2) she was cheating on her first husband at the time so at most Broaddrick and Clinton probably had consensual sex ("If you're cheating on your husband, and then cheat on your boyfriend, do you tell your boyfriend the truth?"); and (3) she attended a Clinton fundraiser and accepted appointment to a government post after the alleged rape ("Why did she still want to support a man who raped her?"). [65]

Former White House special counsel Lanny Davis protested, "Is journalism about reporting facts or not?.... It is not corroborated because her girlfriend saw her with a swollen lip. That doesn't make the charge of rape a fact.... How do we know she didn't lie to all her friends? We know that, voluntarily...she swore out an affidavit that she now says she lied about."[66] His protest might have been a bit more convincing if we hadn't watched a similar affidavit signed by Monica Lewinsky go up in smoke just six months earlier.

Feminists had trouble discounting Juanita Broaddrick's allegations. Gloria Allred, an attorney who filed the first formal charges against Senator Bob Packwood for sexual harassment, is a rape survivor herself who never reported the rape to police.[67] Whether or not anything could be done legally about Broaddrick's rape, Ms. Allred insisted that the public has a right to know if the president is a rapist.[68] Denise Snyder, executive director of the D.C. Rape Crisis Center, cautioned people about viewing Juanita Broaddrick's two-decade delay in coming forward as a slight on her credibility. When the assailant has "a lot of power and a high public profile," such delays are common, she said.[69]

Patricia Ireland—the then-president of NOW who also voiced support for Kathleen Willey—issued a preemptive statement calling on the White House to treat Broaddrick "fairly, respectfully," and not to "trash this woman," whose allegations must be taken seriously.[70] On *Larry King Live* Ireland added that even if President Clinton looked America in the eye and denied the rape, there's a "certain credibility gap" to whatever he'd say.[71] She added that she understood why Juanita Broaddrick felt reluctant to come forward for so many years.[72]

Susan Faludi, author of the influential 1992 feminist tome *Backlash: The Undeclared War Against American Women*, found Broaddrick "credible" but wasn't sure "what Juanita Broaddrick wants done [about her allegations]."[73] So she used Broaddrick to take a swipe at conservatives, for whom "women can be damned" unless "the perpetrator is Clinton."[74] By contrast, feminist author Andrea Dworkin stated flatly, "I believe that Clinton is a rapist. I believe the woman—and if I had doubts about the woman, I trust what I perceive about him."[75] She classified "what he did to Paula Jones" as assault, and from there, she said, "it's a very clear line to rape.... Suddenly, every time you look at this man you have to think about rape. It's harder to sleep, it's hard to work…because this man is the president. That's obscenity—right there."[76] She didn't stop with castigating Clinton, either. "Essentially, while what's left of the women's movement shows any support for Clinton, they're destroying the movement itself as any kind of refuge for women who've been sexually assaulted," Dworkin said cogently.[77] Apparently at least one feminist icon truly believes in feminism's motto—the personal is political—enough to apply it even to a leader who's good on "women's issues" if that same leader mistreats individual women.

Around this time—during and just after the impeachment trial—Clinton's job performance rating remained high, hovering at about 64 percent.[78] However, the percentage of people who believed him to embody the values most Americans try to live up to had plummeted to about 30 percent, and only about 35 percent of the public believed him to be honest and trustworthy.[79] There's nothing schizophrenic about those numbers. A dishonest, untrustworthy man can make official decisions favored even by those who think him dishonest and untrustworthy. Pundit Morton Kondracke argued that nothing should be done about Juanita Broaddrick's story—legally or politically. But as a "cultural test" people should know as much about President Clinton's "personal" behavior as possible, even if it meant considering the possibility that a sitting president is a "monster" who "sexually assaulted a woman, biting her lip to impose himself on her."[80]

One month after Juanita Broaddrick's charges aired publicly, Bill Clinton faced reporters in his first solo press conference in over nine months. One reporter had the audacity to pose this question: If the first president was remembered for never telling a lie, what would be Clinton's legacy in this respect?[81] "Clinton's face tightened. Then, in an edgy voice, he pleaded for people to look just as hard at the veracity and motives of his critics as they have at his own."[82] In a "box score," Clinton went on, "there will be that one negative," but "then there will be the hundreds and hundreds and hundreds of times when the record will show that I did not abuse my authority as president, that I was truthful with the American people, and scores and scores of allegations were made against me and widely publicized without any regard to whether they were true or not."[83] He didn't bother explaining which "allegations" were true and which weren't. And he never directly addressed Juanita Broaddrick's charges. Maybe he feared this was finally a he said, she said battle he might lose.

Broaddrick filed a lawsuit against Clinton in the summer of 1999, to obtain documents the White House may have gathered about her, claiming its refusal to accede to her demand for such documents violated the Privacy Act. The case was dismissed in 2001. In the middle of that lawsuit, Broaddrick's nursing home business found itself audited by the IRS for the first time in its thirty years of existence. "I do not believe this was coincidence," Broaddrick declared, "I do not think our number just came up."[84] For a while Juanita and David Broaddrick returned to their quiet, successful life in rural Arkansas. But, Broaddrick tells me, "My life with David gradually began to deteriorate before and after the interview [on *Dateline*]." Her husband had been "totally against my coming forward and I think the unwanted publicity into our private lives gradually destroyed our marriage." They divorced in 2004. Juanita still owns one of their two nursing home facilities, and their home and acreage, and David owns the other facility. "We are both very happy now," she says, "but I will always wonder if we would be together and happy had I not come forward."

This is a woman of tremendous strength, whose zest for life and self-confidence shines through her voice as we talk. She loves to play tennis and is on two teams. She is financially comfortable and has even begun to date again. "Man, that is a trip at sixty-two," she laughs. She baby-sits her "new, precious grandson" and has a "very happy life." She remains an outspoken critic of former President Clinton, but tells me, "Life goes on, and it is a great life."

◊

The National Center for Injury Prevention and Control, a division of the Center for Disease Control, reports that about 40 percent of rape victims described their attacker as a friend or acquaintance, and that fewer than half of all rapes are reported to authorities.[85] Juanita Broaddrick fits within those statistics. Whatever the circumstances of the rape, most victims experience some level of psychological trauma. Juanita Broaddrick didn't walk us step by step through the long days and nights she must have spent processing what happened to her, but the Rape Treatment Center at UCLA Medical Center tells rape victims that common reactions to the psychological trauma of rape include: shock and disbelief; intense emotions of anger, anxiety or depression; unwanted memories, flashbacks, or nightmares; physical symptoms like sleeplessness, headaches, or stomach pains, fear for personal safety even in situations that didn't previously cause any concern; and feelings of guilt and shame.[86] Acquiring information about all the "normal" reactions does little, though, to actually help a woman feel better about experiencing the brutal act of rape.

I'd rather disclose my limitations in looking at Juanita Broaddrick's story than wonder quietly to myself if I managed to pull off neutrality in writing about her experience. These pages aren't intended for my own life story, but I doubt my ability to write about Juanita Broaddrick without imposing some of my own experience onto my interpretation of hers.

Many years ago I was sexually assaulted...raped—the word still sticks uncomfortably in my throat. I don't think I've said it out loud for years, and I'm even grateful to be writing this instead of speaking it. Reading the transcript of Broaddrick's interview with *Dateline* I noticed immediately that Broaddrick got through her narrative of her encounter with Clinton without saying the word "rape." She answered "yes" when Lisa Myers asked if Clinton raped her, but she never did utter the word herself. A Clinton defender used that omission to insinuate that maybe Broaddrick wasn't really alleging rape;[87] I tend to see it as understandable reluctance to "own" rape as a personal experience.

In my own case, the offender was a person I'd known since childhood. I told no one for months, and when I eventually confided in a few close friends it was through a cloud of alcohol rather than deliberate disclosure. It took a long time working with dear friends and a wonderful therapist before I could accept the word "rape" for what had happened to me. It took many more months to shed the guilt I felt in believing I had caused it to happen, and for the recurring nightmares to stop. It took even longer to let go of the anger that eventually surfaced in my consciousness. In fact, by the time I reached the height of my anger phase, the statute of limitations had passed, precluding me from attempting revenge or remedy through civil or criminal action.

Even if the statistic floated by feminists that one in four women suffers rape overestimates the actual number, even one is too many. The trite phrase "Whatever doesn't kill you makes you stronger" truly means something when it comes to experiencing rape, because for a while you feel as if a part of you has died, and recovering means finding a new, stronger life and identity.

I have my own theories now about what might have made my attacker treat me the way he did, and my best guesses explain a lot about why I was convinced for a long time that I'd brought it on myself. The guilt was soul-crushing. Broaddrick says her attacker left the scene with the words "You'd better get some ice on that." Mine left with the words, "Love you." You don't forget those words in a moment like that, and no matter what they are, they tend to leave you feeling somehow degraded, dirty, and disposable.

Broaddrick talked about not coming forward because she didn't think anyone would believe her, and because she felt shame and fear about being perceived dishonorably due to the affair she was having at the time with the man who would later become her second husband. My reasons—instincts, more like— for keeping silent were a bit different, but also centered on shame and fear. I don't think I worried that family or friends wouldn't believe me, but I did feel entirely responsible and hated the thought of anyone I cared about thinking of me in some way tainted by involvement in something so ugly. Nor was I eager to invite conversations or questions about my sex life. The thought of going to the police was humiliating, and anyway, it was my word against his. I had no proof.

Broaddrick says she and her now-husband talked about whether she should come forward while her rapist was running for president. They decided it was better for her not to. On balance, she thought, it could bring nothing good to her life. Though I've never heard rumors of the person who raped me aspiring to be president of the United States, I have no desire now to hold him accountable in a public way. I still feel like I knew this person very well, and I long ago trekked the road of forgiveness and arrived with a sense of confidence that this person would never repeat that behavior. If I had been raped by a more-or-less stranger, maybe I wouldn't have that kind of confidence and would feel a sense of responsibility to other actual or potential victims to step forward and make his past behavior public knowledge.

I'd known this person for such a long time that we had many mutual acquaintances, and for quite a while I heard his name and saw his face much too often. Juanita Broaddrick had to live in a country where her rapist's face, voice, and image surrounded her all through the '90s. That kind of constant reminder might have pushed me over the edge to full disclosure, too.

She admits to lying under oath, denying the rape in an affidavit for the Paula Jones case. I wasn't under oath, but I once lied to protect the person who raped me—to a federal investigator doing a background check on this person for a job.

Broaddrick says her rapist once confronted her in person and apologized for what he'd done. She told him to go to hell. The person who raped me apologized too, many months later, over the phone. I just cried.

Most mentions of her experience also included the criticism that she can't remember the month of the alleged rape. Neither can I. You'd think a person would remember the exact hour, day, month, and year of something like that. You'd think. Except that's just it; you're not navigating through the experience with your head. You go through it with your body and your heart and soul. So I can say with certainty precisely where I was, the colors in the room, the tone of his voice, what I felt in each moment. But I cannot for the life of me say with certainty whether it happened in October, November, or December. I guess that's just me. Well, and Juanita Broaddrick.

It's just her word against his. No possibility of legal action for the rape itself, so no possibility of any evidence other than her story. None of us were present that fateful day, and I realize that some people falsely accuse others of crimes, but I also recognize sparks of authenticity in Broaddrick's story.

No one wants to think of Bill Clinton as a monster. But the possibility or plausibility of Juanita Broaddrick's story doesn't force a conclusion as black and white as that. Rape is always a horrific crime, but not all rapists are horrific people. Women consistently describe Clinton as charming, boyish, good-natured, fun-loving. That can be a genuine side of a person coexisting with a darker side of the same person. Years after the incident, Clinton took Broaddrick's hands in his and tried to apologize for what he'd done, assuring her he was now a different person. Hopefully that's true. I don't believe the person who assaulted me is a monster. Far from it; I'd known him as a kind, even-tempered, patient man with an easy sense of humor, and before the actual assault I'd never seen a clue of that kind of contempt or rage from him. Believing Juanita Broaddrick doesn't mean painting Bill Clinton as an evil human being who doesn't deserve to draw another breath. Very few people are entirely good or entirely evil. Believing Juanita Broaddrick, or even conceding that she *might* be telling the truth, for our purposes adds a final dimension to our look at how liberal politics influenced Clinton's behavior.

◊

The core mistreatment aspect of Juanita Broaddrick's experience with Bill Clinton is almost the polar opposite of his mistreatment of women like Elizabeth Ward Gracen, Sally Perdue, and Gennifer Flowers. The latter three women didn't suffer mistreatment *sexually*, but found themselves variously mistreated in the aftermath. Paula Jones and Kathleen Willey experienced unwanted sexual *advances*, but neither alleged unwanted *sex*. Juanita Broaddrick isn't the only woman ever rumored to accuse Bill Clinton of rape, but she is the only woman who has confirmed her claims publicly. Clinton didn't go through the trouble of smearing Broaddrick's reputation as he did with other women, but he didn't really have to; with no fear of legal or political repercussions, he ignored her and moved on, and he surely hopes we will ignore her, too. Her story faded quickly from the front pages, though—in the words of Charles

Krauthammer—it is still "lingering, subterranean."[88] What does it mean that we may have permitted a rapist to run the free world for eight years? Former Clinton political consultant Dick Morris may have had the most incisive one-liner in the wake of Juanita Broaddrick's public allegations: "If you're going to be a sexual predator, be pro-choice."[89]

A credible accusation of rape against any ostensible leader should be devastating, but against a leader held up as a champion for women it should have been shocking. As we've seen, though, not many were shocked by Juanita Broaddrick's story. Sickened, perhaps, and maybe even angrier at Republicans for attacking Clinton than at Clinton himself, but few people found themselves so stunned that they could dismiss the story out of hand. One journalist said bluntly, "The president is accused of rape and nobody is shocked."[90] Of course, the appropriate adjectives were used to report Broaddrick's story: horrific, terrible, monstrous; but after about two weeks her name and story faded into near-oblivion, even though the name and story of her attacker remained one of the most visible in all the world.

Not that equal fame or celebrity is what Juanita Broaddrick wanted for herself. In fact, she did all she could for two decades to avoid reliving or being questioned about her attack. But since she did come forward, I'm on the side of Dorothy Rabinowitz, who intoned that history has the right and responsibility to take her story into account when it evaluates the man who became our forty-second president. In some ways, Juanita Broaddrick is like all other rape victims, but in other ways, the identity of her rapist places her in a category of her own, with unique burdens. Most rape victims don't face the knowledge that their attacker is poised to grace the pages of history books, possibly painted as some kind of hero, for generations to come. Most rape victims don't have to stomach their attacker being heralded as the best thing to happen to women since the right to vote, much less hear about him selling 400,000 copies of his legacy-obsessed memoirs in just one day.

With Juanita Broaddrick's story, we find ourselves back where we started: is it pure hypocrisy, driven solely by personal weakness, that propels a person so devoted to so-called women's issues in the political realm to be such a calloused abuser of women in his individual relations with them? Bill Clinton's victimization of Juanita Broaddrick certainly manifests psychological, emotional, and personal issues on Clinton's part, but it also illustrates a central feature of liberalism that can induce such raw, violent mistreatment of women.

Modern liberalism paradoxically aligns itself with force to bring about goals of peace. This intrinsic paradox dooms liberalism's goals of world peace and global equality from the start. The rhetorical aims of leftism actually comport nicely with the message of Jesus Christ and other religious figures. *Love your neighbor, care for the widows and orphans among you, make no distinctions between "Jew nor Gentile, male nor female," turn the other cheek, judge not lest ye be judged,* and so forth. Imagine how beautiful our world today could be if we had spent the past two thousand years practicing those lofty principles (regardless of whether every one of us revered Christ as God). As a code of morality, those principles encourage us to treat each other with genuine kindness, respect, and love. We cannot prevent every natural disaster or calamity, but we bear responsibility for creating much of the trauma that fills our modern world by refusing to practice love, tolerance, and kindness.

But Christ spoke to people's hearts; he didn't suggest that his teachings ought to become the law of the land *imposed* on people by force. In fact, he recognized that such an effort is ultimately futile: you can use force to bully people into changing their *acts,* but you can't force people to change their innermost desires, intents, thoughts, or feelings. A change in the latter is only possible through an individualized, conscience-driven spiritual process. It cannot be imposed by other people; Christ made this clear when he proclaimed, "Render to Caesar that which is Caesar's, and to God that which is God's." Yet the use of force to try to change people's hearts is precisely what political ideologues have attempted to do throughout history, sometimes out of a raw, inhumane desire for power but often out of good intentions to improve society by forcing people to do the right thing.

Many admirable parallels exist between liberalism's central values and those propounded by Jesus Christ. Liberalism's exaltation of equality, fairness, and peace echo St. Paul's exhortation of "faith, hope, and love." The core values espoused by liberalism comprise an ancient set of *moral* tenets that, whenever they have been practiced, make the world a better place. But here's the harsh reality that makes liberalism a dangerous ideology: politics isn't about morality.

Genuine morality must be voluntary, or it's no longer morality. Forcing you to choose correctly is no moral victory on your part because you had no real choice. And politics is *always* a discussion about how and when to use force. To pass a law, regulation, tax increase, or program always involves using force or the threat of force to bring it about. If politics is about enforcing morality, the paradox emerges: genuine morality cannot be achieved by force. To liberal ideology, politics is about enforcing values. Therein lies the problem.

The values of leftism fit comfortably within a moral code, but they have no place in a political ideology. Liberalism's morality finds itself inevitably corrupted by association with political force, just as Christ's message has at times found itself corrupted by an unholy alliance between church and state. This is not to say that politics doesn't involve ethics. But there is a crucial distinction between morality and ethics. Every individual person needs a moral code to guide her beliefs and actions, but selection and practice of such a code needs to remain solely the province of her own conscience or else it isn't genuine morality. Every political system needs a code of ethics to guide it, but political ethics differ from personal morality. Personal morality tells us what we *should* choose; political ethics tell us what we are *permitted* to choose.

When it comes to political ethics, the rules should be made according to the rights of everyone involved—and each of us possesses identical rights to own and use our own lives and property. That leaves each of us free to apply our own moral precepts to the problems of life and strive to make the world a better place using every nonviolent means at our disposal. No matter how noble the purpose, advocating the initiation of force against our fellow human beings can only perpetuate a culture of violence, dominance, and control, placing a world based on peace, partnership, and cooperation further out of reach.

In a person psychologically or emotionally predisposed to mistreat women, attachment to liberal ideology can reinforce misogyny because of liberalism's advocacy of political force as an appropriate way to impose values. The political conviction that your ideology permits you to initiate force against citizens in order to mold their behavior can translate into a personal conviction that you can justifiably initiate force against a woman to wrangle submission from her.

It does not require a stretch of the imagination to surmise that Clinton's political convictions instilled in him a belief that he could justifiably initiate force against a woman if she somehow threatened his ability to impose acceptable values on society. Juanita Broaddrick knows in her heart that Bill Clinton found himself capable of using the most egregious display of force possible against a woman. Many who have spoken with Juanita—including this author—believe her. Her credible accusation should leave us all disturbed at the thought that we put a rapist in the White House. Her story should encourage us all to think carefully about the connection between misogyny and liberalism, and whether we really want another Clinton presidency.

ANOTHER CLINTON PRESIDENCY?

T HROUGH THE STORIES of seven different women with sadly similar experiences of crossing paths with Bill Clinton, this book has discussed some of the ways liberalism contributes to Clinton-style misogyny. That is not to say that other ideologies can't foster their own special brands of misogynistic behavior. The focus here has been on *liberal* misogyny because unlike conservatism, liberalism cherishes gender equality as a core value, yet liberalism has produced advocates like Bill Clinton who betray those values in their personal interactions with women.

Generally, the reaction to this apparent hypocrisy split along liberal and conservative lines: the left half-heartedly chastised Clinton's behavior but insisted that his personal misdeeds had nothing to do with his exemplary political values; the right pointed to Clinton's personal immorality as evidence that he didn't have character worthy of a national leader. Both sides missed the causal relationship between Clinton's liberalism and his treatment of women. Ignoring the connection leaves unexplained the reasons for the astonishing discrepancy between

Clinton's political championship of women's rights and his disturbing mistreatment of women on a personal level. Exploring the connection might help us rise above arguments over liberal and conservative values long enough to engage in political discourse over whether *anyone's* moral values deserve enforcement through the political system.

Liberalism's influence on Bill Clinton's sordid mistreatment of women shouldn't be interpreted as a reason to reject liberal values out of hand. Rather, it should encourage a deeper understanding about the connection between politics and personal behavior, and alert us to the dangers inherent in joining moral values with political methods. Even the purest moral values necessarily become corrupted—with life-damaging consequences to real victims like Juanita Broaddrick—when force is an acceptable method of attaining those values.

My core objection to liberalism lies not with its values but with its methods. I support gender, racial, and sexual orientation equality in all aspects of life. I support a healthy balance between commerce and protection of the ecosystem. I support nonviolent solutions to global conflict. I support using economic resources to provide material comforts to as many people as possible. What I cannot support is trying to accomplish any of that through the power of political force.

The cause of liberal misogyny is liberalism's acceptance and perpetuation of dominance and control rather than partnership and cooperation. In a fundamental sense, any division among human beings along lines of dominance tends to leave women on the losing end, simply because of the biological fact of men's superior physical strength. If the "two halves of humanity,"[1] males and females, are ranked instead of linked, women will land on the lower rung.

Drawing on cultural transformation theory, feminist scholar Riane Eisler posits that there are two fundamental ways to organize society, variously phrased as: ranking or linking; domination or partnership; control or cooperation. In her widely acclaimed book *The Chalice and the Blade,* Eisler argues that throughout prehistory and history, society has arranged itself mostly along a dominator model, but persistent attempts recur to align it along a partnership model.[2] Eisler views efforts to establish a partnership model as critical for the survival of humanity because a dominator society leads to male dominance over women, violence, and authoritarianism.[3]

Borrowing Eisler's terminology,[4] modern liberalism promotes *values* that would urge society to rearrange along a partnership model but it promotes *methods* that perpetuate our alignment based on a dominator model. Even with respect to eliminating gender discrimination, liberalism's fundamental internal contradiction precludes it from achieving what it seeks. Using the state (even when it is a representative democracy like our own) to enforce notions of gender equality will perpetuate violence over peace, domination over partnership, control over cooperation. That ideological flaw will continue to assist liberal misogynists like Bill Clinton in degrading and dominating women on a personal level, even as he promotes so-called women's rights on a political level.

Is there any way to advance liberal values like gender equality while avoiding the paradox of modern liberalism? Yes. It may feel like a slower, less efficient route, but it is possible. Our political system must accept a limited but vital role in human affairs. It must establish some basic ground rules designed to protect and vindicate our rights vis-à-vis each other, leaving us free to work with each other on mutually agreed-upon terms toward whatever goals we choose, including gender equality. That process doesn't guarantee progress because it leaves progress in the hands of millions of individual people, some of whom won't care to work for it. But banning force from the process ensures that the results which emerge are the product of voluntary, cooperative action rather than compelled behavior, giving us each the right and responsibility to develop and practice our own moral values.

For truly moral precepts like gender equality to have a shot at actualization in our society, those of us who cherish that ideal must use every nonviolent method of persuasion at our disposal to reach the hearts and minds of men and women. We must have the courage to resist using the political system as a short cut for imposing on others the moral precept of gender equality. The same holds for all other moral values, whether they are espoused by liberals, conservatives, moderates, libertarians, or anyone else.

So long as the people who hold our political offices insist on utilizing political force to impose their moral values, we will not escape our current political climate: a perennial battle over *whose* moral values get imposed. The left will continue to use politics to force us to adopt moral values like gender and racial equality and sanctity of the environment, while the right will use the same system to advance an anti-abortion platform and unequal treatment of gays and lesbians. What gets lost in this process is the realization that neither liberals nor conservatives have the right to force their moral values upon the nation, and any attempt to do so negates the existence of genuine morality because it strips us of our ability to *choose* our morality.

◊

Responsibility for electing leaders who will advance genuine morality by restraining use of the political system falls on each of us as informed citizens. Responsibility for eradicating the disturbing misogyny demonstrated by former President Clinton (and practiced by many men and women less prominent than he) also belongs to each of us. If you're not part of the solution, you're part of the problem. The women profiled in this book have done what they can to be part of the solution by calling attention to Clintonian misogyny and encouraging appropriate public response to it. There are others, however, who have chosen to remain silent.

Revisiting the stories of Elizabeth Gracen, Sally Perdue, Gennifer Flowers, Paula Jones, Kathleen Willey, Monica Lewinsky, and Juanita Broaddrick, omits the stories (and rumors) of others who have had similar experiences with Bill Clinton. One such woman (we'll call her "Mary") has never personally given interviews about her experience with Bill Clinton. Her name has been linked to his by other journalists and in the Paula Jones lawsuit, but she refuses to tell her story. One can only surmise that she has learned from watching Elizabeth, Sally, Gennifer, and the others suffer through smear campaigns that it is not advisable to cross swords with the former leader of the free world. Through a close friend, "Mary" declined an interview for this book, choosing instead to remain one of the countless women whose lives have been impacted by romantic involvement with Clinton, outside the glare of public and media scrutiny.

It's hard to blame her for keeping quiet. If she truly loved Clinton and desires personal security and a peaceful existence, staying silent is the best course of action. Her silence, however, and the silence of so many other women, is part of the problem that permits misogyny to linger and damage to be done to the women brave enough to speak out about their experiences with men like Clinton. But we cannot be too critical of "Mary." There is one other woman who could have done far more to stop Bill Clinton's misogynistic behavior, but has instead chosen to join him in attacking his female conquests.

◊

The only politician on the horizon who could mean more to left-wing feminism and politicized "women's rights" than Bill Clinton is his wife. Perceived by most as even more liberal than her husband, Hillary Rodham Clinton has a realistic shot at winning the Democratic Party's nomination in 2008.

The thought of Hillary being nominated as a presidential candidate by a major political party gives me mixed feelings.

From a feminist perspective, I want desperately for this particular glass ceiling to be shattered. Sometimes symbolism is valuable, and the symbolism of an American electorate ready and willing to put into the Highest Office in the Land a qualified person who is not a white male will, I believe, stand as a triumphant advance for gender equality in our country. But as Rush Limbaugh says trenchantly, liberals too often champion symbolism over substance.

When it comes to electing our first female president, we can do better than Hillary Clinton. We *need* to do better than Hillary Clinton, or the symbolism of a woman as president will be marred by electing a woman who has done almost as much to inflict mistreatment on real-life women as her misogynist husband.

By all accounts, Hillary Clinton is not a hapless wife victimized by her husband's philandering. Rather, it appears she long ago accepted his "weakness" and consciously decided to go the distance to protect their political careers. When this required public appearances hand in hand with Bill, she obliged. When it required solo television interviews deflecting attention away from Bill and onto his Republican enemies, she stepped up. Why did she make these choices? Should she have denounced his misdeeds publicly, or perhaps divorced him? It really isn't our place to judge her, her marriage, or her relationship with Bill. But it is our responsibility to pay attention to the choices she's made, particularly since she appears to be angling for our presidential vote in the near future.

When it comes to mistreatment of women, Hillary Clinton's behavior seems to be motivated by fear of losing power and prestige, not by misogyny per se. You'll understand, however, if women like Kathleen Willey and Juanita Broaddrick fail to appreciate this fine distinction, because the results on the lives of real-life women are the same. Hillary Clinton's choices and actions severely impacted the women whose stories we've looked at in this book. She *always* defended her husband publicly against each and every woman who leveled charges against him or disclosed consensual affairs with him. She *never* gave these women a shred of credibility or expressed anything but contempt for them. That much is, perhaps, excusable. She was married to Bill, after all, and had no personal attachment to any of the women profiled in this book. It is not surprising that she would stand by his side.

Yet a paradox emerges. Hillary Clinton, standing alone, appears to be a solid feminist, committed to gender equality and respect for women's independence and autonomy. But she is married to a man who mistreats women on a regular basis, and that marriage is the cornerstone of her own political success. Thus she faces a conflict of values. On the one hand, her intellectual belief in women's rights; on the other hand, the importance of her own political career. Her choices consistently seem to favor the latter at the expense of the former. Not only will she excuse Bill's behavior, she will lead the smear team in discrediting and ruining women who come forward against him.

If Bill were not in her life, I doubt Hillary Clinton would mistreat her fellow women or act out misogynistically. But her choice to stand by a man who does—to protect, defend, and even facilitate that behavior—leaves her vulnerable to charges of misogyny by association. Those of us with no personal connection to the Clintons have had only our voices and votes with which to influence Bill's behavior. But a wife has far more influence than even a voting booth. Hillary could have ameliorated the negative effects of Bill's misogyny by calling attention to it, chastising him privately and publicly, and encouraging all of us to recognize it for what it was and fight it. But Hillary opted not to use her position for that purpose. Instead she chose, at various times, to stay quiet, defend him ardently, trash talk his accusers, and deflect the public's attention from Bill's misogyny onto the motives of Bill's political enemies.

Eight years of President Hillary Rodham Clinton would mean eight more years of losing the fight for genuine gender equality. It would mean eight more years with the leader of this country selling out the interests of real-life, individual women whenever they threaten political damage. It would mean eight more years of symbolic political measures designed to advance women's rights by a First Couple who don't hesitate to mistreat women who get in their way. Ask Paula Jones, Kathleen Willey, or Juanita Broaddrick which means more to them: a politician who fights for passage of stricter equal pay laws, or a leader who truly treats women with dignity and respect. With the Clintons, you can't have both. With the Clintons, you get leftist policies that supposedly advance women's rights hand in hand with leaders who have demonstrated intense disrespect for women in their personal lives. Voting for Hillary Clinton as a way of breaking the glass ceiling in American politics shatters the glass in the name of biology, but not in the name of meaningful advancements for women.

Before rushing into another Clinton Administration, I hope we take some time to reflect on what Bill Clinton brought to our culture in terms of women's rights. For all his political support for left-wing feminists' goals, he did nothing to promote a culture of respect for women as individuals. Hillary Clinton's defense of her husband and refusal to acknowledge his behavior leave her in an uncomfortable bind: she's either as misogynistic as he is, or she's content to sell out gender equality for her own political career. Either way she is hardly a woman who deserves to carry the torch lighting the way to America's first female president.

Supporting Hillary, the politician closest to liberal misogyny's brightest star (Bill), is a slap in the face to women like Paula Jones, Kathleen Willey, and Juanita Broaddrick. And if you find their stories half as credible as I do, it's a slap in the face to all women and to the very concept of true gender equality. Just as those women deserved better than Bill Clinton, we deserve better than Hillary. We can let another Clinton expand the use of political force knowing she has little compunction about her husband using personal force on women, or we can insist on leaders who actually walk the walk and demonstrate respect for women in their personal lives. It's our choice, and it's an important one.

NOTES

Chapter One

1. David Liep, *Dave Liep's Atlas of U.S. Presidential Elections*, http://www.uselectionatlas. org (accessed June 11, 2004). In 1920, Harding won with 60.32%; in 1936, FDR won with 60.80%; in 1964, Johnson won with 61.05%; and in 1972, Nixon won with 60.67%.

2. Hillary Rodham Clinton, *Living History* (New York: Scribner, 2003), 52.

3. David Maraniss, *First In His Class: The Biography of Bill Clinton* (n.p.: Touchstone, 1996), 460.

4. Ibid, 439-440.

5. Ibid.

6. Melanie C. Falco, "Comment: The Road Not Taken: Using the Eighth Amendment to Strike Down Criminal Punishment for Engaging in Consensual Sexual Acts," 82 N.C.L. Rev. 723 734, 744 (2004). "Today, adultery remains a crime in 23 states and the District of Columbia." Ibid,744.

7. Bill Clinton, *My Life* (New York: Random House, 2004), 332.

8. Ibid, 332-333.

9. Ibid, 460-461.

10. Ibid, 372-73.

11. Ibid, 372.

12. Arizona Department of Public Safety's Crime Victim Services Unit Web site, http://www.dps.state.az.us/azvictims/assault/myths.asp (accessed June 12, 2004).

13. Richard Goldstein, "Bush's War on Women: Stealth Misogyny," *The Village Voice*, March 5-11, 2003, http://www.villagevoice.com/print/issues/0310/goldstein.php (accessed June 12, 2004.)

14. Psychiatric Times, October 1998, Volume XV, Issue 10.

15. Joe Sharkey, "The Nation; 'Enabling' Is Now a Political Disease," *The New York Times*, September 27, 1998.

16. Counseling Net, Web Information for Psychological Wellness Presented by the Adirondack Institute and Dr. Don Fava, "Sex Addiction," http://www.counselingnet. com/clinton.html (accessed June 11, 2004).

17. Letter from Patricia Ireland to the media about portrayal of NOW. Reprinted in *USA Today*, April 4, 1998, and *The New York Post*, April 9, 1998, http://now.org/press/04-98/letter-ed.html (accessed June 11, 2004).

Chapter Two

1. Clinton, *My Life*, 86.
2. Ibid, 40.
3. Ibid, 46.
4. Ibid, 58. Ellipses in original.
5. Ibid, 73.
6. Ibid, 173.
7. Ibid, 209.
8. Ibid, 821.
9. Suzi Parker, *Sex in the South: Unbuckling the Bible Belt* (Boston: Justin, Charles & Co., 2003), xiii.
10. Ibid, xii.
11. Ibid, xiii.
12. Rodham Clinton, *Living History*, 21. On page 27, she writes, "I arrived at Wellesley carrying my father's political beliefs and my mother's dreams and left with the beginnings of my own."
13. Ibid, 56.
14. Ibid.
15. Statement by Senator George McGovern (D.-South Dakota) announcing candidacy for the 1972 Democratic presidential nomination, January 18, 1971, http://www.4president.org/speeches/mcgovern1972announcement.htm (accessed June 13, 2004).
16. Ibid.
17. Ibid.
18. Ibid.
19. Joe Klein, *Primary Colors* (New York: Warner Books, 1996).
20. Daniel Frankel, "'I Had Sex With Clinton,' Says TV Actress," *E!Online*, March 31, 1998.
21. Jean Sonmor, "Beauty Queen Trapped in 'Zippergate," *The Toronto Sun*, April 12, 1998, http://www.canoe.ca/CNEWSClinton/apr12_gracen.html (accessed June 13, 2004).
22. Tom Squitieri, "Kantor had talks in '92 about Clinton, beauty queen," *USA Today*, April 1, 1998.
23. Ibid.
24. Ibid.
25. Helen Kennedy, "Former Miss American Tells N.Y. Daily News She Had Sex With Clinton," *Daily News* (New York), March 30, 1998.
26. Alastair Robertson, "The Playboy Highlander," *Sunday Times* (London), November 22, 1998.
27. Carl Limbacher, "Clinton's Next Kathleen Willey?" *The Washington Weekly*, March 23, 1998, reprint available at http://www.chuckbaldwinlive.com/willey.html (accessed June 13, 2004).
28. Helen Kennedy. "Former Miss American tells N.Y. Daily News she had sex with Clinton," *Daily News* (New York), March 30, 1998.
29. "Women in the Clinton era: Abuse, intimidation and smears," *Capitol Hill Blue*, June 1999, http://www.capitolhillblue.com/June1999/061099/clintonwomen061099.htm (ac-

cessed June 13, 2004).

30. "Ex-Miss America's Clinton Encounter," *Time*, March 31, 1998, http://www.time.com/time/daily/scandal/miss_america.html (accessed June 13, 2004).

31. Kennedy, "Former Miss American Tells N.Y. Daily News She Had Sex with Clinton."

32. Ibid.

33. "Former Miss America Elizabeth Gracen Admitting She Had a One-Night Stand with Bill Clinton 15 Years Ago," *CNBC's Rivera Live*, March 31, 1998 (airdate).

34. "Former Miss America Apologizes to First Lady," *CNN.com*, April 25, 1998, http://images.cnn.com/ALLPOLITICS/1998/04/25/clinton.gracen/ (accessed June 13, 2004).

35. Ibid.

36. Tracy Connor, "Actress Who Claimed Sex with Bill Says IRS is Hounding Her," *The New York Post*, January 13, 1999.

37. Ibid.

38. Brian Blomquist, "Juanita Latest Bill Foe to be Audited," *The New York Post*, May 31, 2000.

39. Steve Dunleavy, "I Was Victim of Clinton Reign of Terror: Actress Harassing Phone Calls After One-Night Stand," *The New York Post*, September 27, 1998.

40. "I'm not Xena, quoth The Raven," *The Toronto Star*, August 16, 1998.

41. Jean Sonmor. "Beauty queen trapped in 'Zippergate,'" *The Toronto Sun*, April 12, 1998, http://www.canoe.ca/CNEWSClinton/apr12_gracen.html (accessed June 13, 2004).

42. Claire Bickley, "Gracen Paid Her Bill: On Clinton, Encounter is Ancient History for Star of TV's Highlander: The Raven," *The Toronto Sun*, September 17, 1998.

43. Jean Sonmor, "A Tangled Tale Among the Jet Set," *The Toronto Sun*, October 25, 1999.

44. "Jail's Home to 'Raven' Star's Ex," *The New York Post*, December 16, 1999.

45. Suzi Parker, "Blood Money," *Salon.com*, December 24, 1998, http://archive.salon.com/news/1998/12/cov_23news.html (accessed February 13, 2005).

46. Ibid.

47. Ibid.

48. Ibid.

49. Ibid.

50. Suzi Parker, "Dumping Scandal: The Export of Bad Blood," *Salon.com*, February 25, 1999, http://archive.salon.com/news/1999/02/25news.html (accessed February 13, 2005).

51. Will Gibson, "The Arkansas connection," *Alberta Report* (Canada), August 16, 1999.

52. Ibid.

53. Alastair Robertson, "The Playboy Highlander," *Sunday Times* (London), November 22, 1998.

54. The National Center for Self-Esteem, http://www.self-esteem-nase.org/whatisself esteem.shtml (accessed June 14, 2004).

55. Ibid.

56. Available online at http://www.pinn.net/~sunshine/book-sum/seneca3.html (accessed June 14, 2004).

Chapter Three

1. Howard Rosenberg, "It's Raphael's Patriotic Duty to Tell," *Los Angeles Times*, July 20,

1992.

2. Ibid.

3. Ibid.

4. Ibid.

5. Ibid.

6. Michael Isikoff, "Clinton Team Works to Deflect Allegations on Nominee's Private Life," *The Washington Post*, July 26, 1992.

7. Karen Ball, "Curtain Call," *The Washington Post*, January 28, 2001.

8. Isikoff, "Clinton Team Works to Deflect Allegations on Nominee's Private Life."

9. Ibid.

10. Ibid.

11. Ibid.

12. Ibid.

13. Ibid.

14. "Former beauty queen says she had an affair with Clinton," *Agence France Presse*, January 23, 1994.

15. Ibid.

16. Dave Shiflett, "Media Selective With Its Scandals," *Rocky Mountain News* (Denver), February 21, 1994.

17. Tony Gallagher, "Clinton 'Mistress' Demands Inquiry Into His Sex Trysts." *Daily Mail* (London), January 24, 1994.

18. Ibid.

19. "The Press and Whitewater; Shhhh," *The Economist* (U.K. edition), February 26, 1994, 62.

20. Geordie Greig, "Fornigate," *Sunday Times* (London), May 1, 1994.

21. Alex Beam, "Whitewater: What It Boils Down To," *The Boston Globe*, March 9, 1994.

22. Howard Kurtz. "Brits Keep Tabs on Clinton Sex Life; London Papers Trumpet Tawdry Allegations about the President," *The Washington Post*, May 3, 1994.

23. Roger Morris, *Partners in Power: The Clintons and Their America* (Washington, D.C.: Regnery Publishing, 1996).

24. Discussed at length in a review of *Partners in Power* by Kevin Phillips, "Prelude to a Presidency," *The Washington Post*, June 16, 1996.

25. "The Politics of Sex in Clinton's America; U.S. President Has a Long History of Womanizing, Says New Bestseller," *The Toronto Sun*, July 28, 1996.

26. Paul Sperry, "A Bully in the White House?" *Investor's Business Daily*, March 11, 1999.

27. Ibid.

28. Ibid.

29. Ibid.

30. Joe Conason and Gene Lyons, *The Hunting of the President: The Ten-Year Campaign to Destroy Bill and Hillary Clinton* (New York: St. Martin's Press, 2000).

31. Matt Labash, "Women of the Clinton Scandals; Whatever happened to Paula and Gennifer and Monica and Connie and Sally and Dolly and Susan and [. . .]," *The Weekly Standard*, January 15, 2001.

32. Russell Miller, "Indecent Exposure," *The Australian*, June 3, 1996.

33. Jim Smith, "Suit: Clinton Tryst Cost Me My Job; Claims Affair Led to Abuse by

Quakers," *Philadelphia Daily News*, October 29, 2004.

34. Ibid.

35. Maraniss, *First In His Class*, 440.

36. Ibid, 440.

37. Ibid, 441.

38 .Ibid.

39. Chuck Baldwin, interview of David Horowitz, June 6, 1997, http://www.chuck baldwinlive.com/horowitz.html (accessed June 17, 2004).

40. For a fascinating account of David Horowitz's life experience and transformation from Communist radical to conservative icon, see David Horowitz, *Radical Son: A Generational Odyssey* (New York: Touchstone, 1997). The book also tells the story of the far left's walk-out on the Democratic Party in 1948 (due to anger at Harry Truman's international efforts to resist Communism), Communists' formulation of the Progressive Party in 1948 and re-entry into the Democratic Party through candidate George McGovern in 1972. McGovern's first big political campaign involvement had been as an activist campaigning for Henry Wallace, the Progressive Party candidate against Truman in 1948. McGovern gave Bill Clinton and Hillary Rodham their first taste of national politics and remained a hero to Bill Clinton throughout his political life.

41. Chuck Baldwin, interview of David Horowitz.

42. Ibid.

43. Ludwig von Mises, *Bureaucracy* (Spring Mills, PA: Libertarian Press, 1993), 99. This is a reprint of the famous book originally published by Yale University Press in 1944.

44. John W. Burns and Andrew J. Taylor, "A New Democrat? The Economic Performance of the Clinton Presidency," *The Independent Review*, Winter 2001, 387-408.

45. Ibid, 403.

46. Ibid.

47. Ibid.

48. Ibid, 404.

49. Maraniss, *First In His Class*, 381, 376-381.

50. Ibid, 416.

51. Mises, *Bureaucracy*, 6.

52. Ibid.

Chapter Four

1. Maraniss, *First In His Class*, 462.

2. David Maraniss, "Image Questions Bewilder Clinton, Longtime Friends; Allies Describe Candidate's 'Constancy,'" *The Washington Post*, April 12, 1992.

3. David Lauter, "Clinton: Healer or Waffler?" *Los Angeles Times*, January 14, 1992.

4. Ibid.

5. Maraniss, First In His Class, 398-399.

6. Ibid, 400-401.

7. Ibid.

8. Adam Pertman, "Bill Clinton: Mediator Who Loves Politics." *The Boston Globe*, January 10, 1992.

9. Steve Daley, "Clinton Challenging Long-Time Party Ideals," *The Chicago Tribune*, October 6, 1991.

10. Maraniss, "Image Questions Bewilder Clinton, Longtime Friends; Allies Describe Candidate's 'Constancy.'"

11. Ibid.

12. Lauri Githens, "Buzz," *The Buffalo News* (New York), November 5, 1992.

13. David Maraniss and Bill McAllister, "For Clinton, the Toughest Character Tests Seemed Past," *The Washington Post*, February 16, 1992.

14. Official Web site for the city of Brinkley, Arkansas, http://www.brinkleyar. com/index.html (accessed June 19, 2004).

15. Ibid.

16. Maraniss and McAllister, "For Clinton, the Toughest Character Tests Seemed Past."

17. Gennifer Flowers, *Passion and Betrayal* (Del Mar, CA: Emery Dalton Books, 1995), 7.

18. Glynn Wilson, "Gennifer Flowers Readies New Club for First Mardi Gras," *The Southerner*, 2002, Vol. 3, No. 1.

19. Ibid.

20. Mark Mayfield, "Anger in Arkansas," *USA Today*, January 31, 1992.

21. Lorraine Adams, "Into the Spotlight," *The Washington Post*, August 9, 1998.

22. Transcript, *Larry King Weekend*, August 5, 2001 (airdate), http://cnnstudentnews. cnn.com/TRANSCRIPTS/0108/05/lklw.00.html (accessed June 20, 2004).

23. Declaration of Gennifer G. Flowers, March 12, 1998, Jones v. Clinton, Civil Action No. LR-C-94-290 (E.D. Ark.).

24. Ibid.

25. C. Rempel and Douglas Frantz, "Troopers Say Clinton Sought Silence on Personal Affairs; Arkansas: The White House Calls Their Allegations About The President's Private Life 'Ridiculous,'" *Los Angeles Times*, December 21, 1993.

26. *Larry King Weekend*, August 5, 2001.

27. Flowers, *Passion and Betrayal*.

28. Ibid.

29. Ibid.

30. Ibid.

31. Marilyn Schwartz, "Repentance Not Enough to Sell Flowers," *The Dallas Morning News*, August 15, 2000.

32. Ibid.

33. Flowers, *Passion and Betrayal*.

34. Ibid, 77.

35. Ibid.

36. Schwartz, "Repentance Not Enough To Sell Flowers."

37. Ibid.

38. "Clinton: That Other Woman Won't Go Away," *Sunday Herald Sun* (Australia), July 26, 1992.

39. Martin Kasindorf, "Ex-Boyfriend's Story; Says He, Flowers Broke Up Over Her Affair with Clinton," *Newsday* (New York), January 26, 1992.

40. Ibid.

41. Ibid.

42. Dan Balz and Howard Kurtz, "Clinton Calls Tabloid Report Of 12-Year Affair 'Not True,'" *The Washington Post*, January 24, 1992.

43. Timothy Clifford and Shirley E. Perlman, "The Flowers Job; Officials' Changes Gave Her an Advantage," *Newsday* (New York), February 6, 1992.

44. Balz and Kurtz, "Clinton Calls Tabloid Report of 12-Year Affair 'Not True.'"

45. Declaration of Gennifer G. Flowers.

46. Ibid.

47. Ibid.

48. Clifford and Perlman, "The Flowers Job; Officials' Changes Gave Her an Advantage."

49. Ibid.

50. Ibid.

51. Ibid.

52. *Larry King Weekend*, August 5, 2001.

53. Ibid.

54. Sperry, "A Bully in the White House?"

55. Timothy Clifford, "Flowers: Clinton's Lying; She insists they were lovers, says tape shows his deceit," *Newsweek* (New York), January 28, 1992.

56. Ibid.

57. "The Politics of Sex in Clinton's America; U.S. President Has a Long History of Womanizing, Says New Bestseller."

58. Maraniss, *First In His Class*, 457-458.

59. Peter Stothard, "Wild Bill Ambushed By Sex Pack on Campaign Trail," *Times* (London), January 18, 1992.

60. Ibid.

61. Howard Kurtz, "Clinton Denies Affairs Report Linked To Suit; Democratic Hopeful Ridicules Tabloid," *The Washington Post*, January 18, 1992.

62. Myron S. Waldman, "Would-Be Prez Denies Affairs; Clinton Calls Allegations Rehash Of Lawsuit 'Trash,'" *Newsweek*, January 18, 1992.

63. Kurtz, "Clinton Denies Affairs Report Linked To Suit; Democratic Hopeful Ridicules Tabloid."

64. James Adams, "Wild Bill dogged by the affairs of state," *Sunday Times* (London), January 19, 1992.

65. Clinton, *My Life*, 360.

66. Ibid, 385.

67. Basil Talbott and Lynn Sweet, "Dem Opponents Pounce on Clinton in Debate," *Chicago Sun-Times*, January 20, 1992.

68. Ibid.

69. Elaine K. Swift and Kenneth Finegold, "Has Clinton Said Enough?; A Yes or No Will Do," *The New York Times*, January 23, 1992.

70. Ibid.

71. Ibid.

72. *Larry King Weekend*, August 5, 2001.

73. Ibid.

74. Ibid.

75. Adam Nagourney and David Colton, "Tapes Still Entangle Clinton." *USA Today*,

January 30, 1992.

76. "Ex-L.A. Times Reporter Sues Private Eye," *The Hollywood Reporter*, June 3, 2004, http://www.hollywoodreporter.com/thr/media/article_display.jsp?vnu_content_id=100052 3657 (accessed June 21, 2004).

77. Balz and Kurtz, "Clinton Calls Tabloid Report of 12-Year Affair 'Not True.'"

78. Myron S. Waldman and Susan Page, "Clinton's Crisis; Denies woman's account of sex, lies and audiotape," *Newsday* (New York). January 24, 1992.

79. Ibid.

80. David Lauther and Robert Shogan, "Clinton Denies Tabloid Story of 12-Year Affair," *Los Angeles Times*, January 24, 1992.

81. Susan Yoachum, "New Flareup Over Singer's Claim of Affair With Clinton," *The San Francisco Chronicle*, January 24, 1992.

82. Balz and Kurtz, "Clinton Calls Tabloid Report of 12-Year Affair 'Not True.'"

83. Ibid.

84. Yoachum, "New Flareup Over Singer's Claim of Affair With Clinton."

85. Isikoff, *Uncovering Clinton*, 31.

86. Balz and Kurtz, "Clinton Calls Tabloid Report of 12-Year Affair 'Not True.'"

87. Gwen Ifill, "Clinton Defends His Privacy And Says The Press Intruded," *The New York Times*, January 27, 1992.

88. Dan Balz, "Clinton Concedes Marital 'Wrongdoing'; In TV Interview, Presidential Hopeful Asks Public to Drop Questions," *The Washington Post*, January 27, 1992.

89. Ifill, "Clinton Defends His Privacy And Says The Press Intruded."

90. Timothy Clifford, "Flowers: Clinton's Lying; She insists they were lovers, says tape shows his deceit," *Newsweek*, January 28, 1992.

91. Ibid.

92. Dave Kehr, "'Feed' shows media amid the political frenzy,'" *Chicago Sun-Tribune*, October 16, 1992. This review of the political documentary observed: "Most disturbingly, there is some uncensored footage of Gennifer Flowers at her New York press conference, in which her bemused reaction to a couple of extremely tasteless questions betrays the presence of a formidible [sic] sense of humor. She seems both fun and smart, qualities that didn't come across in print, and qualities that might explain her attractiveness to a powerful politician."

93. Mary McGrory, "Flowers and Dirt," *The Washington Post*, January 28, 1992.

94. Isikoff, *Uncovering Clinton*, 54.

95. David Von Drehle. "Clinton Accuser Defends Story, Plays Tapes," *The Washington Post*, January 28, 1992.

96. Clinton, *My Life*, 386.

97. Ibid.

98. Ibid, 387.

99. "The Specter of Scandal," *Newsweek*, November 1992 (Special Election Issue).

100. Ibid.

101. Waldman and Page, "Clinton's Crisis; Denies Woman's Account Of Sex, Lies And Audiotape."

102. Lauter and Shogan, "Clinton Denies Tabloid Story of 12-Year Affair."

103. Jean Sonmor, "Why Is This Man Smiling? Clinton's Long History Of Sexual Risk-

Taking May Be His Undoing," *The Toronto Sun*, January 25, 1998.

104. Lorraine Adams, "Into the Spotlight," *The Washington Post*, August 9, 1998.

105. Ibid.

106. Lorraine Adams, "Flowers Feels Vindicated By Report; Similarities Seen In Relationships," *The Washington Post*, January 23, 1998.

107. David Von Drehle, "Clinton Accuser Defends Story, Plays Tapes; But Flowers Refuses to Discuss Apparent Discrepancies in Account She Sold to Tabloid," *The Washington Post*, January 28, 1992.

108. Ibid.

109. Paula Span and Laurie Goodstein, "The Bright and Slimy Star; Checking Out the Tabloid That Ran With the Clinton Story," *The Washington Post*, January 28, 1992.

110. Ibid.

111. Ibid.

112. Mayfield, "Anger in Arkansas."

113. Ibid.

114. Michael Sneed, "Tipsville," *Chicago Sun-Times*, February 14, 1992.

115. Ibid.

116. Githens, "Buzz."

117. Martin Kasindorf, "Ex-Boyfriend's Story; Says he, Flowers Broke Up Over Her Affair With Clinton," *Newsday* (New York), January 26, 1992.

118. Gwen Ifill, "The 1992 Campaign: Democrats; Clinton, Cheered by New Polls, Again Assails Bush on Economy," *The New York Times*, January 29, 1992.

119. Ibid.

120. Ibid.

121. Adam Nagourney and David Colton, "Tapes Still Entangle Clinton," *USA Today*, January 30, 1992.

122. Ibid.

123. Maraniss and McAllister, "For Clinton, The Toughest Character Test Seems Past."

124. Kathy O'Malley and Dorothy Collin, "Flower Girl," *Chicago-Tribune*, October 30, 1992.

125. Duncan Campbell, "Gennifer Flowers Discovers Life After Bill In The Big Easy," *The Guardian* (London), February 5, 2002.

126. Jeff Zeleney, "Starting over as a New Orleans Clubowner, Gennifer Flowers Still Has A Knack For Getting Close To People In High Places," *Chicago Tribune*, January 31, 2002.

127. Rick Bragg, "After the Glare of Scandal, The Soft Glow of Celebrity," *The New York Times*, January 15, 2002.

128. Adams, "Into the Spotlight."

129. Ibid.

130. "Daily Briefing," *The Seattle Times*, September 18, 1998.

131. "Clinton's Former Mistress Warns Students Against Affairs," *The Examiner* (Ireland), February 20, 1999, http://archives.tcm.ie/irishexaminer/1999/02/20/fhead.htm (accessed March 17, 2005).

132. *Larry King Weekend*, August 5, 2001.

133. Karen Ball, "Curtain Call," *The Washington Post*, January 28, 2001.

134. Adams, "Flowers Feels Vindicated By Report; Similarities Seen In Relationships."

135. Adams, "Into the Spotlight."

136. Ibid.

137. Ibid.

138. *Larry King Weekend*, August 5, 2001.

139. Ibid.

140. Wilson, "Gennifer Flowers Readies New Club for First Mardi Gras."

141. Ibid.

142. Ibid.

143. Ibid.

144. Les Carpenter, "Bright Lights Big Easy," *The Seattle Times*, January 29, 2002.

145. Zeleney, "Starting over as a New Orleans clubowner, Gennifer; Flowers still has a knack for getting close to people in high places."

146. Ibid.

147. Adams, "Into the Spotlight.".

148. Transcript available through *Washington Post* Web site at http://www.washington post.com/wp-srv/politics/special/pjones/docs/clintondep031398.htm#flowers (accessed June 22, 2004).

149. Ibid.

150. "Clinton's Grand Jury Testimony, Part 10," available at http://www.washington post.com/wp-srv/politics/special/clinton/stories/bctest092198_10.htm (accessed July 17, 2004).

151. Susan Faludi, "The Power Laugh," *The New York Times*, December 20, 1992.

152. Ibid.

153. Ibid.

154. Ibid.

155. Richard Goldstein, "Stealth Misogyny," *The Village Voice*, March 5-11, 2003.

156. Kim Gandy, *National NOW Times*, Summer 2002, http://www.now.org/nnt/summer-2002/viewpoint.html (accessed June 9, 2004).

157. Dina Rabadi, "U.S. drags feet on ratifying UN treaty on women's rights," *Chicago Tribune*, June 13, 2004.

158. Ibid.

159. Goldstein, "Stealth Misogyny."

160. Arianna Huffington, "Suspension of logic is essential in D.C. follies," *Chicago Sun-Times*, March 25, 1998.

161. Ibid.

Chapter Five

1. John King, "Clinton's Star Rises, as Does Cleveland's; Dems Recall Reagan Rhetoric," *The Associated Press*, May 8, 1991.

2. Rodham Clinton, *Living History*, p. 98.

3. Dan Balz and David S. Broder, "Democrats Argue Over Quota Clause; Meeting to Reshape Party Image Opens," *The Washington Post*, May 7, 1991. (Emphasis added.)

4. Ibid.

5. Clinton, *My Life*, 366.

6. Maraniss, *First In His Class*, 456.

7. King, "Clinton's Star Rises, as Does Cleveland's; Dems Recall Reagan Rhetoric."

8. "Clinton's Speech Brings Delegates to Their Feet," *Arkansas Democrat-Gazette* (Little Rock), May 7, 1991.

9. Ibid.

10. Michael Isikoff, Charles E. Shepard, and Sharon LaFraniere, "Clinton Hires Lawyer as Sexual Harassment Suit Is Threatened; Former State Employee in Arkansas Alleges Improper Advance in 1991," *The Washington Post*, May 4, 1994.

11. Isikoff, *Uncovering Clinton*, 41.

12. Ibid, 40.

13. Ibid, 41.

14. Ibid, 78-79.

15. Ibid, 345, n.5.

16. Ibid, 11-12.

17. Ibid, 20.

18. Bill Nichols, "Paula Jones Says She's No Pawn," *USA Today*, June 17, 1994.

19. John M. Broder and Thomas B. Rosenstiel, "Clinton's Accuser Goes on the Interview Circuit," *Los Angeles Times*, June 17, 1994.

20. Clinton, *My Life*, 565.

21. Bill Nichols, "In up-down year, Clinton looked homeward," *USA Today*, December 22, 1993.

22. Ibid.

23. Ibid.

24. "Sexual adventures by Clinton detailed in magazine story," *The Washington Times*, December 21, 1993. (Emphasis added.)

25. "Two Troopers Say Clinton Used Security Staff to Facilitate Trysts," *The Associated Press*, December 19, 1993.

26. Ibid.

27. Ibid.

28. CNN, News 5:57 p.m. ET, Transcript # 619-1, December 19, 1993.

29. "Sex and the art of the 'statement,'" *The Washington Times*, December 21, 1993.

30. Mara Liasson, "Clinton's Christmas woes," *All Things Considered* (National Public Radio), December 21, 1993.

31. Mickey Kaus, "Old News," *The New Republic*, March 7, 1994 (quoting *Newsweek* correspondent Joe Klein). See also Isikoff, *Uncovering Clinton*, 14.

32. Isikoff, *Uncovering Clinton*, 8.

33. Ibid.

34. Ibid, 9.

35. Kaus, "Old News."

36. Ibid.

37. Lloyd Grove, "It Isn't Easy Being Right; At the Conservative Confab, Out of Sorts About Who's in Power," *The Washington Post*, February 14, 1994.

38. Michael Hedges, "Another trooper says he found women for Clinton; Spectator story describes a Hillary-Foster romance," *The Washington Times*, April 12, 1994.

39. Ibid.

40. Ibid.

41. Ibid.

42. Ibid.

43. Isikoff, *Uncovering Clinton*, 73-74.

44. Harold Johnson, "Paula Jones Wants Clinton Exposed," *Orange County Register* (California), April 12, 1994. The article was reprinted there with permission from *National Review*.

45. Ibid.

46. Ibid.

47. Ibid.

48. Ibid.

49. Isikoff, *Uncovering Clinton*, 77-78.

50. Johnson, "Paula Jones Wants Clinton Exposed."

51. Isikoff, Shepard, and LaFraniere, "Clinton Hires Lawyer as Sexual Harassment Suit Is Threatened; Former State Employee in Arkansas Alleges Improper Advance in 1991."

52. Isikoff, *Uncovering Clinton*, 83.

53. Ibid, 48-49.

54. Ibid, 75.

55. Ibid, 82.

56. Isikoff, Shepard, and LaFraniere, "Clinton Hires Lawyer as Sexual Harassment Suit Is Threatened; Former State Employee in Arkansas Alleges Improper Advance in 1991."

57. Isikoff, *Uncovering Clinton*, 62-63.

58. Ibid, pp. 59-61.

59. Clinton, *My Life*, 595.

60. Ibid, 595-596.

61. Ibid, 596.

62. Isikoff, *Uncovering Clinton*, 83-84.

63. Ibid, 88.

64. Ibid.

65. Joel Williams, "Former Arkansas Employee Files Suit Against Clinton," *The Associated Press*, May 6, 1994.

66. Mike Royko, "Talking Trash; The Class Warfare Against Paula Jones Is A Media Disgrace," *Pittsburgh Post-Gazette*, January 19, 1997.

67. Nichols, "Paula Jones Says She's No Pawn."

68. Roger Simon, "Calling Paula Jones a Slut Doesn't Exonerate Clinton," *The Baltimore Sun*, October 26, 1994.

69. Ibid.

70. Ibid.

71. Lynn Rosellini and Greg Ferguson, "The Woman Who Sued the President," *Rocky Mountain News* (Denver), June 12, 1994. Note: The article was reprinted from *U.S. News & World Report*.

72. Ibid.

73. Howard Schneider, "Paula Jones and A House Divided; They Believe Sis. It's Her Motives They Don't Buy," *The Washington Post*, June 9, 1994.

74. "Too Much Immunity in the Jones Case," *The New York Times*, December 30, 1994.

75. Rodham Clinton, *Living History*, 257.

76. Ibid.

77. Ibid.

78. "Vowing He'll Run In '96, Clinton Seeks Middle-Class Tax Aid; President Will Continue Pushing for Health Reform," *Chicago Tribune*, December 30, 1994.

79. Ruth Marcus, "Court Says Suit Against Clinton May Proceed; Appeals Panel Rejects Immunity Claim in Case Alleging Sexual Harassment in 1991," *The Washington Post*, January 10, 1996.

80. Martin Kasindorf, "For Better, Worse / Prez defends Hillary, says legal fees are breaking them," *Newsday* (New York), January 12, 1996.

81. "Whitewater Convictions Bode Ill for Clintons," *The San Francisco Chronicle*, May 30, 1996.

82. "Top Court Clears Way For Jones Lawsuit; Justices Rule That Office Doesn't Shield President," *The New York Times*, May 27, 1997.

83. Peter Baker, "Lawyers for Paula Jones Trying to Prove Pattern by President; Former Clinton Aide's Attorney Denounces Subpoena Tactic," *The Washington Post*, August 1, 1997.

84. Ibid.

85. David G. Savage and Robert L Jackson, "Paula Jones's Lawyers Quit, Citing Disagreement," *Los Angeles Times*, September 9, 1997.

86. "Jones Says She'll Attend Deposition," *Detroit Free Press*, January 8, 1998.

87. Clinton, *My Life*, 769.

88. Isikoff, *Uncovering Clinton*, 165-166.

89. Ibid.

90. Clinton, *My Life*, 769.

91. Ibid.

92. James Bennet, "Pasts Are Prologue as Jones v. Clinton Moves Nearer to Trial," *The New York Times*, November 9, 1997.

93. "Trial of Paula Jones's lawsuit seems inevitable, Clinton says," *Fort Worth Star-Telegram* (Texas), January 14, 1998.

94. Michael Kelly, "The President's Past," *The New York Times*, July 31, 1994 (quoting from Virginia Kelley's memoirs).

95. Peter Baker, "President Faces His Accuser; Clinton Questioned Under Oath for 6 Hours on Allegations of Harassment," *The Washington Post*, January 18, 1998.

96. "President Clinton's Deposition; Cross-Examination by Clinton Lawyer Robert Bennett," available at: http://www.washingtonpost.com/wp-srv/politics/special/pjones/docs/clintondep031398.htm#crossbe (accessed July 17, 2004).

97. Ibid.

98. Peter Baker, "Jones v. Clinton Suit Dismissed; Judge Finds 'No Genuine Issues for Trial,'" *The Washington Post*, April 2, 1998.

99. Clinton, *My Life*, 220-221.

100. Ibid, 221.

101. Peter Baker, "Looms Over Scope of Clinton Trial Inquiry," *The Washington Post*, January 19, 1998.

102. Peter Baker, "Appeals Court Hears Arguments in Jones Harassment Case," *The Washington Post*, October 21, 1998.

103. Ibid.

104. Peter Baker, "Clinton, Jones Reach Settlement; President to Pay $850,000 to End Harassment Suit, Without Admission or Apology," *The Washington Post*, November 14, 1998.

105. Kevin Newman and Lisa McCree, "Paula Jones's Settlement," ABC's *Good Morning America* (Transcript # 98111605-j01), November 16, 1998.

106. Ibid.

107. "Source: Paula Jones' marriage ends in divorce," *CNN.com*, June 8, 1999, http://www. cnn.com/ALLPOLITICS/stories/1999/06/08/jones.divorce/ (accessed July 2, 2004).

108. Tracy Moran, "Seen enough of Paula Jones?" *USA Today.com*, October 25, 2000, http://www.usatoday.com/news/opinion/columnists/tmoran/tm28.htm (accessed July 2, 2004).

109. Jan Crawford Greenburg, Bill Crawford, and John O'Brien, "Paula Jones Perils, Penthouse and a Stopoff in Chicago," *Chicago Tribune*, November 1, 1994.

110. Thane Burnett, "All the president's Women," *The Toronto Sun*, December 10, 1994.

111. "Clinton Accuser Loses Her Case to Penthouse," *The New York Times*, December 2, 1994.

112. "Newsmakers," *The Houston Chronicle*, July 16, 1995.

113. Anita K. Blair and Kate Kennedy, "The Two Faces of Paula Jones," *Women's Quarterly*, Winter 2001, http://articles.findarticles.com/p/articles/mi_m0IUK/is_2001_Wntr/ai_ 71837543/print (accessed July 2, 2004).

114. Ibid.

115. Transcript, *Larry King Live*, "Paula Jones Discusses Why She's Posing For Penthouse", October 24, 2000 (airdate), http://www.cnn.com/TRANSCRIPTS/0010/24/lkl.00.html (accessed July 2, 2004).

116. Josh Grossberg, "Celeb Boxing KO's Ratings," *Eonline.com*, March 15, 2002, http://www.eonline.com/News/Items/0,1,9667,00.html?newsrellink (accessed July 2, 2004). The article reported: "Of the three bouts, the Harding-Jones contest was the most watched, if not the most competitive. As Nancy Kerrigan might have predicted, Harding thrashed Jones, who appeared to be overly protective of her surgically trimmed nose. The fight was over by the second round, a TKO win for the former ice queen, who didn't even need a lead pipe."

117. Simon, "Calling Paula Jones a slut doesn't exonerate Clinton."

118. J.E. Bourgoyne, "Talk Show Host Objects to Ex-Girlfriend's Tales," *Times-Picayune* (New Orleans, LA), July 9, 1994.

119. Ruth Marcus, "Clintons Establish Fund to Meet Legal Expenses; Lobbyists Among Those Allowed to Contribute," *The Washington Post*, June 29, 1994.

120. Ibid.

121. Ibid.

122. Ibid.

123. Lynn Sweet, "Paula Jones complains feminists not on her side," *Chicago Sun-Times*, March 17, 1997.

124. Andy Rooney, "If Election Were This Week, Forget It," *Buffalo News* (New York), April 5, 1997.

125. Ibid.

126. Robin Givhan, "Paula Jones's Revamped Image; Her Sleek Look May Be a Fashion Statement, but It Says a Lot About Power, Too," *The Washington Post*, January 16, 1998.

127. Times Wire Reports, "Papers Report Nose Job for Paula Jones," *Los Angeles Times*, July 20, 1998.

128. Givhan, "Paula Jones's Revamped Image; Her Sleek Look May Be a Fashion Statement, but It Says a Lot About Power, Too."

129. Isikoff, *Uncovering Clinton*, 96-97.

130. Leora Tanenbaum, "Paula Jones's Reputation Was Trashed," *St. Louis Post-Dispatch*, February 3, 1997.

131. Andrew Sullivan, "Is This the Woman to Hit Clinton Where it Hurts?" *Sunday Times* (London), November 17, 1996.

132. Available, among other places, at http://www.courttv.com/archive/legaldocs/government/jones/jones_complaint.html (accessed June 28, 2004).

133. Isikoff, *Uncovering Clinton*, 20-24.

134. Stuart Taylor, "Her Case Against Clinton," *American Lawyer*, November 1996, as reprinted in *Palm Beach Daily Business Review*, November 4, 1996.

135. U.S. Equal Employment Opportunity Commission, http://www.eeoc.gov/facts/fs-sex.html (accessed June 28, 2004).

136. Isikoff, *Uncovering Clinton*, 23.

137. Nina Burleigh, "Can Clinton Get The Venus Vote? Women Worry He's From Mars," *The Washington Post*, May 21, 1995.

Chapter Six

1. Roger Simon, "Ex-Aide: Clinton Fondled Me; Accusation May Be Most Serious Yet Against President," *Chicago Tribune*, March 16, 1998.

2. Michael Isikoff, "A Twist in the Paula Jones Case," *Newsweek*, August 11, 1997.

3. Isikoff, *Uncovering Clinton*, 112.

4. "Final Report of the Independent Counsel In Re: Madison Guaranty Savings & Loan Association," Robert W. Ray, Independent Counsel, May 18, 2001, 88, http://icreport.access.gpo.gov/lewinsky.html (accessed July 5, 2004)

5. Isikoff, *Uncovering Clinton*, 109.

6. Ibid.

7. Ibid, 109-110.

8. Angie Cannon, "Those Who Met Willey Cite the Odd and Classy," *The Philadelphia Inquirer*, March 19, 1998.

9. Ibid.

10. Isikoff, *Uncovering Clinton*, 109.

11. Ibid.

12. Ibid.

13. "Kathleen Willey, 'I Just Thought It Was Extremely Reckless,'" *The Washington Post*, March 16, 1998.

14. Ibid.

15. Isikoff, *Uncovering Clinton*, 109.

16. "Kathleen Willey: 'I Just Thought It Was Extremely Reckless.'"

17. Jeff Leen, "The Other Woman in Jones Case; Kathleen Willey's Chance Encounter with Tripp Changed Her Life," *The Washington Post*, January 29, 1998.

18. Michael Isikoff, "A Twist in the Paula Jones Case," *Newsweek*, August 11, 1997.

19. Isikoff, *Uncovering Clinton*, 110.

20. Leen, "The Other Woman in Jones Case; Kathleen Willey's Chance Encounter With Tripp Changed Her Life."

21. Ibid.

22. Ibid.

23. Ibid.

24. Transcript, *Larry King Live*, "Kathleen Willey Details Sexual Harassment Accusation Against President Clinton," May 12, 1999 (airdate), Transcript # 99051200V22.

25. Isikoff , "A Twist in the Paula Jones Case."

26. Ibid.

27. Leen, "The Other Woman in Jones Case; Kathleen Willey's Chance Encounter With Tripp Changed Her Life."

28. Ibid.

29. Ibid.

30. Ibid.

31. Isikoff, *Uncovering Clinton*, 111.

32. Ibid, pp. 111-112.

33. Ibid, p. 112.

34. Ibid.

35. Ibid.

36. Ibid, p. 113.

37. "Final Report of the Independent Counsel In Re: Madison Guaranty Savings & Loan Association," 90.

38. *Larry King Live*, May 12, 1999.

39. Isikoff, *Uncovering Clinton*, 114.

40. Leen, "The Other Woman in Jones Case; Kathleen Willey's Chance Encounter With Tripp Changed Her Life."

41. *Larry King Live*, May 12, 1999.

42. Ibid.

43. Isikoff, *Uncovering Clinton*, 115.

44. *Larry King Live*, May 12, 1999.

45. Ibid.

46. Clinton testified that he was aware she got a paid position in the White House Counsel's office after her husband's death but had no clue how she got the job; maybe it was Nancy Hernreich who helped her get it, he mumbled. *See* "President Clinton's Deposition; Regarding Kathleen Willey," available at http://www.washingtonpost.com/wp-srv/politics/special/pjones/docs/clintondep031398.htm#willey (accessed July 17, 2004).

47. Amy Goldstein, "Willey's Career Path Had a Sharp Upturn; From Volunteer to U.S. Delegate," *The Washington Post*, March 15, 1998.

48. Leen, "The Other Woman in Jones Case; Kathleen Willey's Chance Encounter With Tripp Changed Her Life."

49. Michael Isikoff, "A Twist in the Paula Jones Case," *Newsweek*, August 11, 1997.

50. Goldstein, "Willey's Career Path Had a Sharp Upturn; From Volunteer to U.S. Delegate."

51. Leen, "The Other Woman in Jones Case; Kathleen Willey's Chance Encounter With Tripp Changed Her Life."

52. Isikoff, *Uncovering Clinton*, 115.

53. Leen, "The Other Woman in Jones Case; Kathleen Willey's Chance Encounter With Tripp Changed Her Life."

54. Isikoff, *Uncovering Clinton*, 115.

55. Leen, "The Other Woman in Jones Case; Kathleen Willey's Chance Encounter With Tripp Changed Her Life."

56. Ibid.

57. Isikoff, *Uncovering Clinton*, 99-100.

58. Ibid, 104.

59. Ibid, 106-113.

60. Ibid, 114-115.

61. Ibid, 116, 126-128.

62. Ibid, 123.

63. *Larry King Live*, February 15, 1999.

64. Isikoff, *Uncovering Clinton*, 134-35.

65. Ibid, 138.

66. Ibid.

67. Ibid, 143.

68. Ibid, 141.

69. Ibid, 144.

70. Peter Baker, "Ex-Clinton Aide Vows to Fight Jones Subpoena," *Newsday* (New York), August 1, 1997.

71. Peter Baker, "Clinton Unveils Agenda Heralding Contentious Fall," *The Washington Post*, August 7, 1997.

72. Ibid.

73. Isikoff, *Uncovering Clinton*, 144-146.

74. Ibid, 147.

75. Ibid.

76. "Final Report of the Independent Counsel In Re: Madison Guaranty Savings & Loan Association," 91 n. 42-44.

77. Isikoff, "A Twist in the Paula Jones Case."

78. Ibid.

79. Ibid.

80. Ibid.

81. Isikoff, *Uncovering Clinton*, 152.

82. Isikoff, "A Twist in the Paula Jones Case."

83. Isikoff, *Uncovering Clinton*, 152-153.

84. Ibid.

85. Ibid.

86. Ibid, p. 212.

87. "Kathleen Willey: 'I Just Thought It Was Extremely Reckless.'"

88. Ibid.

89. Ibid.

90. Ibid.

91. Ibid.

92. Isikoff, *Uncovering Clinton*, 369-370 n. 5. Isikoff also details Kenneth Starr's efforts to identify the threatening thug.

93. Complaint filed on behalf of Kathleen Willey Schwicker in September 2000 in the United States District Court for the District of Columbia, available at http://www.judicialwatch.org/cases/65/willeycomp.htm (accessed July 5, 2004). This case was voluntarily dismissed by the plaintiff (i.e., Willey) in October 2000.

94. Isikoff, *Uncovering Clinton*, 369, n.5.

95. Ibid.

96. Ibid. Also see "The Personal Edge: Kathleen Willey's Story," *The Edge With Paula Zahn*, March 6, 2001 (airdate), Transcript # 030603cb.260.

97. Ibid.

98. Ibid.

99. Ibid.

100. David Stout, "Testing of A President: The Witness; Jones Lawyers Seek New Talk with Accuser," *The New York Times*, March 6, 1998.

101. "Excerpts of Kathleen Willey's Deposition," available at http://www.washington post.com/wp-srv/politics/special/pjones/docs/willey031398.htm (accessed July 6, 2004).

102. Susan Schmidt, Peter Baker, and Toni Locy, "Clinton Accused of Urging Aide to Lie; Starr Probes Whether President Told Woman to Deny Alleged Affair to Jones's Lawyers," *The Washington Post*, January 21, 1998.

103. "Excerpts of Kathleen Willey's Deposition."

104. "President Clinton's Deposition," available at http://www.washingtonpost.com/wp-srv/politics/special/pjones/docs/clintondep031398.htm#willey (accessed July 6, 2004).

105. Isikoff, "A Twist in the Paula Jones Case."

106. Arianna Huffington, "Slick Willie dodges another bullet," *Chicago Sun-Times*, August 10, 1997.

107. Isikoff, "A Twist in the Paula Jones Case."

108. Ibid.

109. R.H. Melton, "Clinton Tie to Va. Woman Led to Probe's Latest Angle," *The Washington Post*, January 22, 1998.

110. Ibid.

111. "Players in the Clinton Scandal," *Pittsburgh Post-Gazette*, January 25, 1998.

112. Leen, "The Other Woman in Jones Case; Kathleen Willey's Chance Encounter With Tripp Changed Her Life.

113. Mark Lacy and Edwin Chen, "Clinton Under Fire," *Los Angeles Times*, January 23, 1998.

114. "Testing of a President," *The New York Times*, February 8, 1998.

115. Ibid.

116. Susan Schmidt and Toni Locy, "Starr Subpoenas Ex-White House Aide Who Said Clinton Groped Her," *The Washington Post*, February 18, 1998.

117. "Witness Comes Forward In Jones Case; Woman Says She Was Asked To Lie To Bolster Charge Against Clinton," *Chicago Tribune*, February 17, 1998.

118. Richard A. Serrano, "3rd Woman in Clinton Saga Maintains Her Silence," *Los Angeles Times*, March 1, 1998.

119. David Jackson and Ray Gibson. "Grand Jury Awaits Key Player," *Chicago Tribune*, February 24, 1998.

120. Richard T. Pienciak, "Willey Tale May Harm Bill," *Daily News* (New York), March 15, 1998.

121. *Larry King Live*, May 12, 1999.

122. Ibid.

123. Pienciak, "Willey Tale May Harm Bill."

124. Ibid.

125. Simon, "Ex-Aide: Clinton Fondled Me; Accusation May Be Most Serious Yet Against President."

126. Ibid.

127. Ronald J. Ostrow, "Willey Details Charge of Clinton Sexual Advance," *Los Angeles Times*, March 16, 1998.

128. Ibid.

129. "Clinton Strikes Back At Willey; White House Releases Letters From Her," *Sun-Sentinel* (Fort Lauderdale, FL), March 17, 1998.

130. "Kathleen Willey: 'I Just Thought It Was Extremely Reckless.'"

131. Simon, "Ex-Aide: Clinton Fondled Me; Accusation May Be Most Serious Yet Against President."

132. Ibid.

133. Ibid.

134. "Kathleen Willey: 'I Just Thought It Was Extremely Reckless.'"

135. Simon, "Ex-Aide: Clinton Fondled Me; Accusation May Be Most Serious Yet Against President."

136. Ibid.

137. "Kathleen Willey: 'I Just Thought It Was Extremely Reckless.'"

138. Ibid.

139. Associated Press. "Clinton: 'I Told Truth' In Willey Encounter; 'Nothing Improper Happened' Between Them, President Says," *Chicago Tribune*, March 16, 1998.

140. Ibid.

141. Ibid.

142. Joanne Jacobs, "Defining Harassment: Will We Ever Get It Right? Find A Middle Ground Between Workplace Vixens And Virgins," *San Jose Mercury News* (California), March 5, 1998.

143. CNN's *Crossfire*, October 10, 1991 (airdate), Transcript # 418.

144. Ibid.

145. Associated Press. "Willey Correspondence For 'Context': McCurry," *Chicago Tribune*, March 17, 1998.

146. Ibid.

147. *Larry King Live*, May 12, 1999.

148. Ibid.

149. "Clinton Strikes Back At Willey; White House Releases Letters From Her," *Sun-Sentinel* (Fort Lauderdale, FL), March 17, 1998.

150. *Larry King Live*, May 12, 1999.

151. Pierre Thomas, "Starr quietly continues White House investigation," *CNN.com*, February 19, 1999, http://edition.cnn.com/ALLPOLITICS/stories/1999/02/19/grand.jury/ (accessed January 26, 2005).

152. Ibid.

153. Brian McGrory, "White House fires back over Willey; Shows she wrote to Clinton after 1993 encounter," *The Boston Globe*, March 17, 1998.

154. Prose, Francine. "Facing Up to It; Distinctions That Women Draw," *The Washington Post*, March 22, 1998.

155. Ibid.

156. McGrory, "White House fires back over Willey; Shows she wrote to Clinton after 1993 encounter."

157. Maureen Dowd, "Liberties; Sinners and Spinners on the Equator," *The New York Times*, March 25, 1998.

158. Byron York, "A Courageous Man: Michael Kelly, R.I.P.," *National Review On-Line*, April 4, 2003, http://www.nationalreview.com/york/york040403.asp (accessed July 5, 2004).

159. Michael Kelly, "I Believe," *The Washington Post*, February 4, 1998.

160. Ibid.

161. Michael Kelly, "I Still Believe," *The Washington Post*, March 18, 1998.

162. Simon, "Ex-Aide: Clinton Fondled Me; Accusation May Be Most Serious Yet Against President."

163. Thomas B. Edsall and Terry M. Neal, "Strains in a Key Constituency; Some Women Reassess Clinton in Light of Willey Accusations," *The Washington Post*, March 17, 1998.

164. Ibid.

165. Ibid.

166. Ibid.

167. Ibid.

168. Jonathan Weisman, "Scandal throws women a curve; Democrats' reaction raises a question of double standard," *The Baltimore Sun*, March 17, 1998.

169. Ibid.

170. "Anita Hill, Steinem Make Case For Clinton," *Buffalo News* (New York), March 23, 1998.

171. Ibid.

172. Ibid.

173. Barbara A. Serrano, "Steinem Fires Back—The Feminist Icon Replies To Criticism Of Her Remarks Regarding The President, Monica, Paula And Others," *The Seattle Times*, April 17, 1998.

174. "Law in the Clinton Era; A Feminist Dilemma," *The New York Times*, March 24, 1998.

175. Ibid.

176. "White House Aides Are Trying To Undermine Willey With Quiet Attacks," *St. Louis Post-Dispatch* (Missouri), March 18, 1998.

177. Ibid.

178. John F. Harris, "Quick Shift, White House Brandishes Facts; A Sudden Blitz of Facts About Willey," *The Washington Post*, March 18, 1998.
179. Ibid.
180. Ibid.
181. Ibid.
182. "The President's Testimony: Part Eight of Eight," *The New York Times*, September 22, 1998. (Emphasis added.)
183. Karen Ball, "Curtain Call," *The Washington Post*, January 28, 2001.
184. Steve Campbell, "Collins met privately with a Clinton accuser, book reveals," *Portland Press Herald* (Maine), September 24, 2000.
185. Ibid.
186. Ball, "Curtain Call."
187. Ibid.
188. *Larry King Live*, May 12, 1999.
189. "Final Report of the Independent Counsel In Re: Madison Guaranty Savings & Loan Association," 89, n. 21.
190. Ibid.
191. "Kathleen Willey Joins WND Speakers," *World Net Daily*, May 21, 2001, http://www.worldnetdaily.com/news/article.asp?ARTICLE_ID=22884 (accessed July 5, 2004).
192. For example, see Kathleen Willey, "NOW's the Time to Speak Up," *World Net Daily*, July 31, 2001, http://www.worldnetdaily.com/news/article.asp?ARTICLE_ID=23857 (accessed July 5, 2004).
193. Kathleen Willey, "The Cat's Meow," *The Weekly Standard*, February 19, 2001.
194. The complete text of the OIC's report is available at http://icreport.access.gpo.gov/lewinsky.html.
195. Ibid, p. 87, fn. 2.
196. Ibid, p.94 (emphasis added).
197. Ibid, p. 93, fn. 37 (emphasis added).
198. Ibid, p. 93.
199. Ball, "Curtain Call."
200. Ibid.
201. Associated Press. "Kathleen Willey says she needs a hero as president, supports McCain," February 29, 2000.
202. "Interview with Kathleen Willey Schwicker," Fox News Network, *Hannity & Colmes*, March 1, 2001 (airdate), Transcript # 030103cb.253.
203. "Kathleen Willey: Predator Clinton Will Strike Again," *Federal Observer*, http://www.federalobserver.com/archive.php?aid=5719 (accessed July 5, 2004).
204. "Kathleen Willey Bombs as Radio Talk Show Host—Give Julie Hiatt Steele A Chance!," *Democrats.com*, http://www.democrats.com/preview.cfm?term=Whitewatergate (accessed July 5, 2004).
205. *The Edge With Paula Zahn*, March 6, 2001.
206. "Kathleen Willey Schwicker discusses her allegations against President Clinton and her new radio talk show beginning tonight," *Sunday Today*, NBC News Transcripts, April 7, 2002 (airdate).
207. Melton, "Clinton Tie to Va. Woman Led to Probe's Latest Angle."

208. Thomas Eckes, "Paternalistic and envious gender stereotypes: testing predictions from the stereotype content model," *Sex Roles: A Journal of Research,* August 2002, available at: http://www.findarticles.com/p/articles/mi_m2294/is_2002_August/ai_95514604 (accessed July 6, 2004). This theory is called Ambivalent Sexism Theory, or ABT.

209. Jacob Sullum, "The War on Fat: Is the size of your butt the government's business?" *Reason,* August/September 2004, 20-31.

210. Ibid, 30.

211. Ibid.

212. Ibid, 31.

Chapter Seven

1. Isikoff, *Uncovering Clinton,* 155.

2. Ibid, pp. 155-56.

3. Ibid, pp. 335-36.

4. Despite the ramblings of former U.S. Attorney General Ramsey Clark, who has drafted articles of impeachment against President Bush. See http://www.votetoimpeach.org/ (accessed July 12, 2004).

5. William L. Anderson and Candice E. Jackson, "Law as a Weapon: How RICO Subverts Liberty and the True Purpose of Law," *The Independent Review: A Journal of Political Economy,* Summer 2004, 85-97. See also Anderson and Jackson, "Washington's Biggest Crime Problem," *Reason* magazine, April 2004; and Anderson and Jackson, "Derivative Crimes and Federal Injustice," *Freedom Daily,* March 2004, http://www. fff.org/freedom/fd0403f.asp (accessed July 22, 2004).

6. William L. Anderson and Candice E. Jackson, "Martha Stewart and Our Shadow Legal System," March 10, 2004, http://www.lewrockwell.com/anderson/anderson88.html (accessed July 22, 2004). See also Anderson and Jackson, "Wealthy Beyond A Reasonable Doubt," March 6, 2004, http://www.mises.org/fullstory.asp?control=1467 (accessed July 22, 2004).

7. "Arkansas disciplinary panel recommends Clinton disbarment," *CNN.com,* May 23, 2000, http://www.cnn.com/2000/ALLPOLITICS/stories/05/22/clinton.disbarred/ (accessed July 22, 2004). Judge Susan Webber Wright, who presided over (and dismissed) the Paula Jones lawsuit, must have felt especially annoyed by Clinton's intentional deceptions; she cited him for contempt of court and fined him $90,000 in 1999. Clinton accepted a five-year suspension of his Arkansas law license and a $25,000 fine in January 2001 just before leaving office, which took effect in April 2001; in October that year the U.S. Supreme Court suspended Clinton from practicing before it, following, as it usually does, the state court's decision. See Anne Gearan, "Ex-President Clinton suspended from law practice before U.S. Supreme Court," *Associated Press,* October 1, 2001. In November 2001 Clinton resigned from the Supreme Court bar to avoid the spectacle of permanent disbarment. "Investigating the President: The Trial," *CNN.com,* http://www.cnn.com/ALLPOLITICS/resources/1998/lewinsky/ (accessed March 17, 2005).

8. Isikoff, *Uncovering Clinton,* 337.

9. Lynda Gorov, "Ex-Intern: Past of Privilege, Hard Work; The Clinton Allegations," *The Boston Globe,* January 22, 1998.

10. "Lewinsky's Aug. 6 Grand Jury Testimony, Part 1" available at http://www.washing tonpost.com/wp-srv/politics/special/clinton/stories/mltest080698_1.htm (accessed July 7, 2004).

11. Ibid. (one cite 9-13).

12. Ibid.

13. Clinton, *My Life*, 677.

14. "Lewinsky's Aug. 6 Grand Jury Testimony, Part 1."

15. Ibid.

16. Howard Kurtz, "Monica To The Nth; The Deluge: Stay Tuned For Still More," *The Washington Post*, March 4, 1999.

17. Bob Hohler, "Lewinsky Tells All In Book and On TV; Reveals Pregnancy By Pentagon Official," *Seattle Post-Intelligencer*, March 4, 1999.

18. "Lewinsky's Aug. 6 Grand Jury Testimony, Part 4" available at http://www.washing tonpost.com/wp-srv/politics/special/clinton/stories/mltest080698_4.htm (accessed July 8, 2004).

19. "Lewinsky's Aug. 6 Grand Jury Testimony, Part 1."

20. Ibid.

21. "Lewinsky's Aug. 6 Grand Jury Testimony, Part 5" available at http://www.washing tonpost.com/wp-srv/politics/special/clinton/stories/mltest080698_5.htm (accessed July 8, 2004).

22. "Lewinsky's Aug. 6 Grand Jury Testimony, Part 3" available at http://www.washing tonpost.com/wp-srv/politics/special/clinton/stories/mltest080698_3.htm#TOP (accessed July 8, 2004).

23. "Lewinsky's Aug. 6 Grand Jury Testimony, Part 2" available at http://www.washing tonpost.com/wp-srv/politics/special/clinton/stories/mltest080698_2.htm> (accessed July 8, 2004).

24. "Lewinsky's Aug. 6 Grand Jury Testimony, Part 3."

25. Ibid.

26. "Lewinsky's Aug. 6 Grand Jury Testimony, Part 5."

27. Ibid.

28. "Lewinsky's Aug. 6 Grand Jury Testimony, Part 6" available at http://www.washing tonpost.com/wp-srv/politics/special/clinton/stories/mltest080698_6.htm (accessed July 8, 2004).

29. Ibid.

30. Ibid.

31. "Lewinsky's Aug. 6 Grand Jury Testimony, Part 8" available at http://www.washing tonpost.com/wp-srv/politics/special/clinton/stories/mltest080698_8.htm (accessed July 8, 2004).

32. "In Lewinsky's Words," *USA Today*, March 4, 1999.

33. "Lewinsky's Aug. 6 Grand Jury Testimony, Part 10" available at http://www.washing tonpost.com/wp-srv/politics/special/clinton/stories/mltest080698_10.htm (accessed July 8, 2004).

34. Ibid.

35. Ibid.

36. Ibid. See also "Lewinsky's Aug. 6 Grand Jury Testimony, Part 11" available at http://

www.washingtonpost.com/wp-srv/politics/special/clinton/stories/mltest080698_11.htm (accessed July 8, 2004).

37. "Lewinsky's Aug. 6 Grand Jury Testimony, Part 11."

38. Ibid.

39. Ibid.

40. "Lewinsky's Aug. 6 Grand Jury Testimony, Part 12" available at: http://www.washing tonpost.com/wp-srv/politics/special/clinton/stories/mltest080698_12.htm (accessed July 8, 2004).

41. "Lewinsky's Aug. 6 Grand Jury Testimony, Part 11."

42. Ibid.

43. Ibid.

44. "Lewinsky's Aug. 6 Grand Jury Testimony, Part 14" available at http://www.washing tonpost.com/wp-srv/politics/special/clinton/stories/mltest080698_14.htm (accessed July 8, 2004).

45. "In Lewinsky's Words."

46. Ibid.

47. "Lewinsky's Aug. 6 Grand Jury Testimony, Part 14."

48. Ibid.

49. "Lewinsky's Aug. 6 Grand Jury Testimony, Part 15" available at http://www.washing tonpost.com/wp-srv/politics/special/clinton/stories/mltest080698_15.htm (accessed July 8, 2004).

50. "Lewinsky's Aug. 6 Grand Jury Testimony, Part 16" available at http://www.wash ingtonpost.com/wp-srv/politics/special/clinton/stories/mltest080698_16.htm (accessed July 8, 2004).

51. "Lewinsky's Aug. 20 Grand Jury Testimony, Part 2."

52. "Lewinsky's Aug. 20 Grand Jury Testimony, Part 4."

53. Ibid.

54. "Lewinsky's Aug. 20 Grand Jury Testimony, Part 5."

55. Susan Schmidt and Peter Baker, "Ex-Intern Rejected Immunity Offer in Probe; Independent Counsel Sought Her Cooperation; Apartment Is Searched," *The Washington Post*, January 24, 1998.

56. Ibid.

57. Ibid.

58. Ibid.

59. "Monica Lewinsky's Recent Interviews and Book Release," CNBC's *Rivera Live*, March 4, 1999 (airdate).

60. "Lewinsky's Aug. 20 Grand Jury Testimony, Part 7."

61. Schmidt and Baker, "Ex-Intern Rejected Immunity Offer in Probe; Independent Counsel Sought Her Cooperation; Apartment Is Searched."

62. Ibid.

63. "Lewinsky's Aug. 20 Grand Jury Testimony, Part 8."

64. Ibid.

65. Isikoff, *Uncovering Clinton*, 332.

66. Susan Schmidt, Peter Baker, and Toni Locy, "Clinton Accused of Urging Aide to Lie; Starr Probes Whether President Told Woman to Deny Alleged Affair to Jones's Lawyers,"

The Washington Post, January 21, 1998.

67. Roger Simon and William Neikirk, "Cover-Up Charges Embroil Clinton; Taping of Intern Key to Inquiry," *Chicago Tribune,* January 22, 1998.

68. Schmidt, Baker, and Locy, "Clinton Accused of Urging Aide to Lie; Starr Probes Whether President Told Woman to Deny Alleged Affair to Jones's Lawyers."

69. Ibid.

70. Simon and Neikirk. "Cover-Up Charges Embroil Clinton; Taping of Intern Key to Inquiry."

71. Ibid.

72. John Harris, "FBI Taped Aide's Allegations; Clinton Denies Affair, Says He 'Did Not Urge Anyone' to Lie," *The Washington Post,* January 22, 1998.

73. "The President Under Fire; Excerpts From Statements by White House and President on Accusations," *The New York Times,* January 22, 1998.

74. Ibid. (Emphasis added.)

75. "Tell the Full Story, Mr. President," *The New York Times,* January 23, 1998.

76. Simon and Neikirk. "Cover-Up Charges Embroil Clinton; Taping of Intern Key to Inquiry."

77. Schmidt and Baker, "Ex-Intern Rejected Immunity Offer in Probe; Independent Counsel Sought Her Cooperation; Apartment Is Searched."

78. "Testing Of A President: In Her Own Words; What She Has Said," *The New York Times,* August 18, 1998.

79. Simon and Neikirk. "Cover-Up Charges Embroil Clinton; Taping of Intern Key to Inquiry."

80. Ibid.

81. Ethan Bronner, "The President Under Fire: The Media; Reports of Sexual Scandal Have Everybody Talking," *The New York Times,* January 23, 1998.

82. Mimi Hall, "White House tries to ride out the storm[;] Battle-tested staff sticks to routine," *USA Today,* January 22, 1998.

83. "Clinton Cabinet Counterattacks; Four Secretaries Defend Their Boss; Intern's Lawyer Cites 'Pressure' By Starr," *Chicago Tribune,* January 23, 1998.

84. John F. Harris, "FBI Taped Aide's Allegations; Clinton Denies Affair, Says He 'Did Not Urge Anyone' to Lie," *The Washington Post,* January 22, 1998.

85. Ibid.

86. E.J. Dionne, Jr., "Why Hand Them This Lethal Weapon?" *The Washington Post,* January 23, 1998.

87. Ibid.

88. Peter Baker and Susan Schmidt, "FBI Taped Aide's Allegations; Seeking Cooperation, Bureau Confronted Ex-White House Intern," *The Washington Post,* January 22, 1998.

89. Jill Abramson and Don Van Natta, Jr., "The President Under Fire: The Friends; Friendship of 2 Women Slowly Led to the Crisis," *The New York Times,* January 22, 1998.

90. Jeff Leen, "Lewinsky: Two Coasts, Two Lives, Many Images," *The Washington Post,* January 24, 1998.

91. Margery Eagan, "Scandal Rocks Clinton: How will Bill spin out of this alleged bimbo-blunder?" *The Boston Herald,* January 22, 1998.

92. Ibid.

93. Michael Tackett and Jan Crawford Greenburg, "Lewinsky's Lawyer Seeks Immunity; Starr Targets Former Intern," *Chicago Tribune*, January 24, 1998.

94. Leen, "Lewinsky: Two Coasts, Two Lives, Many Images."

95. Ibid.

96. "An Unruly Mess," *The Washington Post*, February 25, 1998.

97. Richard Cohen, "Menace to Society," *The Washington Post*, September 24, 1998.

98. "Privacy—'Sluts and Nuts,'" *Daily Oklahoman* (Oklahoma City, OK), February 3, 1999.

99. "America Is Listening, Mr. President," *Daily News* (New York), January 27, 1998. (Emphasis added.)

100. "In Lewinsky's Words," *USA Today*, March 4, 1999.

101. "Discussion on the Latest Development of White House Crisis," CNN's *Larry King Live*, January 26, 1998 (airdate), Transcript # 98012600V22.

102. John F. Harris and Dan Balz, "Disclosure Lifts Long Siege at White House; As Day to Testify Approached, Clinton Reopened Door to Supportive Confidants," *The Washington Post*, August 18, 1998.

103. Maureen Dowd, "Liberties; D.C. Confidential," *The New York Times*, February 25, 1998.

104. "Investigating the President: What Will Cockell Testify Before the Grand Jury?" CNN's *Larry King Live*, July 20, 1998, Transcript # 98072000V22.

105. Tucker Carlson, "Trashing Kenneth Starr," *The Weekly Standard*, June 29, 1998.

106. Ibid.

107. Roger Simon, "Clinton Admits 'Personal Failure,' Assails Probe Of His Private Life; Statements End Months Of Denials," *Chicago Tribune*, August 18, 1998.

108. Susan Schmidt and Ruth Marcus, "The Legal Gamble: To Say Just Enough; Clinton Relies on a Narrow Definition," *The Washington Post*, August 18, 1998.

109. Debra J. Saunders, "Women Who Talk Too Much," *The San Francisco Chronicle*, July 14, 1998 (quoting Geraldo Rivera).

110. "Testing Of A President: In His Own Words; Last Night's Address," *The New York Times*, August 18, 1998. (Emphasis added.)

111. Clinton, *My Life*, 773-774.

112. Ibid, pp. 772-773.

113. Ibid, pp. 774-775.

114. Dan Balz, "Baring the Soul, Daring Prosecutor," *The Washington Post*, August 18, 1998.

115. Michael Kelly, "A President Who Will Never Stop Lying . . .," *The New York Post*, August 19, 1998.

116. Tom Shales, "Unfortunately Not the Last Word on the Subject," *The Washington Post*, August 18, 1998.

117. "Bill Clinton Speaks, a Little," *The New York Times*, August 18, 1998.

118. Ibid.

119. John C. Henry, "Lewinsky opens up in TV interview; Says she 'felt like...trash,'" *The Houston Chronicle*, March 4, 1999.

120. Lloyd Grove, "Hung Out To Dry; Clinton Loyalists After The Spin Cycle Ends," *The Washington Post*, August 18, 1998.

121. Ibid.

122. Richard Berke and Don Van Natta, Jr., "Testing Of A President: The Friends; One By One, The President Told His Closest Aides The Painful Truth," *The New York Times*, August 18, 1998.

123. Ibid.

124. Ibid.

125. Elizabeth Shogren and Ronald J. Ostrow, "Clinton confesses Lewinsky affair; 'It's nobody's business,' president tells nation," *Chicago Tribune*, August 18, 1998.

126. Michael Duffy and Monica Lewinsky, "Monica Up Close," *Time*, March 15, 1999.

127. Ibid.

128. Ibid.

129. John C. Henry, "Lewinsky opens up in TV interview; Says she 'felt like...trash,'" *The Houston Chronicle*, March 4, 1999.

130. Bob Hohler, "Lewinsky Tells All In Book and On TV; Reveals Pregnancy By Pentagon Official," *Seattle Post-Intelligencer*, March 4, 1999.

131. David Jackson, "Lewinsky blasts Starr's tactics 'Lewinsky's Story' describes thoughts of suicide, Clinton's vulnerability," *The Dallas Morning-News*, March 4, 1999.

132. Hohler, "Lewinsky Tells All In Book and On TV; Reveals Pregnancy By Pentagon Official."

133. Duffy and Lewinsky, "Monica Up Close."

134. Ibid.

135. Ibid.

136. Ibid.

137. "Monica Lewinsky's Recent Interviews and Book Release," CNBC's *Rivera Live*, March 4, 1999 (airdate).

138. Associated Press, "Clinton 'United With Democratic Agenda' / Goal: Shaping A Legislative Plan," *Newsday* (New York), March 4, 1999.

139. Hohler, "Lewinsky Tells All In Book and On TV; Reveals Pregnancy By Pentagon Official."

140. The Don Juan Center, http://www.sosuave.com/ (accessed July 11, 2004).

141. "Don Juan," *MSN Encarta*, http://encarta.msn.com/encyclopedia_761565350/Don_Juan.html (accessed July 11, 2004).

142. Roger Schlobin, "The Femivore: An Undiscovered Archetype," *The Journal of the Fantastic in the Arts* , Spring 1989, http://wpl.lib.in.us/roger/FEM.HTML (accessed July 11, 2004) (quoting Sheri Tepper's 1987 horror novel *The Bones*, which Schlobin credits with naming the "femivore" archetype).

143. Ibid, 179-184.

144. Ibid.

145. Steve Goldstein, "Other Lewinsky Affair Brought A Pregnancy / Her Book Reveals A Liaison With Another Man. Last Night, The Public Heard More," *The Philadelphia Inquirer*, March 4, 1999.

146. Alan Brinkley, "The Assault on Government," in *New Federalism Papers*, ed. Alan Brinkley, Nelson W. Polsby, and Kathleen M. Sullivan (New York: W.W. Norton & Company, 1997), 19.

147. "The Retirement Dilemma of Generation X," *New York Life*, http://www.newyorklife.com/cda/0,3254,11967,00.html (accessed July 13, 2004).

Chapter Eight

1. Maraniss, *First In His Class*, 346.
2. Ibid, 351.
3. Ibid, 352-354.
4. Ibid, 357.
5. NBC's *Dateline*, February 24, 1999 (airdate), available at http://www.capitolhill blue.com/Feb1999/022599/datelinetranscript022599.htm (accessed July 13, 2004).
6. Ibid.
7. Ibid.
8. *Dateline*, February 24, 1999.
9. Lois Romano and Peter Baker, "'Jane Doe No. 5' Goes Public with Allegation; Clinton Controversy Lingers Over Nursing Home Owner's Disputed 1978 Story," *The Washington Post*, February 20, 1999.
10. Dorothy Rabinowitz, "Juanita Broaddrick Meets the Press," *The Wall Street Journal*, February 19, 1999.
11. *Dateline*, February 24, 1999.
12. Rabinowitz, "Juanita Broaddrick Meets the Press."
13. Ibid.
14. Ibid.
15. *Dateline*, February 24, 1999.
16. Rabinowitz, "Juanita Broaddrick Meets the Press."
17. Murray, Frank J. "House impeachment managers forgo using 'Jane Doe' accounts," *The Washington Times*, January 8, 1999.
18. "New Allegations That President Clinton Sexually Assaulted Juanita Broaddrick 20 Years Ago," NBC Nightly News, March 28, 1998 (airdate).
19. Ibid.
20. NBC's *Meet the Press*, March 29, 1998 (airdate).
21. Ibid.
22. William Goldschlag, "Nurse Tied to Latest Claim," *Daily News* (New York), March 29, 1998.
23. Peter Baker and Lena H. Sun, "Starr Seeks Records From Jones Team on Other Women; Four Are Named In Counsel Subpoena," *The Washington Post*, March 26, 1998.
24. Lois Romano and Peter Baker, "'Jane Doe No. 5' Goes Public With Allegation; Clinton Controversy Lingers Over Nursing Home Owner's Disputed 1978 Story," *The Washington Post*, February 20, 1999.
25. Timothy J. Burger, "Clinton Forced Sex On Me—Ark. Nurse Sez She Wants To Set Record Straight," *Daily News* (New York), February 20, 1999.
26. Frank J. Murray, "House impeachment managers forgo using 'Jane Doe' accounts," *The Washington Times*, January 8, 1999.
27. Rabinowitz, "Juanita Broaddrick Meets the Press."
28. Ibid.
29. Ibid.
30. Ibid.

31. Ibid.

32. Ibid.

33. *Dateline*, February 24, 1999.

34. Rabinowitz, "Juanita Broaddrick Meets the Press."

35. *Dateline*, February 24, 1999.

36. Ibid.

37. Ibid.

38. Pete Yost, "Arkansas woman's sexual assault accusation against Clinton denied," *Associated Press*, February 20, 1999.

39. *Dateline*, February 24, 1999.

40. CNN's *Larry King Live*, March 8, 1999 (airdate), Transcript # 99030800V22.

41. Lois Romano and Peter Baker, "'Jane Doe No. 5' Goes Public With Allegation; Clinton Controversy Lingers Over Nursing Home Owner's Disputed 1978 Story," *The Washington Post*, February 20, 1999.

42. Tony Snow, "Parsing the presidential denial," *The Washington Times*, March 1, 1999.

43. Ibid.

44. Howard Kurtz, "Clinton Accuser's Story Aired," *The Washington Post*, February 25, 1999.

45. Richard Cohen, "The Untouchables," *The Washington Post*, February 23, 1999.

46. Neftali Bendavid and Tim Jones, "Allegation Of Rape By Clinton Aired; Interviewed On TV, Arkansas Woman Claims Sexual Assault In 1978," *Chicago Tribune*, February 25, 1999.

47. Ibid.

48. Mary McGrory, "The Senate's Post-trial Glow," *The Washington Post*, February 25, 1999.

49. Michael Kelly, "MO for a President?" *The Washington Post*, February 25, 1999.

50. Richard Cohen, "A Lasting Look at Reagan," *The Washington Post*, June 17, 2004.

51. Cohen, Richard. "Who Is This Guy?" *The Washington Post*, March 2, 1999.

52. Ibid.

53. "Clinton Cabinet Counterattacks; Four Secretaries Defend Their Boss; Intern's Lawyer Cites 'Pressure' By Starr," *Chicago Tribune*, January 23, 1998.

54. John F. Harris, "Looking Past Scandal, Focusing on Future; President Dominates Policy Agenda Despite Issues of Private Behavior," *The Washington Post*, March 4, 1999.

55. Ibid.

56. Carlin Romano, "Critic From the Inside George Stephanopoulos Is Talking, and People Want To Listen To What the Former Presidential Aide and Author Of 'All Too Human' Has To Say," *The Philadelphia Inquirer*, March 15, 1999.

57. David Reinhard, "Feeling Broaddrick's Pain—Or Not," *The Sunday Oregonian*, February 28, 1999.

58. Jeff Jacoby, "Rape? Sounds like our Bill," *The Boston Globe*, March 1, 1999.

59. "The President's Missing Voice," *The New York Times*, February 27, 1999.

60. "Bill Bennett, Susan Estrich and Patricia Ireland Discuss the Allegations of Rape Made by Juanita Broaddrick Against President Clinton," NBC's *Meet the Press*, February 28, 1999.

61. "Mrs. Broaddrick's Story," *The Washington Post*, March 2, 1999.

62. "Dorothy Rabinowitz from Wall Street Journal And Alan Dershowitz, Professor of Law at Harvard University, Discuss The Credibility of Juanita Broaddrick's Story," NBC's *Today*, February 25, 1999 (airdate).

63. Ibid.

64. Ibid.

65. Bill Press, "Clinton Rape Charge Can't Be Proved; Juanita Broaddrick Tells A Familiar Story, But It Suffers In The Details," *Los Angeles Times*, February 26, 1999.

66. Howard Kurtz, "Clinton Accuser's Story Aired," *The Washington Post*, February 25, 1999.

67. Joyce Howard Price, "Feminists find rape claim against Clinton serious, disturbing," *The Washington Times*, February 25, 1999.

68. Ibid.

69. Ibid.

70. "Presidential Legal Troubles," Fox News Channel's *Hannity & Colmes*, February 25, 1999 (airdate), Transcript # 022503cb.253.

71. "Rape Accusation Launches Debate on President Clinton's Morality," CNN's *Larry King Live*, February 25, 1999 (airdate), Transcript # 99022500V22.

72. Ibid.

73. Susan Faludi, "What can we learn from Clinton's accuser," *The Ottawa Citizen*, March 9, 1999.

74. Ibid.

75. Will Self, "The Interview: The Invisible Woman," *The Independent* (London), March 21, 1999.

76. Ibid.

77. Ibid.

78. Morton M. Kondracke, "Broaddrick Story Deserves Attention as Cultural Test," *Roll Call*, February 25, 1999.

79. Ibid.

80. Ibid.

81. John F. Harris, "The Mantra Is 'Move On,' But Past Emotions Linger; President Reacts Strongly to Question on Truth-Telling," *The Washington Post*, March 20, 1999.

82. Ibid.

83. Ibid.

84. Ben Macintyre, "Clinton foes say they are victims of tax witch-hunt," *The Times* (London), June 1, 2000.

85. "Sexual Violence: Fact Sheet," *National Center for Injury Prevention and Control*, http://www.cdc.gov/ncipc/factsheets/svfacts.htm (accessed July 15, 2004).

86. "Impact of Rape: Common Reactions," *Rape Treatment Center, UCLA Medical Center*, http://www.911rape.org/impact/index.html (accessed July 15, 2004).

87. "Presidential Legal Troubles," Fox News Network's *Hannity & Colmes*, February 25, 1999 (airdate), Transcript # 022503cb.253. When host Sean Hannity said that if he'd been accused of rape, he wouldn't just sit on his attorney's dry denial, he'd shout his innocence from the rooftops, Eleanor Clift, a *Newsweek* editor, said: "[F]irst of all, the word 'rape' never passed her lips..." She continued, "Now, that's a fine point, but this is something . . . that went on between two people 21 years ago. . . . I'm not questioning her memory or her

recollection, but it is her memory and her recollection."

88. Charles Krauthammer, "A Hollow Presidency," *The Washington Post*, March 19, 1999.

89. "Presidential Legal Troubles," Fox News Channel's *Hannity & Colmes*, February 25, 1999 (airdate), Transcript # 022503cb.253.

90. Jeff Jacoby, "Rape? Sounds like our Bill," *The Boston Globe*, March 1, 1999.

Conclusion

1. Riane Eisler, *The Chalice and the Blade: Our History, Our Future*, (New York: Harper-Collins Publishers, 1987), 60.

2. Ibid, xv-xvii.

3. Ibid, 153-155.

4. Ibid, 156-171, especially page 169. I should point out that Ms. Eisler would certainly take umbrage at the conclusions I draw using her terminology; she clearly supports leftist ideology, though she argues that it needs a severe shot of feminism before it can eradicate the evils of male domination.

ABOUT THE INDEX

The index for this book can be found at:

www.worldahead.com/theirlives/index